The Politics and
Poetics of
Everyday Life

Kristin Ross is the author of a number of books on modern French politics and culture, all of which have been widely translated: *The Emergence of Social Space: Rimbaud and the Paris Commune*; *Fast Cars, Clean Bodies: Decolonization and the Reordering of French Culture*; *May '68 and Its Afterlives*; and *Communal Luxury: The Political Imaginary of the Paris Commune*. She has also translated works by Jacques Rancière and by the militant collective Mauvaise Troupe. She lives in Stone Ridge, New York, and Paris.

The Politics and Poetics of Everyday Life

Kristin Ross

VERSO

London • New York

First published by Verso 2023
© Kristin Ross 2023

The author and publisher would like to express their gratitude to the original
publishers of these essays.

Every effort has been made to obtain permission for the images reproduced herein.
The publisher will endeavor to rectify any omissions or errors at the earliest
opportunity.

1 3 5 7 9 10 8 6 4 2

Verso
UK: 6 Meard Street, London W1F 0EG
US: 388 Atlantic Avenue, Brooklyn, NY 11217
versobooks.com

Verso is the imprint of New Left Books

ISBN-13: 978-1-83976-831-6
ISBN-13: 978-1-83976-833-0 (US EBK)
ISBN-13: 978-1-83976-832-3 (UK EBK)

British Library Cataloguing in Publication Data
A catalogue record for this book is available from the British Library

Library of Congress Cataloging-in-Publication Data

Names: Ross, Kristin, author.
Title: The politics and poetics of everyday life / Kristin Ross.
Description: First edition paperback. | London ; New York : Verso Books,
2023. | Includes index.
Identifiers: LCCN 2022054480 (print) | LCCN 2022054481 (ebook) | ISBN
9781839768316 (paperback) | ISBN 9781839768330 (ebk)
Subjects: LCSH: Political science—France—Philosophy. | Political
culture—France—History. | France—Politics and government—Social
aspects. | France—Politics and government—History.
Classification: LCC JA84.F8 R66 2023 (print) | LCC JA84.F8 (ebook) | DDC
320.944—dc23/eng/20221214
LC record available at https://lccn.loc.gov/2022054480
LC ebook record available at https://lccn.loc.gov/2022054481

Typeset in Fournier by MJ & N Gavan, Truro, Cornwall
Printed and bound by CPI (UK) Ltd, Croydon CR0 4YY

Contents

Introduction

The essays gathered here were written over a period of more than three decades of reflection on French political and cultural history. In selecting them according to their relevance to the themes of everyday life and what I call the "commune-form," I have given my work more of the form of a trajectory than I was aware of pursuing at the time—a kind of after-the-fact coherence to what I experienced then as the product of three quite distinct encounters that occurred amid a shifting set of political and cultural desires. It is true that when I began my graduate studies in the mid-1970s, only a very few (post-structuralist) theoretical voices were audible, and deconstruction had attained a quasi-liturgical status. The general political environment was darkening quickly and, it seemed to me, quite abruptly, into what we have now come to recognize as the counterrevolution that set in after the emancipatory moment of the long 1960s. These factors helped draw my attention to the antiproductivist Marxism of Henri Lefebvre—my teacher and colleague Fredric Jameson's enthusiasm for it also helped. Working through Lefebvre's theories of the everyday, and helping make his work familiar to an English-language readership, was, for me, a way of creating a solidarity with the recent political past, a way of continuing a form of work, a field of subversion in thought and practice that had been opened by the events of '68, even if for a university context that at times ignored it or sometimes even held it in contempt.

Henri Lefebvre's powerful intuition was that the level of shared existence which society relegates to its margin—its residues, its leftovers—might well furnish the best access to the social as such. Thinking the everyday as residue and as resource was a way of working through and with ideology as a means of working against it. The rites and rituals of Zola's *midinettes* and lady shoppers, no less than the elaborate traffic patterns formed by Jacques Tati's trapped commuters a hundred years later—all those disregarded and unarticulated aspects of shared experience—could now be read as eminently communicable. Everyday life offered a new and welcome vantage point for social analysis for me when I wrote about the consumer society that sprang up during the "second Haussmannization" of Paris in the 1950s and 1960s, years in which France attempted to extricate itself from the weight of its colonization of Algeria—a task never completed, by the way.* Everyday life was a way to understand past and absolutely contemporary alienations at the same time as all the various attempts to overcome them. In the critique of everyday life Lefebvre sustained over several decades, I saw, for the first time, what philosophy looks like when it turns away from building worlds out of abstract ideas (to which it alone holds the key), and instead explores, in collaborative fellowship with other modes of thinking and acting, the concrete, pragmatic reality of a world approached in common with others.

At around the same time, my encounter with the work of another materialist and maverick philosopher, Jacques Rancière,

---

* Kristin Ross, *Fast Cars, Clean Bodies: Decolonization and the Reordering of French Culture* (Cambridge, MA: MIT Press, 1995).

and the *Révoltes Logiques* collective he was a part of, led to my decision to translate and write the preface included here for what remains, I believe, his most significant book, *The Ignorant Schoolmaster*. Little unites Rancière to Lefebvre other than the political culture of 1968, a shared hostility to structuralism, and a belief in the vital role played by the aesthetic in subject-formation and social change. But, in Rancière's rendering of the desires that surface on the edge of the artisanal world among woodworkers and autodidacts, I found a way of thinking about emancipation and the resistance to work. Rancière's conviction that workers' voices from the past are entitled to the same degree of attention we pay to those that make up theories about them afterwards, became a kind of guiding light for me years later when I went about restaging the everyday life—the "actual working existence" as Marx called it—of Communards in Paris in *Communal Luxury* (2015).

The last essays in the volume, on the commune-form, were written after *Communal Luxury* and my first visits to the zad at Notre-Dame-des-Landes. They bear the mark of that encounter. I had been invited to the zad to talk with occupiers there about the continuities and discontinuities their situation bore to that of the 1871 Communards. What I encountered was a model of social sustainability and a strikingly new form of political intelligence among the people accomplishing it. The zad had (and continues to have) the capacity to incarnate and make common pragmatic questions—the future of agricultural land and its usages, the way to build solidarity in diversity to name just two—that extend well beyond the reality of a small corner of farmland in western France.

If the earlier essays in the volume tend to highlight the more normative and rote aspects of a dailiness ruled by the violence of economic logic, the essays on the zad and the commune-form remind us that the everyday harbors rich oppositional resources and the capacity for immanent social creativity as well. In the site-specific, vernacular struggles that have re-emerged in recent times in Notre-Dame-des-Landes and throughout the world, a dynamic conception of everyday life as a making (*poesis*) is put to the test. What this suggests to me is that the commune-form may not only be the most rational way for people in our historical moment to organize their own forces as social forces—it may be the most pleasurable way as well.

Part I. Everyday Life: Theoretical Interventions

1

Introduction to *Yale French Studies* "Everyday Life"

Alice Kaplan and Kristin Ross

To advance a theory of everyday life is to elevate lived experience to the status of a critical concept—not merely in order to describe lived experience, but in order to change it. One of the purposes of this issue is to bring to the attention of an American readership new work informed by such a transformative project: a critique of everyday life elaborated in France in the '50s and '60s which remains underacknowledged and little translated in this country.

The strain of French thought produced in the '50s and '60s which *did* come to be known in American universities with enormous speed and authority was, of course, structuralism and its various derivatives. One of the reasons for the eventual institutional success of structuralism in America was undoubtedly its pedagogical efficiency: techniques of textual analysis could be smoothly transmitted to students who had grown up isolated from French cultural or historical referents. In France, the dazzling technical innovations of structuralism were produced during the same decades that saw an intense intellectual and political critique—both inside and outside academic institutions—of consumer society. This questioning was to culminate in the events surrounding May '68.

Thought so intimately tied up with lived experience and political struggle would obviously not find the same American audience as structuralist discourse, which viewed its arena as textual. Postwar American academics still preoccupied with questions of lived experience and ideological debate tended to formulate those questions within dated existentialist categories involving authenticity and inauthenticity, good faith or bad faith. The critique of everyday life was to concern itself rather with extramoral perceptions; it was to find a small audience in the United States, as in England, Italy, and West Germany, primarily among student activists and anarchist groups.

The critique of everyday life in France achieved notoriety with the activities of a fringe group called the Situationists. In the mid-1950s, the Situationists formed themselves out of the shards of a number of avant-garde groups, including the Dada-inspired International Lettrists, the antifunctionalist Society for an Imaginist Bauhaus, and the Scandinavian CoBrA movement. They proclaimed their own era to be "The Society of the Spectacle"— the historical moment in which the logic of commodities had successfully seized and colonized all social and cultural relations, the totality of everyday life. They took their concept of everyday life from the one first substantially developed in the first volume of Henri Lefebvre's *Critique de la vie quotidienne*, published in 1947 (two more volumes would follow in subsequent decades). Everyday life, defined elliptically as "whatever remains after one has eliminated all specialized activities," is, Lefebvre argues, a limited historical phenomenon. It is inextricably tied to two parallel developments: first, to the rise of a middle class and the demise of the great "styles" formerly imposed in Western societies by Church and Monarch; second, to the vast migration of those middle classes to urban centers, spaces where their everyday activities would become increasingly organized—hence perceptible.

Cultural interventionists rather than academics, the Situationists interpreted Lefebvre's concept of everyday life in an essentially spatial way. They initiated a series of empirico-utopian experiments under the general rubric *psychogeography:* the active study of mental states and spatial ambiances produced by the material organization of the urban terrain. They proposed a division of the city into affective zones or microclimates; in more or less organized and only carelessly documented traipses through Paris, they surveyed the city for what might be salvaged and used in a utopian reconstruction of social space. To link them to French utopian/spatial tradition, we might mention several ghost intellectual figures hovering about Situationist activities: the Fourier of a *Nouveau Monde amoureux*; the Lafargue of a *Droit à la paresse*; the Elisée Reclus of a radical anticolonialist geography.

Perhaps the best way to appreciate the force of Situationist activities is to compare them to traditional Marxist blueprints for action. We can outline two interrelated areas of difference. In their attempts to disrupt the dominant organization of social space, that is, in their essentially synchronic sensibility, the Situationists mark a significant departure from the diachronically oriented Marxism of the nineteenth century. Staying within a specifically Marxist vocabulary, we might say that Situationists shifted their attention from the relations of production within the factory to that basic yet undertheorized problem of *social reproduction*—the myriad activities and conditions for existence that must be satisfied in order for relations of production to take place at all. Social reproduction—what we are calling here everyday life—has, of course, become, in our own time, the urgent issue on a host of political and cultural agendas, most significantly on that of feminism. For everyday life has always weighed heavily on the shoulders of women.

Quotidie: How many times a day? How many days? The quotidian is on the one hand the realm of routine, repetition, reiteration: the space/time where constraints and boredom are produced. Far from being an escape from this realm, segmented leisure time such as the weekend is rather a final cog permitting the smooth functioning of the routine. Even at its most degraded, however, the everyday harbors the possibility of its own transformation; it gives rise, in other words, to desires which cannot be satisfied within a weekly cycle of production/consumption. The political, like the purloined letter, is hidden in the everyday, exactly where it is most obvious: in the contradictions of lived experience, in the most banal and repetitive gestures of everyday life—the commute, the errand, the appointment. It is in the midst of the utterly ordinary, in the space where the dominant relations of production are tirelessly and relentlessly reproduced, that we must look for utopian and political aspirations to crystallize.

At this point, it should be clear how our conception of everyday life differs from that great accumulation and inventory of detail undertaken by the Annales school of historiography. Like that of the Annales school, the critique of everyday life we represent here veers away from canonical events and personages. But, while the discourse of permanence produced by the Annales school would recenter history in an immutable village life or in climatic durée, we would insist on the mutable, and specifically on the power of the city both to constrain and to alter consciousness. For this reason, the articles we have included here bear little resemblance to the mimetic effort of cataloging or describing "daily living" that has come to be associated with a title like ours.

What does it mean to approach cultural production from the

vantage point of everyday life? It means attempting to grasp the everyday without relegating it either to institutional codes and systems or to the private perceptions of a monadic subject. Between, for example, the traffic court and the angry driver who has received a moving violation, we would need to evoke a complex realm of social practice and to map out not merely a network of streets, but a conjunction of habit, desire, and accident.

When it is successful, everyday life analysis offers a new alternative to a subject/object opposition so basic to postwar continental thinking as to correspond to its two major intellectual movements: phenomenology and structuralism. By this we mean that everyday life is situated somewhere in the rift opened up between the subjective, phenomenological, sensory apparatus of the individual and reified institutions. Its starting point is neither the intentional subject dear to humanistic thinking nor the determining paradigms that bracket lived experience. Institutions, codes, and paradigms are not abstract constructs confronting us in some official "out there." Nor do we come to institutions alone. We live them in historically specific ways, and we live them—we must insist on this now, when it has become all the more difficult to do so—as collective or as virtually collective subjects.

To read everyday life, what Hegel called "the prose of the world," is therefore to become engaged in an act of *poesis*. This means, for instance, that the everyday should not be assumed to be some quality inherent only in the great realist or mimetic narratives of the nineteenth and early twentieth centuries. Nor, as we suggested earlier, should it be located only in those specifically mimetic moments in a given text. It means, more importantly, that we understand *poesis* in the sense of a transformative or creative act. Everyday life harbors the texture of social change; to perceive it at all is to recognize the necessity of its conscious transformation.

2
Lefebvre on the Situationists:
An Interview

In the introduction to a recent anthology of Henri Lefebvre's writings on the city, the editors of the volume comment that the relationship between Lefebvrian and Situationist concepts awaits a serious study.* What follows is less a serious study than an at-times-playful conversation in which Henri Lefebvre recalls his relationship with Guy Debord and the Situationist International. The interview, if it may be called that, took place in 1983 at the University of California at Santa Cruz, where Lefebvre, on the invitation of Fredric Jameson, was a visiting scholar in residence. I had then just begun my own reading of Lefebvre and the Situationists, research that would result in a book on Rimbaud and an issue of *Yale French Studies* coedited with Alice Kaplan on "everyday life."† From the outset of the conversation, it was evident that Lefebvre, then in his eighties, had very clear ideas of the directions he wanted to pursue.

---

* Henri Lefebvre, *Writings on Cities*, ed. and trans. Eleonore Kofman and Elizabeth Lebas (Oxford: Blackwell, 1996), p. 13. This interview and other translations from the French in this volume are, unless otherwise noted, my own; the interview was transcribed by Marie-France Nizet Sangrones.

† See Chapter 1.

H.L. Are you going to ask the questions about the Situationists? Because I have something I'd like to talk about.

K.R. Fine, go ahead.

H.L. The Situationists ... it's a delicate subject, one I care deeply about. It touches me in some ways very intimately because I knew them very well. I was close friends with them. The friendship lasted from 1957 to 1961 or '62, which is to say about five years. And then we had a quarrel that got worse and worse in conditions I don't understand too well myself but which I could describe to you. In the end, it was a love story that ended badly, very badly. There are love stories that begin well and end badly. And this was one of them.

I remember a whole night spent talking at Guy Debord's place where he was living with Michèle Bernstein in a kind of studio near the place I was living on the rue Saint Martin, in a dark room, no lights at all, a veritable ... a miserable place, but, at the same time, a place where there was a great deal of strength and radiance in the thinking and the research.

K.R. They had no money?

H.L. No ...

K.R. How did they live?

H.L. No one could figure out how they got by. One day, one of my friends (someone to whom I had introduced Debord) asked him, "What do you live on?" And Guy Debord answered very proudly, "I live off my wits" [je vie *d'expédients*]. [*Laughter*] Actually, he must have had some money; I think that his family wasn't poor. His parents lived on the Côte d'Azur. I don't think I really know the answer. And also, Michèle Bernstein had come up with a very clever way to make money, or at least a bit of money. Or at least this is what she told me. She said that she did horoscopes for horses, which were published in racing magazines. It was extremely funny. She determined the date of birth of the horses and did their horoscope in order to predict the outcome of the race. And I think there were racing magazines that published them and paid her.

K.R. So the Situationist slogan "Never work" didn't apply to women?

H.L. Yes it did, because this wasn't work. They didn't work; they managed to live without working to quite a large extent—of course, they had to do something. To do horoscopes for race-horses, I suppose, wasn't really work; in any case I think it was fun to do it, and they didn't really work.

But I'd like to go farther back in time, because everything started much earlier. It started with the CoBrA group. They were the intermediaries: the group made up of architects, with Constant in particular (the architect from Amsterdam), and Asger Jorn (the painter), and people from Brussels—it was a Nordic group, a group with considerable ambitions. They wanted to renew art, renew the action of art on life. It was an extremely interesting and active group, which came together in the 1950s, and one of the books that inspired the founding of the group was my book *Critique de la vie quotidienne.* That's why I got involved with them from such an early date. And the pivotal figure was Constant Nieuwenhuys, the utopian architect who designed a utopian city, New Babylon—a provocative name, since in the Protestant tradition Babylon is a figure of evil. New Babylon was to be the figure of good which took the name of the cursed city and transformed itself into the city of the future. The design for New Babylon dates from 1950. And, in 1953, Constant published a text called *For an Architecture of Situation.* This was a fundamental text based on the idea that

---

* Henri Lefebvre, *Critique de la vie quotidienne*, 3 vols. (Paris: L'Arche, 1947–81); English translation of Volume 1, *Critique of Everyday Life* (London: Verso, 1991).

architecture would allow a transformation of daily reality. This was the connection with *Critique de la vie quotidienne*: to create an architecture that would itself instigate the creation of new situations. So, this text was the beginning of a whole new research that developed in the following years, especially since Constant was very close to popular movements; he was one of the instigators of the Provos, the Provo movement.

K.R. So there was a direct relationship between Constant and the Provos?

H.L. Oh yes, he was recognized by them as their thinker, their leader, the one who wanted to transform life and the city. The relation was direct; he spurred them on.

It's important to understand the periodization of the times. Politically, 1956 was an important year because of the end of Stalinism. There was Khrushchev's famous report to the Twentieth Congress of the Communist Party in the USSR, where he demolished the figure of Stalin—a report that was much

Henri Lefebvre, Nepenthe, Big Sur, California, 1983.

© Kristin Ross

discussed, argued about. In France, people claimed that it was false, that it had been invented by the American secret service. In fact, it was entirely the work of the one who succeeded Stalin, Nikita Khrushchev—and who demolished the figure of his predecessor. We have to keep the periodization in mind. During the postwar years, the figure of Stalin was dominant. And the communist movement was *the* revolutionary movement. Then, after '56 or '57, revolutionary movements moved outside the organized parties, especially with Fidel Castro. In this sense, Situationism wasn't at all isolated. Its point of origin was Holland, Paris too, but Holland especially, and it was linked to many events on the world scale, especially the fact that Fidel Castro succeeded in a revolutionary victory completely outside of the communist movement and the workers' movement. This was an event. And I remember that in 1957 I published a kind of manifesto, *Le romantisme révolutionnaire*, which was linked to the Castro story and to all the movements happening a little bit everywhere that were outside of the parties. This was when I left the Communist Party myself. I felt that there were going to be a lot of things happening outside the established parties and organized movements like unions.

There was going to be a spontaneity outside of organizations and institutions—that's what this text from 1957 was about. It was this text that put me into contact with the Situationists, because they attached a certain importance to it—before attacking it later on. They had their critiques to make, of course: we were never completely in agreement, but the article was the basis for a certain understanding that lasted for four or five years—we kept coming back to it.

K.R. And at this point you were working on the second volume of the *Critique de la vie quotidienne?*

H.L. Yes, and also on a book about the Paris Commune.

K.R. You were working on both at once?

H.L. Yes, at the same time, in a state of confusion. It was the moment when I left the party, the moment of the Algerian War. There was a lot going on ... I was almost fired. I went before commissions for having ... I wasn't in the university, I was a research director at the CNRS, and I was almost dismissed for having signed manifestos for the Algerians and for having offered support—a feeble support, of course—to the Algerian cause. It was a moment of intense ferment. But, in France, support for the Algerians didn't happen through the party, nor through the official organizations within the party or through the unions; it went on outside the institutions. The Communist Party only supported the Algerians grudgingly, in appearance only. In fact, they hardly helped them at all, and afterwards the Algerians were very angry with the party. An oppositional group within the party, and also the movement outside of the party—these were the only ones that supported the Algerians, and that played a role in this story, since we have to situate it within the context of the times and the political context.

And then there were the rather extremist movements like that of Isidore Isou and the Lettrists. They also had ambitions on an international scale. But that was all a joke. It was evident in the way that Isidore Isou would recite his Dadaist poetry made up of meaningless syllables and fragments of words. He would recite it in cafés. I remember very well having met him several times in Paris.

But even that showed a certain ferment in French life, which was crystallized in the return of de Gaulle to power in 1958. The Communist Party showed a deep incapacity by not understanding Stalinism, by doing nothing for the Algerians, and by opposing de Gaulle's return to power very ineffectively, limiting itself to calling de Gaulle a fascist, which wasn't exactly the case. De Gaulle wanted to bring order to the Algerian question. He was the only one who could; we realized that later on. But, throughout, the period was one of a great ferment, comparable to 1936.

K.R. Did the Situationist theory of constructing situations have a direct relationship with your theory of "moments"?

H.L. Yes that was the basis of our understanding. They more or less said to me during discussions—discussions that lasted whole nights—"What you call 'moments,' we call 'situations,' but we're taking it farther than you. You accept as 'moments' everything that has occurred in the course of history: love, poetry, thought. We want to create new moments."

K.R. How did they propose to make the transition from a "moment" to a conscious construction?

H.L. The idea of a new moment, of a new situation, was already there in Constant's text from 1953: *Pour une architecture de situation*. Because the architecture of situation is a utopian architecture that supposes a new society, Constant's idea was that society must be transformed not in order to continue a boring, uneventful life, but in order to create something absolutely new: situations.

K.R. And how did the city figure into this?

H.L. Well, "new situations" was never very clear. When we talked about it, I always gave as an example—and they would have nothing to do with my example—love. I said to them: In antiquity, passionate love was known, but not individual love, love for an individual. The poets of antiquity write of a kind of cosmic, physical, physiological passion. But love for an individual only appears in the Middle Ages within a mixture of Islamic and Christian traditions, especially in the South of France. Individual love is Dante's love for Beatrice: *la vita nuova*, new life. It's the love between Tristan and Yseult, tragic love—courtly love in the South of France. Where I come from near Navarrenx, there is the tower of Prince Gaston Phébus, who was the first prince-troubadour to sing songs about individual love: "When I sing, I do not sing for me, but I sing for my friend who is close to me." This is already individual love, the tragedy or individual love which endures throughout the centuries, in *La Princesse de Clèves*, in novels, theaters, in Racine's *Bérénice*, through all of literature.

K.R. But didn't constructing "new situations" for the Situationists involve urbanism?

H.L. Yes. We agreed. I said to them, individual love created new situations; there was a creation of situations. But it didn't happen in a day, it developed. Their idea (and this was also related to Constant's experiments) was that, in the city, one could create new situations by, for example, linking up parts of the city, neighborhoods that were separated spatially. And that was the first meaning of the *dérive*. It was done first in Amsterdam, using walkie-talkies. There was one group that went to one part of the city and could communicate with people in another area.

K.R. Did the Situationists use this technique, too?

H.L. Oh, I think so. In any case, Constant did. But there were Situationist experiments in Unitary Urbanism. Unitary Urbanism consisted of making different parts of the city communicate with one another. They did their experiments; I didn't participate. They used all kinds of means of communication—I don't know when exactly they were using walkie-talkies. But I know they were used in Amsterdam and in Strasbourg.

K.R. Did you know people in Strasbourg then?

H.L. They were my students. But relations with them were also very strained. When I arrived in Strasbourg in 1958 or '59, it was right in the middle of the Algerian War, and I had only been in Strasbourg for about three weeks, maybe, when a group of guys came up to me. They were the future Situationists of Strasbourg—or maybe they were already a little bit Situationist. They said to me: "We need your support, we're going to set up a *maquis* in the Vosges. We're going to make a military base in the Vosges, and from there spread out over the whole country. We're going to derail trains." I replied: "But the army and the police ... you aren't sure of having the support of the population. You're precipitating a catastrophe." So, they began to insult me and call me a traitor. And, after a little while, a few weeks, they came back to see me and told me: "You were right, it's impossible. It's impossible to set up a military base in the Vosges ... We're going to work on something else."

So, I found myself getting along with them, and afterward they became Situationists, the same group that wanted to support the Algerians by starting up military activity in France—it was crazy. But, you know, my relations with them were always very difficult. They got angry over nothing. I was living at the time with a young woman from Strasbourg; I was the scandal of the university. She was pregnant, she had a daughter (my daughter Armelle), and it was the town scandal—a horror, an abomination. Strasbourg was a very bourgeois city. And the university wasn't outside the city, it was right in the middle. But, at the same time, I was giving lectures that were very successful, on music, for example—music and society. I taught a whole course one year on "music and society"; many people attended, so I could only be attacked with difficulty. Armelle's mother, Nicole, was friends with the Situationists. She was always with them; she invited them over. They came to eat at our place, and we played music—this was scandal in Strasbourg. So that's how I came to have close relations, organic relations, with them—not only because I taught Marxism at the university, but through Nicole, who was an intermediary. Guy came to my place to see Nicole, to eat dinner. But relations were difficult, they got angry over tiny things. Mustapha Khayati, author of the brochure, was in the group.

K.R. What was the effect of the brochure [*De la misère en milieu étudiant*]?* How many copies were given out?

H.L. Oh, it was very successful. But, in the beginning, it was only distributed in Strasbourg; then, Debord and others distributed it in Paris. Thousands and thousands were given out, certainly tens of thousands of copies to students. It's a very good brochure, without a doubt. Its author, Mustapha Khayati, was Tunisian. There were several Tunisians in the group, many foreigners who were less talked about afterward, and even Mustapha Khayati didn't show himself very often at the time because he might have had problems because of his nationality. He didn't have dual citizenship; he stayed a Tunisian and he could have had real troubles. But, anyway, in Paris, after 1957, I saw a lot of them, and I was also spending time with Constant in Amsterdam. This was the moment when the Provo movement became very powerful in Amsterdam. With their idea of keeping urban life intact, preventing the city from being eviscerated by autoroutes and being opened up to automobile traffic. They wanted the city to be conserved and transformed instead of being given over to traffic. They also wanted drugs; they seemed to count on drugs to create new situations—imagination sparked by LSD. It was LSD in those days.

K.R. Among the Parisian Situationists too?

H.L. No. Very little. They drank. At Guy Debord's place we drank tequila with a little mezcal added. But never ... mescaline, a

---

* L'Internationale situationniste, *De la misère en milieu étudiant considéré sous ses aspects économique, politique, psychologique, sexuel et notamment intellectuel et de quelques moyens pour y remédier* (1966: Paris: Editions Champ Libre, 1976). An English translation appears in *Situationist International Anthology*, ed. Ken Knabb (Berkeley: Bureau of Public Secrets, 1981).

little, but many of them took nothing at all. That wasn't the way they wanted to create new situations.

K.R. To return to Unitary Urbanism, this way of linking *quartiers* together without creating homogeneity. Each *quartier* retained its distinct aspects, right?

H.L. Yes, they didn't merge together; they're already a whole, but a whole that is in some sense fragmented and is only in a virtual state. The idea is to make of the city a whole, but a whole in movement, a whole in transformation.

The plans for New Babylon were given to the National Museum in The Hague. They were in Constant's studio, which was in a half-demolished brick building. The most striking thing I remember about Constant's studio was what was in an immense cage: an iguana.

K.R. Now, *there's* a new situation.

H.L. He lived on intimate terms with an iguana.

KR. Was Constant's project predicated on the end of work?

H.L. Yes, to a certain extent. Yes, that's the beginning: complete mechanization, the complete automatization of productive work, which left people free to do other things. He was one of the ones who considered the problem.

K.R. And the Situationists too?

H.L. Yes.

K.R. Do you also situate your work in that lineage? From Lafargue to … ?

H.L. Yes, but not from Lafargue. I think my starting point was a science fiction novel called *City*. It's an American novel by [Clifford] Simak in which work is performed by robots. Humans can't stand the situation; they die because they are so used to working. They die, and the dogs that are left take advantage of the situation. The robots work for them, feed them, and so forth. And the dogs are perfectly happy because they aren't deformed by the work habit. I remember the role played by this novel in our discussions. I don't remember when it came out in the United States, but I think it's one of the first science fiction novels that was acclaimed and had influence, but it was maybe only in those years. In any case, that was Constant's starting point: a society liberated from work. And it was in the orientation of Lafargue's *Droit â la paresse*, but renewed by the perspective of automation which began in those years.

And so, a complete change in revolutionary movements beginning in 1956–57, movements that leave behind classic organizations. What's beautiful is the voice of small groups having influence ...

K.R. So the very existence of microsocieties or groupuscules like the Situationists was itself a new situation?

H.L. Yes, to a certain extent. But then again, we mustn't exaggerate either. For how many of them were there? You know that the Situationist International never had more than ten members. There were two or three Belgians, two or three Dutch, like Constant. But they were all expelled immediately. Guy Debord followed André Breton's example. People were expelled. I was never a part of the group. I could have been, but I was careful, since I knew Guy Debord's character and his manner, and the way he had of imitating André Breton, by expelling everyone in order to get at a pure and hard little core. In the end, the members of the Situationist International were Guy Debord, Raoul Vaneigem, and Michèle Bernstein. There were some outer groupuscules, satellite groups, where I was, and where Asger Jorn was too. Asger Jorn had been expelled; poor Constant was expelled as well. For what reason? Well, Constant didn't build anything, he never built anything—he was an architect who didn't build, a utopian architect. But he was expelled because a guy who worked with him built a church, in Germany: expulsion for reason of disastrous influence. It's rubbish. It was really about keeping oneself in a pure state, like a crystal. Debord's dogmatism was exactly like Breton's. And, what's more, it was a dogmatism without a dogma, since the theory of situations, of the creation of situations, disappeared very quickly, leaving behind only the critique of the existing world, which is where it all started, with the *Critique de la vie quotidienne*.

K.R. How did your association with the Situationists change or inspire your thinking about the city? Did it change your thinking or not?

H.L. It was all corollary, parallel. My thinking about the city had completely different sources. Where I come from—an agricultural region—I had been studying agricultural questions for a long time. One bright day, in my region, bulldozers arrived and started leveling the trees—they had discovered oil there. There are oil wells in my region, not very many, but still a significant number; one of the biggest refineries in Europe was at Mourenx, Lacq-Mourenx.

So then I saw a new city being built where before there were only fields and oak forests. This began in 1953–54. Little by little, I left the agricultural questions behind, saying to myself, now here's something new, something important. I didn't expect the very brutal urbanization that followed. That new city was called Lacq-Mourenx, "ville nouvelle." Since I was at the CNRS, I sent some people there right away to watch the development. I even wanted to write a book—which I never did, like so many projects—entitled *Birth of a City*. That was the starting point. But, at the same time, I met Guy Debord, I met Constant, I knew that the Provos in Amsterdam were interested in the city, and I went there to see what was going on, maybe ten times. Just to see the form that the movement was

taking, if it took a political form. There were Provos elected
to the city council in Amsterdam. I forget which year, but
they pulled off a big victory in the municipal elections. Then,
after that, it all fell apart. All this was part and parcel of the
same thing. And, after 1960, there was the great movement in
urbanization. They abandoned the theory of Unitary Urbanism, since Unitary Urbanism only had a precise meaning for
historic cities like Amsterdam that had to be renewed, transformed. But, from the moment that the historic city exploded
into peripheries, suburbs—like what happened in Paris, and in
all sorts of places, Los Angeles, San Francisco, wild extensions
of the city—the theory of Unitary Urbanism lost any meaning.
I remember very sharp, pointed discussions with Guy Debord,
when he said that urbanism was becoming an ideology. He was
absolutely right, from the moment that there was an official
doctrine on urbanism. I think the urbanism code dates from
1961 in France—that's the moment when urbanism becomes an
ideology. That doesn't mean that the problem of the city was
resolved—far from it. But, at that point, they abandoned the
theory of Unitary Urbanism. And then I think that even the
dérive, the *dérive* experiments were, little by little, abandoned
around then too. I'm not sure how that happened, because that
was the moment I broke with them.

After all, there's the political context in France, and there
are also personal relations, very complicated stories. The most
complicated story arose when they came to my place in the
Pyrenees. And we took a wonderful trip: we left Paris in a
car and stopped at the Lascaux caves, which were closed not
long after that. We were very taken up with the problem of the
Lascaux caves. They are buried very deep, with even a well
that was inaccessible—and all this filled with paintings. How
were these paintings made, who were they made for, since they

weren't painted in order to be seen? The idea was that painting started as a critique. All the more so in that all the churches in the region have crypts. We stopped at Saint-Savin, where there are frescoes on the church's vaulted dome and a crypt full of paintings, a crypt whose depths are difficult to reach because it is so dark. What are paintings that were not destined to be seen? And how were they made? So, we made our way south; we had a fabulous feast in Sarlat, and I could hardly drive—I was the one driving. I got a ticket; we were almost arrested because I crossed a village going 120 kilometers per hour. They stayed several days at my place, and working together, we wrote a programmatic text. At the end of the week they spent at Navarrenx, they kept the text. I said to them, "You type it," (it was handwritten) and afterwards they accused me of plagiarism. In reality, this was complete bad faith. The text that was used in writing the book about the Commune was a joint text, by them and by me, and only one small part of the Commune book was taken from the joint text.

I had this idea about the Commune as a festival, and I threw it out into debate, after consulting an unpublished document about the Commune which is at the Feltrinelli Foundation in Milan. It's a diary about the Commune. The person who kept the diary, who was deported, by the way, and who brought back his diary from deportation several years later, around 1880, recounts how, on March 28, 1871, Thiers's soldiers came to look for the cannons that were in Montmartre and on the hills of Belleville; how the women who got up very early in the morning heard the noise and all ran out in the streets and surrounded the soldiers, laughing, having fun, greeting them in a friendly way. Then they went off to get coffee and offered it to the soldiers, and these soldiers who had come to get the cannons were more or less carried away by the people. First the

women, then the men, everyone came out, in an atmosphere
of popular festival. The Commune cannon incident was not
at all a situation of armed heroes arriving and combating the
soldiers taking the cannons. It didn't happen at all like that. It
was the people who came out of their houses, who were enjoy-
ing themselves. The weather was beautiful, March 28 was the
first day of spring, it was sunny: the women kiss the soldiers,
they're relaxed, and the soldiers are absorbed into all of that,
a Parisian popular festival. But this diary is an exception. And,
afterwards, the theorists of the heroes of the Commune said
to me, "This is a testimonial, you can't write history from a
testimonial." The Situationists said more or less the same thing.
I didn't read what they said; I did my work. There were ideas
that were batted around in conversation, and then worked up
in common texts. And then afterwards, I wrote my study on
the Commune. I worked for weeks in Milan, at the Feltrinelli
Institute; I found unpublished documentation, I used it, and
that's completely my right. Listen, I don't care at all about
these accusations of plagiarism. And I never took the time to
read what they wrote about it in their journal. I know that I
was dragged through the dirt.

And then, as for how I broke with them, it happened after
an extremely complicated story concerning the journal *Arguments*. The idea had come up to stop editing *Arguments* because
several of the collaborators in the journal, such as my friend
Kostas Axelos, thought that its role was over; they thought
they had nothing more to say. In fact, I have the text by Axelos
where he talks about the dissolution of the group and of the
journal; they thought it was finished and that it would be better to end it rather than let it drag along. I was kept informed
of these discussions. During discussions with Guy Debord,
we talked about it and Debord said to me, "Our journal, the

Internationale situationniste, has to replace *Arguments.*" And, so, *Arguments*'s editor, and all the people there, had to agree. Everything depended on a certain man, François Erval, who was very powerful at the time in publishing, he did a literary chronicle for *L'Express,* he was also in with the *Nouvelle Revue française* and the Editions de Minuit. He was extremely powerful, and everything depended on him.

Well, at that moment, I had broken up with a woman— very bitterly. She left me, and she took my address book with her. This meant I no longer had Erval's address. I telephoned Debord and told him I was perfectly willing to continue negotiations with Erval, but that I no longer had his address, his phone number—nothing. Debord began insulting me over the phone. He was furious and said, "I'm used to people like you who become traitors at the decisive moment." That's how the rupture between us began, and it continued in a curious way.

This woman, Eveline—who, I forgot to mention, was a longtime friend of Michèle Bernstein—had left me, and Nicole took her place, and Nicole was pregnant. She wanted the child, and so did I: Armelle. But Guy Debord and our little Situationist friends sent a young woman to Navarrenx over Easter vacation one year to try to persuade Nicole to get an abortion.

K.R. Why?

H.L. Because they didn't know, or they didn't want to know, that Nicole wanted this child just as I did. Can you believe that this woman, whose name was Denise and who was particularly unbearable, had been sent to persuade Nicole to have an abortion and leave me, in order to be with them? Then I understood—Nicole told me about it right away. She told me, "You know, this woman is on a mission from Guy Debord; they want me to leave you and get rid of the kid." So, since I already didn't much like Denise, I threw her out. Denise was the girlfriend of that Situationist who had learned Chinese—I forget his name. I'm telling you this because it's all very complex, everything gets mixed up: political history, ideology, women ... but there was a time when it was a real, very warm friendship.

K.R. You even wrote an article entitled "You Will All Be Situationists."

H.L. Oh yes, I did that to help bring about the replacement of *Arguments* by the *Internationale Situationniste* ... Guy Debord accused me of having done nothing to get it published. Yes, it was Erval who was supposed to publish it. Lucky for me that it didn't appear because, afterwards, they would have reproached me for it.

But there's a point I want to go back to—the question of plagiarism. That bothered me quite a bit. Not a lot, just a little bit. We worked together *day and night* at Navarrenx, we went to sleep at nine in the morning (that was how they lived, going to sleep in the morning and sleeping all day). We ate nothing. It was appalling. I suffered throughout the week, not eating, just drinking. We must have drunk a hundred bottles. In a few days—five ... and we were working while drinking. The text was almost a doctrinal résumé of everything we were thinking, about situations, about transformations of life; it wasn't very long, just a few pages, handwritten. They took it away and typed it up and afterwards thought they had a right to the ideas. These were ideas we tossed around on a little country walk I took them on—with a nice touch of perversity I took them down a path that led nowhere, that got lost in the woods, fields, and so on. Michèle Bernstein had a complete nervous breakdown, she didn't enjoy it at all ... It's true, it wasn't urban, it was very deep in the country.

K.R. A rural *dérive*. Let's talk a bit about the *dérive* in general. Do you think it brought anything new to spatial theory or to urban theory? In the way that it emphasized experimental games and practices, do you think it was more productive than a purely theoretical approach to the city?

H.L. Yes. As I perceived it, the *dérive* was more of a practice than a theory. It revealed the growing fragmentation of the city. In the course of its history, the city was once a powerful organic unity; for some time, however, that unity was becoming undone, was fragmenting, and they were recording examples of what we all had been talking about, like the place where the new Bastille Opera is going to be built. The Place de la Bastille is the end of historic Paris—beyond that it's the Paris of the first industrialization of the nineteenth century. The Place des Vosges is still aristocratic Paris of the seventeenth century. When you get to the Bastille, another Paris begins, which is of the nineteenth century, but it's the Paris of the bourgeoisie, of commercial, industrial expansion, at the same time that the commercial and industrial bourgeoisie takes hold of the Marais, the center of Paris—it spreads out beyond the Bastille, the rue de la Roquette, the rue du Faubourg Saint-Antoine, etc. So, already, the city is becoming fragmented. We had a vision of a city that was more and more fragmented without its organic unity being completely shattered. Afterwards, of course, the peripheries and the suburbs highlighted the problem. But, back then, it wasn't yet obvious, and we thought that the practice of the *dérive* revealed the idea of the fragmented city. But it was mostly done in Amsterdam. The experiment consisted of rendering different aspects or fragments of the city simul- taneous, fragments that can only be seen successively, in the same way that there exist people who have never seen certain parts of the city.

K.R. While the *dérive* took the form of a narrative.

H.L. That's it; one goes along in any direction and recounts what one sees.

K.R. But the recounting can't be done simultaneously.

H.L. Yes, it can, if you have a walkie-talkie; the goal was to attain a certain simultaneity. That was the goal—it didn't always work.

K.R. So, a kind of synchronic history.

H.L. Yes, that's it, a synchronic history. That was the meaning of Unitary Urbanism: unify what has a certain unity, but a lost unity, a disappearing unity.

K.R. And it was during the time when you knew the Situationists that the idea of Unitary Urbanism began to lose its force?

H.L. At the moment when urbanization became truly massive; that is, after 1960, and when the city, Paris, completely exploded. You know that there were very few suburbs in Paris; there were some, but very few. And then, suddenly, the whole area was filled, covered with little houses, with new cities, Sarcelles and the rest. Sarcelles became a kind of myth. There was even a disease that people called the "sarcellite." And around then Guy Debord's attitude changed—he went from Unitary Urbanism to the thesis of urbanistic ideology.

K.R. And what was that transition, exactly?

H.L. It was more than a transition, it was the abandonment of one position in order to adopt the exact opposite one. Between the idea of elaborating an urbanism and the thesis that all urbanism is an ideology is a profound modification. In fact, by saying that all urbanism was a bourgeois ideology, they abandoned the problem of the city. They left it behind. They thought that the problem no longer interested them. While I, on the other hand, continued to be interested; I thought that the explosion of the historic city was precisely the occasion for finding a larger theory of the city, and not a pretext for abandoning the problem. But it wasn't because of this that we fell out; we fell

out for much more sordid reasons. That business about sabo-
taging *Arguments*, Erval's lost address—all that was completely
ridiculous. But there were certainly deeper reasons.

The theory of situations was itself abandoned, little by little,
And the journal itself became a political organ. They began to
insult everyone. That was part of Debord's attitude, or it might
have been part of his difficulties—he split up with Michèle
Bernstein. I don't know, there were all kinds of circumstances
that might have made him more polemical, more bitter, more
violent. In the end, everything became oriented toward a kind
of polemical violence. I think they ended up insulting just about
everyone. And they also greatly exaggerated their role in May
'68, after the fact.

The '68 movement didn't come from the Situationists. At
Nanterre, there was a little groupuscule known as *"les enragés."*
They were insulting everyone too. But they were the ones who
made the movement. The movement of March 22 was made
by students, among them Daniel Cohn-Bendit, who was not
a Situationist.

It was an energetic group that took form as the events
developed, with no program, no project—an informal group,
with whom the Situationists linked up, but it wasn't they
who constituted the group. The group took shape apart from
them—Trotskyists joined up with the March 22 group, every-
body ended up joining with them little by little. We called it
"getting aboard a moving train." So, even though the Situationists at Nanterre may have joined up with the group from
the outset, they weren't the animators, the creative element.
In fact, the movement began in a big, crowded amphitheater
where I was giving a course, and where students whom I knew
well asked me if we could name some delegates to go to the
administration to protest the blacklist. (The administration was

insisting on establishing a list of the most disruptive students in order to sanction them.) "Of course," I said. So it was on that podium that the election took place of delegates to protest the blacklist business. And all sorts of people participated in that election, Trotskyists as well as Situationists.

The group of March 22 was formed after these negotiations and arguments with the administration, and then the group occupied the administration building. The stimulus was this business about the blacklist, and I was the one who concocted the blacklist. What actually happened was that the administration phoned my office and asked for a list of the most politically disruptive students. I told them to get lost; I frequently had to say to the dean in those days, "Sir, I am not a cop." So, the blacklist never existed, in black and white. But they were trying to do it, and I told the students to defend themselves; I stirred things up a bit. One has one's little perversities, after all.

I always tell the story. On Friday evening, May 13, we were all at the Place Denfert-Rochereau. Around the Belfort lion, there were maybe seventy or eighty thousand students discussing what to do next. The Maoists wanted to go out to the suburbs toward Ivry; the anarchos and the Situationists wanted to go make noise in the bourgeois quarters. The Trotskyists were in favor of heading for the proletarian districts, the eleventh arrondissement, while the students from Nanterre wanted to go to the Latin Quarter. Then some people cried out, "We've got friends in the Prison de la Santé—let's go see them!" And then the whole crowd started off down the Boulevard Arago toward the Prison de la Santé. We saw hands at the windows, we yelled things, and then we headed off toward the Latin Quarter. It was chance. Or maybe it wasn't chance at all. There must have been a desire to go back to the Latin Quarter; to not get too far away from the center of student life.

There must have been some obscure feeling of attachment to the Latin Quarter ... it was curious, after that hour of floating around, not knowing which way to go. And then, in the Latin Quarter, the television was there, until midnight, that is. Then there was just the radio, Europe No. 1. And, at about three in the morning—in complete bedlam, there was noise from all directions—a radio guy handed the microphone to Daniel Cohn-Bendit, who had the brilliant idea of simply saying: "General strike, general strike, general strike." And that was the decisive moment; it was then that there was action. That was what took the police by surprise. That students were making trouble, that there was a little violence, some wounded, tear gas, paving stones, barricades, and bombs—that was all just the children of the bourgeoisie having a good time. But a general strike, well, that was no laughing matter.

3

The Sociologist and the Priest

One of the achievements of Brian Rigby's history of the discourse surrounding twentieth-century French popular culture is the way his narrative points to the 1970s as a moment of transformation, a turning point in that history.[*] His work has helped me clarify the directions I'd like to take in this essay toward a more focused study of some of the key aspects and figures of the French '70s—a decade that saw not only a resurgence of and transformation of older debates surrounding conceptions of *le peuple*, "the popular," and the relation of rural to urban, but also the end of the postwar economic boom (the *Trente Glorieuses*) and the installation of a worldwide—not merely French—economic crisis. That crisis is, of course, still with us a quarter of a century later; its manifestations include a massive and tenacious recurrence of unemployment in the West, the collapse of the Soviet Union, and a catastrophic level of indebtedness lived chronically by certain regions of the Third World.

When did "popular culture" cease to be a class category? At what point in French postwar history did popular culture become

---

[*] Brian Rigby, *Popular Culture in Modern France: A Study of Cultural Discourse* (London and New York: Routledge, 1991).

detached from the ties that had formerly bound it to particular class constituencies—to urban working-class culture, for one, or to traditional peasant culture, for another? When, in other words, and under what conditions did French popular culture become mass culture?

Today, when a field of French cultural studies is beginning to emerge and distinguish itself from more established British and American variants, posing these kinds of historical questions about the object of study itself is, I think, all the more crucial. I like to think that, by keeping a historicizing project at the forefront, French cultural studies can avoid the presentist tendencies and errors that have marked the development of cultural studies in the United States (tendencies begotten largely, I might add, under the influence of the 1970s French theorists I focus on in this paper).

The years following May '68 are also now widely viewed as a period of accelerated flight on the part of French intellectuals from historical materialism, from the national, political spheres more generally—in short, a decade of depoliticization. And, as the author of an earlier, explicitly political work on popular culture, *Mythologies*, once advised, I think it is important when considering this period to give an active value to the prefix "de" in "depoliticized," to see how it represents an action, how it actualizes a continuous defection.

In the case of one of the writers then at the forefront of popular culture analysis, Michel de Certeau, that defection is made manifest by a palpable anxiety in his work surrounding the use of certain vocabulary, notably the words that named the very object of his study, words like *le peuple* or *populaire*. De Certeau is certainly not alone among analysts of popular culture in exhibiting this anxiety. A recent book by Jean-Claude Passeron and Claude Grignon, for example, was written, according to the authors' preface, entirely as an attempt to deal with and analyze the embarrassment they felt whenever they or anyone else they knew evoked *le peuple.* Rigby and others have charted the use of scare quotes around the expression "popular" as a map of anxiety, or, at the very least, as a sign of the need to indicate the author's distance from any naive or sentimentalized notion of the lower classes. At an earlier historical moment, in the writing of explicitly political postwar figures best represented by Sartre, the dilemma was not so much one of vocabulary as it was that of the intellectual's relation to the people. This was the question that was brought to the forefront in an urgent manner by the revolutionary urbanism of students and workers during May '68, a form of urbanist praxis which, as Henri Lefebvre wrote after the events had subsided, "restored the term political to its oldest meaning—the theoretical and practical knowledge of the social life of the community."[†] In the immediate period after the insurrection, the question of the intellectual/worker relationship gave rise to the *établi* experiments, when intellectuals literally "went to the people" by taking up positions on the Renault assembly lines.[‡] And it was that political dilemma too that informed the analyses of nineteenth-century popular culture produced by a group of historians and philosophers formed, so to speak, by the events of May: Jacques Rancière and the editorial collective of the journal *Révoltes Logiques*. Throughout the 1970s, *Révoltes Logiques* published the most sustained theoretical and historical analyses of the problem of workers' knowledge and its relation

---

* Claude Grignon and Jean-Claude Passeron, *Le Savant et le populaire: Misérabilisme et populisme en sociologie et en littérature* (Paris: Seuil, 1989).

† Henri Lefebvre, *The Explosion: Marxism and the French Upheaval* (New York: Monthly Review Press, 1969), p. 155. Trans. A. Ehrenfeld from *L'Irruption de Nanterre au sommet* (Paris, 1968).

‡ See, for example, Robert Linhart, *L'Etobli* (Paris: Editions de Minuit, 1978); trans. Margaret Crosland as *The Assembly Line* (Amherst: University of Massachusetts Press, 1981).

to bourgeois culture. In his own studies of worker-poets and worker-philosophers, Rancière, in effect, took the great *gauchiste* theme—the relations between intellectual and manual work—and put it in reverse: "not the re-education of intellectuals, but the eruption of negativity, of *thinking,* into a social category always defined by the positivity of *doing.*"*

But de Certeau's anxiety in the 1970s around the problem of *le peuple* is of a different order from that of Sartre or Rancière. In an article entitled "Pratiques quotidiennes" that appeared in 1979 in a collection on "popular cultures" and that essentially laid out the groundwork for his book *L'Invention du quotidien,* published the following year, de Certeau appears to think that, by eliminating the term, he will eliminate the problem. Casually, almost in passing, but nevertheless explicitly, he targets several key analytic terms for annihilation or substitution. Thus, he prefaces his discussion by writing:

> I would simply like to present to you some work-in-progress on "ways of doing" and "everyday practices" to which I would like to give the name of *ordinary culture,* in order to avoid the accepted expression "popular culture," in which the word popular carries too many ideological connotations.†

"Ordinary culture," sanitized of any ideological content, emerges in this article, and in the book which grew out of it, as the deviations and maneuvers of a more or less "authentic" modern urban folk, the authenticity of whose daily practices derives not from

---

*   Jacques Rancière, interview with Francois Ewald, "Qu'est-ce que la classe ouvrière?," in *Magazine litteraire* 175 (July–Aug. 1981).

†   Michel de Certeau, "Pratiques quotidiennes," in Geneviève Poujol and Raymond Labourie, eds., *Les Cultures populaires: Permanence et émergences des cultures minoritaires, locales, ethniques, sociales et religieuses* (Toulouse: Privat, 1979), p. 23. Translation is Brian Rigby's.

any specific class identity, but rather from their sheer, unknowing ordinariness. In French, the ideological connotations of "popular culture" are twofold: the term is associated either with traditional peasant culture or with urban working-class culture. De Certeau, in effect, wants to move the "folk" to the city: his urban dwellers are not a combative working class but, rather, the historically indeterminate, abiding "folk," complete with their repetitive and accumulative customs. By abandoning the term "popular culture," de Certeau dismisses any political or ideological perception of the working class and helps clear the way for a classless, socially cohesive, consensus portrait of "ordinary culture." And, by erasing or negating the term *peuple*, he in effect masks the specific history of workers' movements: that long, frequently combative battle to reverse domination, to claim dignity, and to improve the conditions of not just cultural, but socio-economic life as well.

De Certeau, in fact, went on to dedicate his book *L'Invention du quotidien* to the emblematic figure of "the ordinary man." "To the ordinary man," he writes, "a common man, a ubiquitous character, walking in countless thousands on the streets."* To the pedestrian, in other words, and not the militant; the stroller, not the street fighter. This was a dedication meant to bridge definitively the gap that once separated those who think from those who do. For not only does the term "ordinary man" paper over any specificities inherent to working-class culture, militant or otherwise, it appears to do the same for intellectual culture. The intellectual is henceforth free to shed his privileges and inhibitions and fuse himself seamlessly into the same ordinary, everyday bath of culture, into a unique and same human nature, neither

---

* Michel de Certeau, *The Practice of Everyday Life* (Berkeley: University of California Press, 1984), preface. Trans. Steven Randall from *L'Invention du quotidien: Arts de faire* (Paris: Union Général d'Editions, 1980).

proletarian nor bourgeois. Where previous efforts to forge cultural alliances between French intellectuals and *le peuple* recognized a difference to be overcome, negotiations to be made, and conflicts to be acknowledged in the building of that alliance, de Certeau's "ordinary man" simply and magically erases the difference from the outset.

Heroic in his very ordinariness, de Certeau's pedestrian is endowed with the means of maneuvering within the urban grid; this ability *seems* to make the pedestrian, to a certain extent, a subject who knows, and this semblance of agency is undoubtedly what is appealing to writers and critics who make use of de Certeau. But what is the nature of this agency? The street confers and confirms subjectivity; the street itself, or at least the backstreets, byways and detours, the roads less traveled by, are the site of deviance or (to use the word preferred by followers of de Certeau) "resistance." But resistance to what? Power, in de Certeau's analysis, is extra-ordinary, on another sphere, on high, in its panoptical towers and atop the girders and skyscrapers devoted to rational planning and urban regulation. The pedestrian is excluded from the workings of power, yet achieves a kind of aesthetic equality or compensation by virtue of his exclusion. Power is extraordinary and thus far away; for that reason, the streets cannot be the site of a struggle—power operates elsewhere, behind closed doors, in the office buildings and the town halls. Power has left the back streets to the ordinary folk, to their "multiform, resistant, tricky and stubborn procedures"*—to the tactical maneuvers, that is, of the relatively powerless, a group disabused of any hope for a change in their circumstances: "The actual order of things," writes de Certeau in *L'Invention du quotidien*, "is precisely what 'popular' tactics turn to their own ends, without any illusion that it is about

---

*   Ibid., p. 96.

to change."* Confrontation, contradiction, change—all these are ruled out in advance. What remains are "tactics and strategies," a vocabulary de Certeau seems to have borrowed from Clausewitz if not from Gramsci's "wars of maneuver," but a vocabulary effectively depoliticized, stripped of all of its connotations of collective struggle, military for Clausewitz, political for Gramsci, and made to denote a series of circular, highly individualized activities that lead nowhere.

In the sentence I just quoted, we note that the word "popular," once banished, has snuck back into de Certeau's writing. In fact, he cannot do without it. Once cleansed of ideology it can be allowed back in, and De Certeau uses the term frequently. Once the "popular," as he puts it, can no longer be seen as the distinguishing quasi-exotic characteristic of a single economic class, then it simply becomes what most people do. "The popular" can then function in his analyses as an unstable term used tautologically to separate a culturally "productive" minority from a vast majority of seemingly passive (though in de Certeau's view, heroically resourceful) consumers.†

But "consumers" is my word, not de Certeau's. In the same article in which he declared his preference for the term "ordinary culture" as a means of avoiding "popular culture," de Certeau makes another important substitution: "For this word consumer, tainted by a cultural and social bias whose meaning is all too clear, I substitute the word user [*pratiquant*]."‡ Are we wrong to detect a quasi-Catholic or at least religious connotation surrounding this establishment of a community of humble *pratiquants*? In any case, a veil has effectively been thrown over the crass economic

---

*   Ibid., p. 26.

†   See Jeremy Ahearne, *Michel de Certeau: Interpretation and its Other* (Stanford: Stanford University Press, 1995), pp. 160–1.

‡   De Certeau, "Pratiques quotidiennes," p. 24.

connotations of "consumer." That veil is perhaps what gives free reign to criticism deriving from de Certeau (much of US cultural studies today) to take the economic, which is to say capitalism, for granted as a kind of naturalized forcefield or switchboard for the processing of meaning—the Salvadoran or Guatemalan selling oranges on the freeways of Los Angeles, for example, becomes a figure of "resistance": someone who has appropriated urban space and is using it to his own devices, someone thumbing his nose at the "master planners." But resistance to what? In de Certeau, tactics add up to no larger strategy, cultural practices, in other words, are not made to refer back to capital nor to offer any means of understanding the system as a whole. And, of course, tactics not authorized by a larger strategy or conception of the whole merely delay strategy into infinity. By concentrating on the periphery and only on the periphery, cultural analysis derived from de Certeau ends up with what Henri Lefebvre, in another context, called "a lot of pinprick operations separated from each other in time and space."* Leaving considerations of power to the center—where, like all good functionalists, de Certeau believes it belongs in the interest of social stability—what is left is life on the periphery which rarely gets incorporated into the division of labor (or so Durkheim believed) but is still allowed to exist because it is no threat to the center's hold. De Certeau's version of the everyday highlights the nondiscursive, non-coded areas that have escaped the grids of planning. But these add up to nothing, except perhaps to the distressing vision of a power everywhere and at all instances present, the heroic vision of politics as resistance, or the ludic vision of mystical spaces of affirmation created by those who turn their back on politics and its games of power. In

---

* Henri Lefebvre, *The Survival of Capitalism* (London: Allison and Busby, 1976), p. 116. Trans. Frank Bryant from *La Survie du capitalisme* (Paris: Editions Anthropos, 1973).

the end, de Certeau's active retreat from the national, political level into a mystical celebration of localisms and *quartierismes* comes to resemble the path taken by the "user," the *pratiquant*, the ordinary man, as he appears in a description by one of de Certeau's collaborators, Pierre Mayol: "Faced with the whole complex network of the city, entangled as it is with codes over which the user has no control ... he succeeds in creating places to which he can withdraw.*

"Ghettos of creativity." This is the way Henri Lefebvre described the same set of homey rituals, local practices, and hobbies held up by de Certeau as so many "resistances": "Ghettos of creativity," writes Lefebvre, "scaled down, hygienic and functional."[†] This should not surprise us. In Lefebvre's work the quotidian is not synonymous, as it is in de Certeau's, with the local or the peripheral. But what might be surprising, at least initially, is that Lefebvre is willing to grant everyday, popular practices a value that de Certeau does not: that of creativity. The problem with such practices, as Lefebvre sees it, is their isolation from each other and their distance from the center of power, as well as the functionalized role they are forced to play, as a kind of commodified leisure, in supporting the rhythm of capitalist production. Nevertheless, he does not deny them creativity. It is de Certeau, on the other hand, the defender of a new level of activity or what some call agency, on the part of the ordinary man, who wants to erase the term "creativity." "I purposely avoid the term of everyday 'creativity,'" he writes in "Pratiques quotidiennes," "because of its elitism and its ambiguities."[‡]

---

* Luce Giard and Pierre Mayol, *L'invention du quotidien*, vol. 2, *Habiter, cuisiner* (Paris: Union générale d'éditions,1980), p. 18.

† Henri Lefebvre, *La Vie quotidienne dans le monde moderne* (Paris: Gallimard, 1968), cited in Rigby, p. 36.

‡ De Certeau, *Pratiques*, p. 26.

If "consumer" was too economic and herdlike, "creativity" suffers from the opposite problem: its connotations are at once too productive and too individualistic—qualities, it seems, that belong uniquely to the elite. The problem is that of borrowing a term from the realm of elite or high art and applying it to the activities of the common folk—activities that de Certeau must sometimes resort to a neonaturalist vocabulary to describe, as when he describes their movements as "cette activité fourmilière"—that hive of activity.* But might it not also be the problem of the subjectivity of the popular classes, their knowledge, their capacity as thinking subjects as agents? Who makes culture? Concerning the movement of ordinary people in the street, de Certeau writes that their bodies "follow the thicks and thins of an urban 'text' they write without being able to read."† A popular text is being written, but only on the condition that its authors cannot read or interpret it. In "Pratiques quotidiennes," de Certeau defines popular knowledge with a striking phrase: "une pensée qui ne se pense pas."‡ A thought that is unthought. A thought that does not think itself. But the distance from "a thought that does not think itself" to "a thought that exists on the condition that it does not (or cannot) think itself" is not very far at all. It is as though their very humility, marginality, and downtroddenness, their antlike swarming, makes them candidates for redemption—their unthinkingness is synonymous with "resistance." Brian Rigby suggests that de Certeau's concern with resistance, with celebrating the ways in which popular culture actively manipulates dominant culture, emerged from a desire to throw off the determinism exerted by sociologist Pierre Bourdieu. Certainly, Bourdieu's vision of popular culture as a desert of deprivation, a handicap or

---

* Ibid.

† De Certeau, *Practice*, p. 93.

‡ De Certeau, "Pratiques quotidiennes," p. 28.

symptomatology of backwardness, provides a stark contrast to the
cunning triumphs of the meek and the small depicted by de Certeau. It is as if Bourdieu is directly addressing de Certeau when,
in an article entitled "Vous avez dit 'populaire,'" he asks: "When
the search for distinction on the part of the dominated leads the
dominated to affirm that which distinguishes them—that is to say,
that very thing in the name of which the dominated are constituted as vulgar—must we speak of resistance?* Resistance is not
resistance, in other words, if it is simply a call for the recognition
of the validity of those practices—Bourdieu's example is the use
of slang—which are objectively responsible for keeping one in
a dominated situation. From Bourdieu's perspective, de Certeau
was guilty of rehabilitation—rehabilitating a handicapped lifestyle
or set of practices considered inferior or marginal, rather than
emphasizing the exclusion and alienation that objectively—the
word is Bourdieu's—accompany that lifestyle.

Rigby may be right that the sociologist and the priest are locked
in a vicious battle, their views of *le peuple* and popular culture
diametrically opposed. But I think it would be more accurate
and more productive to see those views as the flip side of the
same coin. De Certeau's classless portrait of a cohesive and ludic
"ordinary culture" is nothing more than the flip side of Bourdieu's
determinism—that virtually naturalizing schema whereby the
dispossessed, trapped in a culture of deprivation from which
they can never escape, excluded by definition from access to the
cultural capital wielded by the elites, are dispossessed in the end
even of the consciousness of their own dispossession.

How do the priest and the sociologist join hands? They come
together in that both propose a virtually immobile social landscape, and a vision of the popular stripped of violence, struggle,

---

* Pierre Bourdieu, "Vous avez dit 'populaire'?," in *Actes de la recherche en
sciences sociales* 46 (1984), p. 101.

and revolt. The opening sentences of Bourdieu's article "Les usages du peuple" are, on this subject, emblematic. Here, the words *peuple* and *lutte* appear as they have traditionally appeared (at least in France) in close proximity to each other. But in Bourdieu's phrase the *lutte* no longer belongs to the people, it has passed completely into the realm of the intellectuals: "The fact of being authorized to speak about 'the people,'" he writes, "can constitute in itself a force in the struggles internal to the different fields [*champs*], political, religious, artistic, etc."* He goes on to argue that intellectuals position themselves on the issue of "the people" as part of a strategic struggle to gain mastery within their own *champ*, as well as to assert the mastery of their particular *champ* in the struggle for supremacy among the various *champs*! The terrain of struggle, in other words, is now completely that of the intellectual career, and "the people" are rhetorical cannon fodder, pawns, in that battle, and not actors in their own.

But this act of dispossession on the part of Bourdieu is entirely in keeping with his caricature-like reduction of the popular classes elsewhere in his work. In *Distinction*, for example, published like de Certeau's "Pratiques quotidiennes," in 1979, the originary drama of the popular classes is that of the experience of deprivation, of a constitutive lack, one which begins as an economic lack, but that soon penetrates into every pore of their being, effecting every dimension of their individual formation: "These classes, as they say, have no future, and in any case have little to expect from the future."† Definitively situated in a temporality that could best

---

    *   Pierre Bourdieu, "Les usages du peuple," in *Choses dites* (Paris: Minuit, 1987), p. 178.

    †   Pierre Bourdieu, *Distinction: A Social Critique of the Judgement of Taste* (Cambridge, MA: Harvard University Press, 1984); trans. by Richard Nice of *La Distinction* (Paris: Minuit, 1979), p. 183. The argument that follows owes much to Patrick Cingolani's discussion of class in *Distinction*; see his "*lppur si muovel* Classes populaires et structures de classes dans *La Distinction*," in Collectif

be called purgatorial, they are given over entirely to repetition, to beginning their task again anew, their lives destroyed, absorbed, eaten up in a movement that cannot change. Lest the abjection of their lives should cause some dialectical move toward liberation to emerge, Bourdieu *saturates* the popular classes with their lack, enclosing them eternally within the realm of matter and material, chaining them to the order of production and reproduction. And since all symbolic creation, or even efforts at symbolization or abstract thought, evaporate at the contact with the material world, the popular classes are, by definition, foreclosed from the symbolic. Popular *culture,* in this schema, can amount to nothing more than "the sparse fragments of a more or less ancient elite culture ... selected and obviously reinterpreted in function of the fundamental principles of class *habitus*"*—the shards, in other words, and fragments of the symbolic production of the dominant classes that have somehow drifted or wended their way into the irreversible torpor of popular life, where they are chewed over and masticated for centuries by the popular taste of the class *habitus*.

Bourdieu originally formulated the concept of *habitus* in his early studies of traditional folk cultures in Kabylia; like de Certeau, then, he has taken a mechanism he has used for studying the social life of rural villages and transported it to study urban popular culture. What are the implications of this critical displacement? Within the *habitus,* individuals are the found objects that a structure constantly disposes and moves about. ("A structured structure predisposed to functioning as a structuring structure," is the way Bourdieu puts it.)† The *habitus* acts as a "shelter from crisis," implying both the fixity of place and the regularity and

---

"Révoltes Logiques," *L'Empire du sociologue* (Paris: Editions La Découverte, 1984), pp. 89–102.

* Bourdieu, ibid., p. 395.

† Ibid., pp. 170–5.

repetition that allow people to put into practice an accumulation
of collective experiences without knowing they are doing so, a
sheltered space where events or eventfulness are held at bay. If
the *habitus* is anything, it is a guaranteed force for maintaining
social stability. For the popular classes, the *habitus* thus adds an
additional burden to the objective conditions already assigned
them: the principle of conformity. "They accept what they have
to be," writes Bourdieu in *Distinction*; "They tend to attribute
to themselves what distribution attributes to them." Or, "They
define themselves the way the established order defines them."*
Subjected to their social or collective destiny, the popular classes
have no horizon other than that of being in perfect conformity to
their condition; they have the inertia of a dead body.

But it is that dead body which in Bourdieu's schema causes
conflicts and struggles in the *other* classes. "The people" is the
catalyst for the dialectic of pretension and distinction that animates
the petite bourgeoisie and the bourgeoisie, just as, in the article I
cited earlier, "Les usages du peuple," "the people" engendered the
struggle for supremacy within the various intellectual *champs* and
career trajectories. "The people" mobilize a kind of struggle in the
other classes (the struggle to define themselves over and against
the popular classes in terms of taste) but all this movement and
frenzy on the part of the others only serves to reinforce the unity
and immobility of the popular classes. The horizon of the popular
classes for both Bourdieu and de Certeau is thus constrained to a
kind of static repetition. But the social immobility each produces
cannot be explained completely by the way that both theorists
emphasize spatial determinations—*habitus* and *champ* for Bourdieu, panopticon and detour for de Certeau—at the cost of other
determinations. (It is, however, interesting to note how much of

---

*   Ibid., p. 471.

the much-vaunted "spatial turn" in cultural studies is just a disguised continuation of the structuralist paradigm, the "linguistic turn" of the 1960s and 70s). Bourdieu and de Certeau share a mode of reasoning as well, one that Roland Barthes in *Mythologies* diagnosed as itself productive of an "immobilizing effect": the bourgeois fondness for reasoning by tautology. Tautology, Barthes writes, defining the same by the same, amounts to a kind of spatialized thinking: it is the foundation of a dead world, an immobile world.* Over the course of de Certeau's work, the "popular," as we have seen, stripped of its historical ideological connotations, comes to constitute a somewhat unwieldy and thoroughly tautological tool through which to categorize the cultural practices of the majority. Bourdieu's recourse to tautology is more intricate, but it has been wonderfully laid bare by Jacques Rancière in an analysis of what he calls "the Bourdieu effect."† It is, for example, all too obvious to say that working-class youth are almost entirely excluded from the university system, and that their cultural inferiority is a result of their economic inferiority. The sociologist attains the level of "science" by providing a tautology whose systemic workings, veiled to the agents trapped within its grip, are evident to him alone. In so doing, the sociologist places himself in the position of denouncing a system granted the ability to hide itself forever from its agents; the social critic sees what others cannot. His authority derives from the unknowingness of his objects of study. The sociologist, in other words, certifies his realm, legitimates its scientific status, through naturalizing and objectifying his other, in this case, the popular classes. He becomes the only legitimate denouncer of both the mechanisms of

---

* See Roland Barthes, *Mythologies* (New York: Hill and Wang, 1972), pp. 152–3. Trans. Annette Lavers from *Mythologies* (Paris: Seuil, 1957).

† See Jacques Rancière, "L'Ethique de la sociologie," in *Collectif Révoltes Logiques, L'Empire du sociologue* (Paris: Editions La Découverte, 1984).

domination and the illusions of liberation. This priestly sociology can only be matched by the sociological priestliness of de Certeau, who defines the job of the historian (what he himself once was) as lying outside of any concern with explaining change: "For the historian, as for the ethnologist, the goal is to make function a cultural whole, to make its laws appear, to listen to its silences, to structure a landscape."*

The unusual phenomenon of Bourdieu's themes of reproduction and distinction being, so to speak, inside everyone's head derives entirely from their being in keeping with their historical moment, embedded in the post-'68 dissipation of hopes for social change. Bourdieu's Marxian-inflected structuralist analysis cataloged class division as it is manifested in posture, behavior, and attitude, while saying nothing at all about the question of social transformation. The resistance de Certeau celebrates, that of an escapee from the panopticon, can only be individual, or at best part of a culture of consolation. At the end of the 1970s, the sociologist and the priest provided the most influential examples of the French intellectual world attempting, once again, to come to terms with *le peuple*, but in this instance more than most in the long history of that relationship, actually eliminating them.

The influence wielded by Bourdieu and de Certeau would only increase in the decade that followed, as English translations of both writers appeared in great quantity. But it is important to remember that, even then, the sociologist and the priest did not have the monopoly on the discourse surrounding "popular culture." The unthinkable for Bourdieu and de Certeau in their conception of popular culture and the popular classes—whether we call it change, transformation, struggle, or dialectic—forms the very basis of another tradition of cultural analysis, whose

* Michel de Certeau (with Dominique Julia and Jacques Revel), "La beauté du mort," in de Certeau, *La Culture au pluriel* (Paris: Christian Bourgois, 1980), p, 69.

traces can be found in the work of Raymond Williams, for example, or that of Henri Lefebvre or Jacques Rancière. Here culture is conceived not as a value or an allotment of symbolic capital, nor as a consoling ritual, but as formation, as the production, or, in the words of Francis Mulhern, the integrally historical making of sense and of subjects, always both, always together.* For these writers, cultural practices, symbols, representations, and creations are linked inextricably to a social struggle against domination as well as to the formation of a cultural project—even if it be the project of forming a new culture.

It is difficult to say what it means to evoke this counter-tradition—the "culture as formation" tradition—today, in the mid-1990s, when the library shelves are full of narratives about the shattering of class and the decomposition of workers' consciousness and forms of sociability, when Bourdieu and his *école* effectively control all of the *champs* of intellectual production in France, and when de Certeau and his model of ludic resistance through consumption provide the direction for a great portion of current Anglophone cultural studies. To begin to do so, we would have to ask ourselves whether the 1970s debates about the popular have not now been rendered definitively obsolete, in the wake of the virtually universal saturation of merchandise itself, and we would have to ask what the effect of that saturation might be on a "separate realm" of culture—be it elite or popular. We would have to wonder whether it is possible to even speak of popular culture today, when the fact that culture has become more and more of a commercial business implies that a large part of what we used to think of as specifically economic and commercial has itself become cultural. Does retaining an explicit class resonance for popular culture, in other words, relegate popular culture itself

---

* Francis Mulhern, "Message in a Bottle: Althusser in Literary Studies," in *Althusser: A Critical Reader*, ed. Gregory Elliott (Oxford: Blackwell, 1994), p. 170.

to a definitive past, to some mausoleum of cultural artifacts; does it make of our study a purely historical one, one that has no purchase on the present, and by this very fact is granted all the poignancy of any search for authentic traditions which—*hélas*—are always being lost, like the last beret-wearing, cigarette-smoking artisan hammering out bells for the last goats of the Haute-Savoie? We would have to ask ourselves whether arguing in favor of retaining some notion of the class resonance of "popular culture" in the French case—the set of representations and social symbolisms surrounding the myth of the worker—does not run the risk of populist naiveté on the one hand or a quasi-Sorelian mysticism on the other.

These are difficult questions which we can only raise today, but I will venture so far as to say that the very fanfare with which consensual democracies like France have celebrated the end of the "myths" of class conflict is in itself symptomatic of the continuing existence of a subjectivizing, emancipatory, political process that has historically taken form—even as recently as last winter in Paris*—around the name or figure of "workers," "the people."

---

* I am referring here to the mass labor strikes of the winter of 1995.

4
Introduction to Jacques Rancière, The Ignorant Schoolmaster

In *The Ignorant Schoolmaster*, Jacques Rancière recounts the story of Joseph Jacotot, a schoolteacher driven into exile during the Restoration who allowed that experience to ferment into a method for showing illiterate parents how they themselves could teach their children how to read. That Jacotot's story might have something to do with the post-1968 debates about education in France was not immediately apparent to most of the book's readers when it appeared in 1987. How could the experiences of a man who had lived all the great pedagogical adventures of the French Revolution, whose own utopian teaching methods knew a brief—if worldwide and perfectly serious—flurry of attention before passing rapidly into the oblivion Rancière's book rescues them from—how could these experiences "communicate" with administrators face-to-face with the problems of educating immigrant North African children in Paris, or with intellectuals intent on mapping the French school system's continued reproduction of social inequalities? Rancière's book explained nothing about the failures of the school system;* it entered directly into none of

---

* French journalism of the 1980s spoke frequently about "l'echec de l'ecole";

the contemporary polemical debates. Its polemics, dramatically recounted in the second half of the book, were rather those of the era of the ignorant schoolmaster, Joseph Jacotot: the effects of Jacotot's unusual method; its fate at the hands of the reformers and pedagogical institutions it undermined; its effacement by the educational policies put into effect, under the auspices of François Guizot and Victor Cousin, by the July Monarchy during the 1830s. The names of the most listened-to theoretical voices on post-'68 education—those of Pierre Bourdieu and Jean-Claude Milner—are not mentioned by Rancière. Yet the book's subject was obviously education. Key words like "lessons" and "intellectual," "ignorant" and "schoolmaster" appeared, if in a somewhat paradoxical arrangement, in its title. And education was again, in the 1980s, under scrutiny in France.

Readers in France had difficulty situating the book, as they have had difficulty, generally speaking, keeping up with the maverick intellectual itinerary of its author. For although, in 1965, Rancière published *Lire le Capital* with his teacher Louis Althusser, he was better known for his celebrated leftist critique of his coauthor, *La Leçon d'Althusser* (1974), and for the journal he founded the same year, *Révoltes logiques*. Trained as a philosopher, a professor of philosophy at the University of Paris, but immersed rather unfashionably since 1974 in early nineteenth-century workers' archives, Rancière wrote books that eluded classification—books that gave voice to the wild journals of artisans, to the daydreams of anonymous thinkers, to worker-poets and philosophers who

---

this failure was usually certified by comparing the percentage of French students who attain the *baccalauréat* (30 percent in 1985) with the percentage of high school graduates in Japan (75 percent) and the United States (85.6 percent). Given the advanced nature of the French *bac*—it includes something like two years of what Americans view as college-level work—these statistics perhaps indicate the elite nature of French schooling, its system of professional and vocational "tracking." From nearly a quarter to a third of working-class and rural students fail the preparatory course for the *bac*, against under 3 percent for those from professional families.

devised emancipatory systems alone, in the semi-unreal space/ time of the scattered late-night moments their work schedules allowed them.* Were these books primarily history? The philosophy of history? The history of philosophy? Some readers took *Le Maître ignorant* to be a fragment of anecdotal history, a curiosity piece, an archival oddity. Educators read it—some quite anxiously, given Jacotot's affirmation that anyone can learn alone—in the imperative, as a contemporary prescriptive, a kind of suicidal pedagogical how-to. A few reviewers read it on the level at which it might, I think, most immediately address an American or British readership only beginning to come to terms with the legacies of a decade of Reaganism and Thatcherism: as an essay, or perhaps a fable or parable, that enacts an extraordinary philosophical meditation on equality.

Bourdieu and the New Sociology

The singular history of each national collectivity plays a considerable role in the problems of education. Though the English translation appears in very different conditions,† it may be useful to begin by discussing the book's French context, a context still profoundly marked by the turbulence of the student uprisings of May '68 and by the confusions and disappointments, the reversals and desertions, of the decade that followed: the all but total collapse of the Parisian intelligentsia of the Left, the "end of politics" amid the triumph of sociology.

---

* Jacques Rancière (with Alain Faure), *La Parole ouvrière* (Paris: Union Générale d'Editions, 1976); Rancière, *La Nuit des prolétaires* (Paris: Fayard, 1981), trans. by Donald Reid as *The Nights of Labor* (Philadelphia: Temple University Press, 1989); Rancière, *Le Philosophe plébien* (Paris: La Découverte, 1983).

† In the United States today, for example, arguments about equality invariably turn on the subject of race—not surprisingly in the only major industrial nation built on a legacy of domestic slavery.

For it was perhaps as a reaction to the unexpectedness of the May uprisings that the 1970s favored the elaboration of a number of social seismologies and above all energized sociological reflection itself: the criticism of institutions and superstructures, of the multiform power of domination. In the wake of the political failure of '68, the social sciences awoke to the study of power: to the New Philosophers' self-promotional media takeover, to Michel Foucault, but most importantly, perhaps, to the sociology of Pierre Bourdieu—the enormous influence of whose work would, given the time lag and ideology of translation, begin in earnest in the English-speaking world only in the early 1980s. No less than the New Philosophers, Bourdieu could be said to have profited from both the success and the failure of the May movement, the first granting his work the energy and posture of critique, the second reinforcing in it the gravitational pull of structure.

If Bourdieu's work had little serious impact on methodological debates among professional sociologists, its effect on historians, anthropologists, professors of French, educational reformers, art historians, ghetto high school teachers, and popular journalists was widespread. In the introduction to *L'Empire du sociologue* (1984), a collection of essays edited by Rancière and the *Révoltes Logiques* collective, the authors attribute the extraordinary success of Bourdieu's themes of reproduction and distinction to the simple fact that they *worked*, which is to say that they offered the most thorough philosophy of the social, the one that best explained to the most people the theoretical and political signification of the last twenty years of their lives. Bourdieu had produced, in other words, a discourse entirely in keeping with his time, a time that combined, in the words of the editors, "the orphaned fervor of denouncing the system with the disenchanted certitude of its perpetuity."*

---

* *Révoltes Logiques* collective, *L'Empire du sociologue* (Paris: La Découverte, 1984), p. 7.

Before May 1968, steeped in the theoretical and political atmosphere of the Althusserian battle for revolutionary science against ideology, Bourdieu and Jean-Claude Passeron published *Les Héritiers* (1964), an analysis of the University that helped fuel the denunciation of the institution by showing it to be entirely absorbed in the reproduction of unequal social structures. The post-May dissipation of hopes for social change, however, served only to amplify the influence of that work, and particularly of its theoretical sequels, *La Reproduction* (1970) and *La Distinction* (1979).* Bourdieu's structuralist rigor with a Marxist accent permitted an exhaustive interpretive analysis of class division and its inscription—minutely cataloged in the tiniest details of posture or daily behavior—an analysis that could carry on an existence entirely divorced from the practical hypotheses of Marxism or the naivetés of hope for social transformation. It allowed, *Révoltes Logiques* argued, "the denunciation of both the mechanisms of domination and the illusions of liberation."†

Rancière, in his own critical contribution to the volume, attacked Bourdieu and the new sociology as the latest and most influential form of a discourse deriving its authority from the presumed naiveté or ignorance of its objects of study: in the realm of education, the militant instructors in *La Reproduction* who need the legitimacy of the system's authority to denounce the arbitrariness of that legitimacy; and the working-class students excluded from the bourgeois system of favors and privileges, who do not (and cannot) understand their exclusion. By tracing the passage from *Les Héritiers* to *La Reproduction*, Rancière uncovered a logic whereby the social critic gains by showing democracy

---

    *   All three works have been translated into English by Richard Nice: *The Inheritors* (Chicago: University of Chicago Press, 1979); *Reproduction* (London: Sage Publications, 1977); *Distinction* (Cambridge, MA: Harvard University Press, 1985).

    †   *Révoltes Logiques*, L'Empire *du sociologue*, p. 7.

losing. It was, for example, all too obvious, he wrote, to say that working-class youth are almost entirely excluded from the university system, and that their cultural inferiority is a result of their economic inferiority. The sociologist attained the level of "science" by providing a tautology whose systemic workings, veiled to the agents trapped within its grip, were evident to him alone. The perfect circle, according to Rancière, was made "via two propositions":

1. Working-class youth are excluded from the University because they are unaware of the true reasons for which they are excluded (*Les Héritiers*).
2. Their ignorance of the true reasons for which they are excluded is a structural effect produced by the very existence of the system that excludes them (*La Reproduction*).*

The "Bourdieu effect" could be summed up in this perfect circle: "They are excluded because they don't know why they are excluded; and they don't know why they are excluded because they are excluded." Or better:

1. The system reproduces its existence because it goes unrecognized.
2. The system brings about, through the reproduction of its existence, an effect of misrecognition.†

By rehearsing this tautology, the sociologist placed himself "in the position of eternal denouncer of a system granted the ability to hide itself forever from its agents": not only did the sociologist see what teacher (and student) did not, he saw it *because*

---

*   Jacques Rancière, "L'Ethique du sociologue," in *L'Empire du sociologue*, p. 28.

†   Ibid., pp. 28, 29.

the teacher and student could not. Wasn't the ultimate concern evinced by the logic of the new sociology, Rancière suggested, that of reuniting its realm, legitimating its specificity as a science through a naturalizing objectification of the other?

Pedagogical Reforms

The sociological theories of Bourdieu and Passeron offered something for everyone. For the enlightened reader, the disabused Marxist, they offered the endlessly renewable pleasure of lucidity, the frisson of demystification and the unveiling of the clockwork mechanics of a functionalism usually reserved for the structuralist interpretation of fiction. But, for the progressive educator, they offered the justification for a series of attempts to reform the social inequities of the school system—and this especially after François Mitterrand and the socialists were elected in 1981. At the level of governmental education policy, the Mitterrand administration was riven by two warring ideological tendencies, embodied in the persons who successively occupied the position of minister of education, Alain Savary and Jean-Pierre Chevènement.

Savary, imbued with something of the spontaneous, libertarian ethos of May '68 and with the heady early moments of enacting the socialist agenda, saw his mission as that of reducing, through a series of reforms, the inequalities diagnosed by Bourdieu and Passeron. If petit bourgeois instructors, intent on capitalizing on the distinctions conferred on them by their knowledge, were, as Bourdieu and Passeron argued, complacently reproducing the cultural models that acted to select "inheritors" and legitimate the social inferiority of the dispossessed, then, Savary's reformers argued, a new educational community must be established: one based on undoing the rigid stratification of scholars and their knowledge—a kind of leveling at the top—and creating a convivial, open, egalitarian atmosphere in the schools, which would be attentive to the "whole personality" of the child. Savary, for instance, favored a compensatory attitude to unequal opportunity. He had "priority zones" designated that saw supplementary funding, extra teaching positions, and specially designed curricula established in elementary schools and high schools situated in poor neighborhoods.

When Savary's successor, Chevènement (currently minister of defense under Mitterrand), came to power in 1984, he announced a halt to such attempts at egalitarian reform. Under the watchword of "republican elitism," Chevènement underscored the imperatives of technological modernization and competition for France in a period of worldwide economic crisis. Advocating a return to the Encyclopedist, rationalist, Enlightenment principles of Jules Ferry and the Third Republic, he called for the restoration of grammar, rigid examinations, civic instruction—a kind of curricular "back to basics"—and a return to the rhetoric of selection that so long characterized French schooling. That a violent polemic concerning the values of education should erupt in the journalism of the mid-1980s—a moment of profound general anxiety about the question of French "identity" in the face of rising immigration—was not surprising. But the terms of the debate were all too familiar, as were the polarized positions that resulted: the more Rousseauist disciples of Savary arguing that even a "republican" elitism could lead only to the exclusion and marginalization of an important percentage of French youth; the "Enlightenment" followers of Chevènement arguing that a socialist education system must be rational and scientific.

In intellectual circles, the somewhat brutal transition from the warm bath of Savary to the science of Chevènement was facilitated by the publication in 1984 of the linguist Jean-Claude Milner's controversial polemic, *De l'école*. (Milner appeared on

the popular French literary television show *Apostrophes* to talk
about his book and was invited by Chevènement to the ministry
to discuss his ideas on education.) Milner attributed all the ills
of the French system to a plot launched against knowledge by a
"triple alliance" of stingy administrators, hastily accredited par-
venu high school teachers, and well-intended reformers bent on
advancing something they called "pedagogy"—what, for Milner,
amounted to nothing more than the empty science of teaching
how to teach. These pseudo-progressive advocates of the vaguely
religious and virtuous vocation of pedagogy produced, according
to Milner, a purely parasitic discourse: reform after reform whose
ends lay in sacrificing true scholarly research and passion for a
"convivial schoolroom atmosphere." Not the least provocative
of his assertions was that a teacher did not have to like children to
be a good teacher. Hearkening back approvingly to the rigors of
the Third Republic, he argued that schools and teachers should
dispense with modeling the "whole person" and view their task
instead simply and unequivocally as that of transmitting knowledge, as "instructing," not "educating." The unequal relation
between teacher and student was not to be dismantled but rather
celebrated, for in its inequality, as in that of psychoanalyst and
patient, lay the key to success. Inequality produced in the student
the desire to know. True equality in schooling meant transmitting
the same knowledge to each student.

In his review of Milner's book, Rancière concurred with the
linguist's frank characterization of the reformist programs as
"obscurantist" in their assumption that the best way to reduce
inequalities in the realm of formally transmitted knowledge was
to cut back on knowledge itself; "racist" in their supposition that
the children of the working class—and especially of immigrants
—should be provided with a less "abstract" or "cultural" cur-
riculum; and "infantilizing" in their ideology of school as a vast,

vaguely maternal enterprise based on "nurturing."* But the solution to all this was not, Rancière argued, a return to some notion of pure, scientific transmission à la Jules Ferry, for such a thing had never existed. Wasn't schooling under the Third Republic tainted by, if not obsessed with, a hygienic project of moral formation? The terms of the debate—Rousseau vs. Ferry—were misleading. Equality might reside in teaching the same thing to everyone, but it was simply not true that every child in France now—or at any time in the past—had a right to participate in the community of knowledge. Similarly, Milner's notion of pure scholarly passion, Rancière suggested, masked the interests of the aristocrats of education, the mandarins at the top of the university and grant-funding hierarchies, whose concern lay in preserving, in the face of a rising tide of hastily accredited instructors, the traditional privileges of the possessors of culture.

The Lesson of Althusser

Milner and Rancière shared a student activist past, a friendship, a teacher—Louis Althusser—and a theoretical formation; twenty years previously, they had both belonged to the Union des Etudiants Communistes, the famous "cercle d'Ulm": the small group of young theorists including Etienne Balibar, Pierre Macherey, Jacques-Alain Miller, and Régis Debray, who attended Althusser's early seminars on Marx at the Ecole Normale. Rancière and Milner were among the signatories of the first—mimeographed—issue of the group's journal, the *Cahiers marxistes-léninistes*, an issue whose title, "The Function of Theoretical Formation," reveals its authors' early preoccupation with questions of education and the status of intellectual discourse.

---

* Jacques Rancière, review of J. C. Milner, *De l'école*, in *La Quinzaine littéraire*, 422 (Aug. 1984).

A vast historical chasm separates Milner's *De l'école* from "The Function of Theoretical Formation"—a chasm filled with the momentous political defeat of European worker movements in France, Italy, Portugal, Greece, and Spain; the defeat of Althusserianism itself on the barricades of May; the Right's recuperation of May and its anarcho-libertarian ideology for the free market; and the virtual suppression of historical materialism in France after 1975 at the hands of the intellectual currents of the New Philosophy and post-structuralism. And yet, in certain of Milner's pronouncements about education, about questions of authority and equality, for instance, an echo of the old master's voice, that of Louis Althusser, can be heard: "The function of teaching," Althusser wrote in 1964, "is to transmit a determinate knowledge to subjects who do not possess this knowledge. The teaching situation thus rests on the absolute condition of *an inequality between a knowledge and a nonknowledge*."* For Milner, as for Althusser, the fundamental pedagogical relation is the one between knowledge and ignorance. The same historical chasm separates Rancière's *Le Maître ignorant* from his *La Leçon d'Althusser*, but Rancière's subject—education, or more broadly, the status of those who possess knowledge versus the status of those who don't—and orientation toward authority remain unchanged; both books, in fact, announce themselves as "lessons."

By writing *La Leçon d'Althusser*, Rancière performed what he called "the first clearing of the terrain" for the kind of reflection that has preoccupied him ever since: the consideration of the philosophical and historical relations between knowledge and the masses. Althusserianism, in *La Leçon d'Althusser*, emerges first and foremost as a theory of education. For Rancière, Althusser's only political—in the strict sense of the word—intervention

---

* Louis Althusser, "Problèmes étudiants," *La Nouvelle Critique* 152 (Jan. 1964).

occurred during the early moments of student unrest, when a controversy regarding higher education arose between the student union (UNEF) and the Communist Party. Student discontent had begun at that point to focus on the *forms* of the transmission of knowledge—the pedagogical relation of magisterial professors and docile students—as well as its ends: forming the future auxiliaries of the bourgeoisie. Already in the early 1960s, students had begun to question the arbitrariness of examinations and the ideology of individual research. In these early, tentative efforts—their slogan was "La Sorbonne aux étudiants"—politics appeared in a new form: in the questioning of knowledge and its relation to political power and in the introduction of a new line of division among intellectuals between the producers and the consumers of knowledge. Althusser's intervention was swift and clear. In an article entitled "Problèmes étudiants" (1964), he outlined the correct priorities for Communist students. They must first develop their knowledge of Marxism-Leninism and then conduct scientific analyses that would yield objective knowledge of the University. What should matter to Marxists was less the form—the pedagogical relation in which knowledge was disseminated—than "the quality of knowledge itself." Their task must be that of "discovering new scientific knowledge capable of illuminating and criticizing the overwhelming illusions in which everyone is imprisoned," and the privileged vehicle for performing this task was individual research. The real locus of class division in the University was not in the inequitable relations between teachers and students, but in the *content* of the teaching: "It is by the very nature of the knowledge that it imparts to students that the bourgeoisie exerts … the profoundest influence over them."

For Rancière, the Althusserian concept of science—in fact, the science/ideology distinction itself—had ultimately no other function than that of justifying the pure being of knowledge, and, more important, of justifying the eminent dignity of the possessors of that knowledge. For if science (theory) forms an enclave of freedom in a world of ideological enslavement, if science belongs to the intellectuals—the masters—and the critique of bourgeois content is reserved for those who already know, then there is only one way for students to criticize their masters' knowledge from the point of view of class, and that is to become their peers. If everyone dwells in illusion (ideology), then the solution can only come from a kind of muscular theoretical heroism on the part of the lone theorist. Rancière recounted what was for him the most graphic illustration of this: Althusser's need to deny the antiauthoritarian May revolt as it was happening in order to pretend later to "discover," through chance and solitary research, and to propose as a risky hypothesis, what the mass student action had already revealed to everyone—the function of the school as an ideological apparatus of the state.[*]

Confronted with the events of May, the logic of Althusserianism reacts according to the predictable temporality of *the one who knows*. May '68 was not the *proper* moment. Empirical politics and theory must be dissociated from each other, and the position that enacted that dissociation was that of the educator—he who knows how to wait, how to guard his distance, how to take the time of theory. The last resource of philosophy is to eternalize the division of labor that grants it its place.[†]

---

[*]   Louis Althusser's "Ideology and Ideological State Apparatuses" appeared originally in *La Pensé* in 1970. It was translated the following year in *Lenin and Philosophy*, trans. Ben Brewster (New York: Monthly Review Press, 1971), pp. 127–86.

[†]   Rancière, *La Leçcon d'Althusser* (1974), p. 35.

The Practice of Equality

If the philosophical tradition is itself a product of the division between mental and manual labor, then what authority is to be granted the testimony of this tradition? And particularly when philosophy sets itself the task, as it delights in doing, of speaking for those whose presumed ignorance grants it its domain? Since *La Leçon d'Althusser*, Rancière's investigation of the origin, continuation, and occasional subversion of the hierarchical division of head and hand has been launched on two fronts. The first might be called the archival level, the documenting, chronicling, essentially recounting, of the experiences and voices of early nineteenth-century workers who "transgressed the boundaries set for them": figures both marginal and central to workers' communities whose emancipation took the form of claiming for themselves what the middle classes assumed to be theirs alone, a realm of existence outside the one defined by the circle of material necessity. He focused on workers who claimed the right to aesthetic contemplation, the right to dead time—and, above all, the right to think. "I took the great *gauchiste* theme—the relations of intellectual and manual work—and put it in reverse: not the re-education of intellectuals, but the eruption of negativity, of *thinking*, into a social category always defined by the positivity of *doing*."[*]

This archival, narrative work has run parallel to—and entertains a crucial dialogue with—the second, more polemical and discursive front: Rancière's critique of the claims of bourgeois observers and intellectuals (philosophers, social historians, New Philosophers, sociologists) to know, and thus "speak for" or explicate, the privileged other of political modernity, the worker.[†]

---

[*]   Jacques Rancière, *interview* with François Ewald, "Qu'est-ce que la classe ouvrière?," *Magazine littéraire* 175 (July–Aug. 1981).

[†]   See, in particular, Rancière, *Le Philosophe et ses pauvres* (Paris: Fayard, 1983).

Rancière's critique of the educational theories of Bourdieu, Althusser, and Milner shows them to have at least one thing in common: a lesson in inequality. Each, that is, by beginning with inequality, proves it, and by proving it, in the end, is obliged to rediscover it again and again.* Whether school is seen as the reproduction of inequality (Bourdieu) or as the potential instrument for the reduction of inequality (Savary), the effect is the same: that of erecting and maintaining the distance separating a future reconciliation from a present inequality, a knowledge in the offing from today's intellectual impoverishment—a distance discursively invented and reinvented so that it may never be abolished. The poor stay in their place. The same temporal and spatial distance separates the pedagogue from the student as separates the "explicator of the social" from the worker.

But, what if equality, instead, were to provide the point of departure? What would it mean to make equality a *presupposition* rather than a goal, a *practice* rather than a reward situated firmly in some distant future so as to all the better explain its present infeasibility? This is the lesson provided by Joseph Jacotot's experience—*expérience* in the French Enlightenment sense of both "experiment" and "experience"—and the lesson whose political and philosophical timeliness Rancière affirms by recounting Jacotot's story.

All people are equally intelligent. This is Jacotot's startling (or naive?) presupposition, his lesson in intellectual emancipation. And from this starting point (the result of an accidental discovery occasioned by the peculiar circumstances of exile), Jacotot came to realize that knowledge is not necessary to teaching, nor explication necessary to learning. "Explication," he writes, "is the myth of pedagogy." Rather than eliminating incapacity, explication, in

---

* See Rancière, *Aux bords du politique* (Paris: Osiris, 1990).

fact, creates it. It does this in part by establishing the temporal structure of delay ("a little further along," "a little later," "a few more explanations and you'll see the light") that, writ large, would become the whole nineteenth-century myth of Progress: "the pedagogical fiction erected into the fiction of the whole society," and the general infantilization of the individuals who compose it. The pedagogical myth divides the world into two: the knowing and the ignorant, the mature and the unformed, the capable and the incapable. By the second half of *The Ignorant Schoolmaster*, the homology of delay that links the popular classes, the child, and the poor within the discourse of the republican "Men of Progress" surrounding Jacotot is all too clear.

The pedagogical fiction works by representing inequality in terms of velocity: as "slowness," "backwardness," "delay." Perhaps this homology of delay, the whole temporality of the "lag" that the book exposes, will provide the means for readers who have pondered the forms taken by the ideology of progress since Jacotot's time to trace the constellation (the term is Walter Benjamin's) that our own era forms with Jacotot's. For hasn't the pedagogical fiction of our own time been cast on a global scale? Never will the student catch up with the teacher; never will the "developing" nations catch up with the enlightened nations. Are even the critiques of "dependency theory" free of pedagogical rhetoric in their discussions of the Third World? To say this is to claim that a reading of *The Ignorant Schoolmaster* can suggest how today's much-heralded "democratization" of the globe— our own contemporary institutionalization and representation of progress—is just the new name for inequality.

In *The Ignorant Schoolmaster*, Rancière has found the means of illustrating and defending equality that extends to the very level of formal risks he has taken recounting the story. It is above all the book's formal procedures that have allowed Rancière to think the social itself in such a distinctly original fashion. For, as Benjamin was not alone in realizing, "the concept of the historical progress of mankind cannot be sundered from the concept of its progression through a homogenous, empty time. And a critique of such a progression must be the basis of any criticism of the concept of progress itself."* The critique of progress, in other words, must intervene at the level of the progression, the speed or pacing, the practice of historical writing itself. Viewed from this perspective, the gradualist, "additive" notion of writing history—the slow, reasoned accumulation of data with which the historian fills an empty, homogenous time—begins to bear a distinct resemblance to the gradual, step-by-step acquisition of understanding through explication that Jacotot's method so dramatically explodes.†

If the historian's relation to the past—and to his or her readers—is not to be one of explication, then what can it be? Early writings of the *Révoltes Logiques* collective announce its project to be that of creating an "alternative historical memory." This, I think, suggests a motivation akin to that of Benjamin's to blast, as he put it, "a unique experience of the past" out of the "continuum of history" for the purpose of wresting meaning from the past for the present. As the collective put it:

---

* Walter Benjamin, "Theses on the Philosophy of History," in *Illuminations,* ed. Hannah Arendt (New York: Schocken, 1969).

† Rancière is in fact best known in the United States among historians for his polemical interventions concerning social history as a *métier,* and for his debates with particular social historians over the identity and consciousness of the artisan. See, especially, his exchange with William Sewell, Jr., and Christopher Johnson in "The Myth of the Artisan," *International Labor and Working-Class History,* 24 (Fall 1983). See also what is the most thorough discussion of Rancière's relation to the practice of history, and of his work in general: Donald Reid's introduction to the translation of *La Nuit des prolétaires* (*Nights of Labor;* Philadelphia, 1989). Important essays by Rancière originally published in *Révoltes Logiques* are available in *Voices of the People,* ed. Adrian Rifkin and Roger Thomas (London: Routledge, 1988).

An episode from the past interests us only inasmuch as it becomes an episode of the present wherein our thoughts, actions, and strategies are decided … What interests us is that ideas be events, that history be at all times a break, a rupture, to be interrogated only from the perspective of the here and now, and only politically.[*]

The motivation is clear. But what are the formal or rhetorical strategies, what are the writing practices, that allow an episode from the past to become an episode in the present? In the case of *The Ignorant Schoolmaster,* the story of Jacotot opens and ends without Rancière doing, on one level, anything other than narrating it. Storytelling then, in and of itself, or *recounting*—one of the two basic operations of the intelligence according to Jacotot —emerges as one of the concrete acts or practices that verifies equality. (Equality, writes Jacotot, "is neither given nor claimed, it is practiced, it is *verified*.") The very act of storytelling, an act that presumes in its interlocutor an equality of intelligence rather than an inequality of knowledge, posits equality, just as the act of explication posits inequality.

But another, more unusual effect is created by the narrative style of the book: a particular kind of uncertainty that readers may experience concerning the identity of the book's narrator. The reader, in other words, is not quite sure where the voice of Jacotot stops and Rancière's begins. Rancière slips into Jacotot's text, winding around or worming in; his commentary contextualizes, rehearses, reiterates, dramatizes, elaborates, *continues* Jacotot; the effect is one of a complex echoing taking place between the author and Jacotot at the level of voice, as though an enormously sympathetic disciple of Jacotot's had, by some time-travel device familiar to readers of science fiction, turned up in the twentieth

---

[*]   *Révoltes Logiques* collective, "Deux ou trois choses que l'historien ne veut pas savoir," *Le Mouvement social,* 100 (July–Sept. 1977).

century. One existential grounding for such an echoing may be surmised. Jacotot's relation to post-Revolutionary France (his experiments, in a sense, *prolong* the revolutionary energies of 1789 into the France of the 1820s and 1830s) is doubled by Rancière's relation to 1968. The two are united by something like a shared lived relation to cycles of hope, then to cycles of discouragement, and on to the displacement of hope—a sequence that marks the experience of periods of revolutionary ferment and their aftermath. That such periods are also ones of productive ferment around the question of education—or *transmission*—goes without saying. But, in the end, it is emancipation—not education—that has drawn Rancière to Jacotot.

For the reader, this narrative uncertainty will prove productive, I think, for it has the effect of facilitating—creating the means for—the book's (nonexplicit, unexplicated) intervention into the present. Without explanation, the political timeliness of Jacotot's "naiveté" is affirmed. For Rancière, this particular book becomes the means by which his two previously separated activities—the archival, situated in the past, and the polemical, situated for the most part in the present of contemporary theory—are merged, a merging that in turn confounds any attempt to classify the book generically. Are the nineteenth-century republican Men of Progress, the founders of public education, the sociologists of today? And, if so, is the book a satire? Does a satirist's rage at the fallen reality of postmodernism, our own society of experts, drive the recitation of Jacotot's utopian experience? It is certainly clear, for example, that Rancière's (and Jacotot's) distinctive "untimeliness" stands in agonistic relation to the perfect timeliness and seamlessness of the "Bourdieu effect," the whole contemporary sociology of "systems of representation." Can Jacotot and his series of concrete practices verifying equality be marshaled to do battle with the dominant discourse of our own time, the discourse of a hidden truth and its demystification by the master explicator, the discourse that asserts that "there is no science but of the hidden"?*

The Ignorant Schoolmaster forces us to confront what any number of nihilistic neoliberal philosophies would have us avoid: the founding term of our political modernity, *equality*. And in the face of systematic attacks on the very idea, powerful ideologies that would relegate it to the dustbin of history or to some dimly radiant future, Rancière places equality—*virtually*—in the present. Against the seamless science of the hidden, Jacotot's story reminds us that equality turns on another, very different logic: in division rather than consensus, in a multiplicity of concrete acts and actual moments and situations, situations that erupt into the fiction of inegalitarian society without themselves becoming institutions. And in this, my rendering of the title of the book as *The Ignorant Schoolmaster* is perhaps misleading. For Jacotot had no school. Equality does not, as they say in French, *faire école*.

---

*   Bourdieu, *Reproduction*, p. iv.

5

Historicizing Untimeliness

In an essay written shortly after the American war in Iraq began, Jacques Rancière wrote about the seamless integration of capital, state, military, and media power achieved in the United States during the months preceding the invasion. He called the fusion "a perfecting of the plutocratic System."* Certainly, those of us who lived through those months in the United States (or—again—the months preceding the 2004 presidential election) can testify to the background noise we heard. It wasn't bombs—these we saw and heard very little of—but rather the media's relentless litany of repeated phrases: "weapons of mass destruction," "Afghani women voting," "evil dictator," and one or two others. But I want to begin by evoking an earlier moment in the history of that seamless integration: the moment in 1983 when Ronald Reagan set up a covert CIA operation bearing a name I think Rancière might appreciate: "Perception Management." Perception Management, unlike other CIA operations, was directed domestically and was, for all intents and purposes, the now-forgotten origin of the media

---

* Jacques Rancière, "On War as the Ultimate Form of Advanced Plutocratic Consensus," trans. Lucy R. McNair, *Contemporary French and Francophone Studies: Sites* 8, no. 3 (2004), p. 256–7.

techniques later to be perfected by the George W. Bush administration. Reagan wanted to swing public opinion to support his
Central American policies in Nicaragua and El Salvador, and
to that end polling was conducted to determine which precise
buzzwords and concepts would best turn US citizens against
the Sandinistas and get them to support the Contras and the
Salvadoran government. In the face of the latest great "third-
worldist" cause, the solidarity movements with the peoples of
Nicaragua and El Salvador, the idea was to saturate the media
with phrases repeated over and over like mantras: the Sandinistas
are anti-Semitic, they're drug runners, they discriminate against
indigenous peoples, they're terrorists, and so forth—to enormous
effect.* It is during these years, I think—the early 1980s—that
consensus first comes to be taken for granted as the optimum
political gesture or goal, with "Perception Management" its more
than adequate figure. And it was around this time that I first began
to read Rancière's work. Against this ideological backdrop, the
untimeliness of his project was strongly perceptible. This is why
I'll not focus on *Dis-agreement* and the recent intellectual developments which, as conferences held in the United Kingdom, Berlin,
Cerisy, and elsewhere suggest, are now placing Rancière's work at
the center of contemporary discussions. I want to go back, rather,
to the earlier stages of the project: to Jacotot and *The Names of
History.* For it was in the late 1970s and early 1980s that a generalized offensive against equality, under the cover of a critique of
egalitarianism, began to make of equality a synonym for uniformity, for the constraint or alienation of liberty, or for an assault
on the free functioning of the market.† It is in this context that

---

* For a discussion of "Perception Management" and its relation to contemporary US policy, see Chapter 4 of Greg Grandin, *Empire's Workshop: Latin America,
the United States, and the Rise of the New Imperialism* (New York: Metropolitan,
2006).

† In France this offensive, which I discuss in Chapter 3 of *May '68 and its*

Rancière's preoccupation with, or recurrent staging of, equality and its verification could be called untimely, or that my own experience reading a book like *The Ignorant Schoolmaster* could be one of delighted shock—only initially really graspable for me, teaching in central California, as a kind of echo of certain Latin American utopian pedagogical experiments of the 1960s. So, although the introduction I wrote to my translation of *The Ignorant Schoolmaster* created a kind of context for the book out of the French educational policies and debates of the first period of Mitterrand, my own enthusiasm, what made me want to do the translation, was the way Rancière's book seemed to me to resonate, however slightly, with earlier interventions like Ivan Illich's *Deschooling Society* or Paolo Freire's *Pedagogy of the Oppressed*.

Now France, of course, like Germany, had no Reagan or Thatcher, which is to say no full-scale ultraconservative restructuring of its economy in the 1980s. Then, as now, a difference can be detected between governments where systems of social protection and solidarity have not been completely dismantled and those, like the United States, where they have. But the 1980s in France were nevertheless what Serge Halimi might call an intensely philo-American time,* as France began to accommodate itself to the ascendancy of an American liberal orthodoxy, an orthodoxy in which equality came to be seen as a body of principles which, at best, can be interpreted by a court rather than what Rancière's work insisted on showing it to be: a profoundly political problem, *the* problem, in fact, of politics per se.

Perhaps the best way to talk about Rancière's untimeliness in those years, though, is to remember how the interdisciplinary

---

Afterlives, was part of an effort to sever the leftist activism of May '68 from its real content and to unlink that event from an immanent politics of equality.

   *   Serge Halimi, "Un mot de trop" and "Les 'philo-américains' saisis par la rage," *Le monde diplomatique*, May 2000.

terrain had begun to be taken over and inundated, then, with a
kind of cobbled-together "spatiality," as the human sciences came
to embrace insights, perspectives, and methodologies imported
from the "spatial sciences" of urbanism, architecture, ethnology,
and geography. The spatial turn was reinforced by an appeal to
culturalism, based on the category of culture as a static, spatial
countenance—culture that cannot be seen as an agent of time.
This spatial turn—the imbalance in humanistic and cultural studies that consisted in a privileging of space over considerations of
temporality or change—is apparent in the still-manifest preoccupation in the critical literature (in its popular forms as much
as in its more scientific uses) with the description of territories,
movements, and relations in space. Students today—and not only
students—shy away from large diachronic questions and from
any attempt to conceptualize change, preferring instead to nest
within a set of spatially determined cultural units of comparison.
From the outset, I think it's fair to say that Rancière's project
worked against the grain of this spatial turn, both thematically
and in its polemical attacks on the inherent functionalism that
undergirded some of the principal thinkers associated with the
turn. Functionalism, in all its guises, affirms the status quo by
presenting a social system that is complete, achieved, from which
nothing is lacking. Social systems or cultures appear as fixed and
complete—fully formed. In the case of critics concerned with
postmodernism and the spatial fix, such as David Harvey or
Fredric Jameson, neither of whom figure in Rancière's polemics
(though Lyotard, another postmodernist, does), the static fixity of
the contemporary "postmodern" social system means some sort
of arrival of what Marx called "real subsumption." Rancière's
polemics have targeted a hyphenated structuralism-functionalism
whose powerful hold on not only social anthropology and sociology, but also history and the social sciences generally, testifies to

a kind of unbroken reign of evolutionist epistemology. Polemic, after all, is just a synonym for untimeliness. And to be untimely means to be about time, not outside of it, or beyond it. Rather than participating in the spatial fix, Rancière preferred to think the way time gives form to relations of power and inequality and how its denaturalization shatters those relations: his thinking concerns itself with both the temporal rhythms and schedules of work and ideology, as well as the temporality of emancipation. "Ideology," he wrote in *The Philosopher and His Poor*, "is just another name for work."* Rancière is not alone, of course, in being a thinker of differential temporalities. But to characterize him this way is to place him in a constellation of thinkers that might at first seem incongruous and that I'm not entirely sure he'd appreciate: in the company of the Marx of *Zeitwidrig* or contretemps, of his old teacher Louis Althusser's articulation of multiple times and the irreducibility of various levels to a single common history, of Ernst Bloch's "contemporaneity of the non-contemporaneous," of Maurice Halbwachs's plurality of social times, or even of a conservative thinker like Reinhart Koselleck's recurrent insistence that the archaic persists, and even thrives, at the core of the most advanced modernity.

But, if we return to the dominant spatial discourse of the period, we can see how a kind of all-pervasive functionalism informed the work of even those progressive thinkers who were called upon to form the bridge, so to speak, between an earlier linguistic/structural moment and the new explicit focus on exploring the mechanisms of living societies. I'm thinking of Pierre Bourdieu and Michel de Certeau, two thinkers whose principal works, *Distinction* and *The Practice of Everyday Life*, were translated into English during the 1980s and frequently assigned in classes,

---

* Jacques Rancière, *The Philosopher and His Poor*, trans. John Drury, Corinne Oster, and Andrew Parker (Durham: Duke University Press, 2004), p. 76.

in the States at least. In the United States and Australia, critics
attuned to developments in British cultural studies and weary
of post-structuralism were looking for works they hoped would
help them break out of the corral of epistemology to reach the
social, and these books seemed to respond to that demand. These
critics were particularly drawn to the spatialized dynamics of
power and resistance that de Certeau derived from Foucault, and
to the figure of his wily pedestrian, twisting and turning along
backstreets and byways, "turns" that were tropological as well as
geographic—de Certeau conflating the two in a whole celebratory
rhetoric of nonconformist walking.* All the liberatory values and
frissons of mobility once associated, in the earlier moment of the
linguistic paradigm, with the slippage of meaning in a literary
text, are now attributed to the pedestrian's cunning tactics: the
maneuvers and resistance of the relatively powerless. Leaving
considerations of power to the center—where, like all good functionalists, de Certeau believes it belongs in the interest of social
stability—what remains is life in the margins, which is allowed
to exist precisely because it poses no threat to the center's hold.
In a striking formulation that reading Rancière makes us alert to,
de Certeau writes, "Their bodies follow the thick and thins of
an urban text they write without being able to read."† A popular
text is being written, in other words, but only on the condition
that its authors cannot read or understand it. These, then, are the
maneuvers of a more or less authentic urban folk, the authenticity
of whose daily practices derives from their sheer, unknowing
ordinariness, as well as their sheer unknowingness. "The actual
order of things," de Certeau writes, "is precisely what popular
tactics turn to their own ends, without any illusion that it is about

---

* Michel de Certeau, *The Practice of Everyday Life* (Berkeley: University
of California Press, 1984. See especially the chapter entitled "Walking the City."
    † Ibid., p. 93.

to change."* Unlike, say, a more nuanced thinker of the everyday like Henri Lefebvre, de Certeau cannot imagine how the everyday can be about history—any tension between experience and antic- ipation for him has been erased. Change having been precluded and temporality effectively frozen, the way is now cleared for a socially cohesive consensus portrait of what de Certeau called "ordinary culture"—unchanging, repetitive customs, hobbies, and dispositions that form what might at best be called a culture of consolation. And the historian's role is completely assimilated to that of the ethnologist: "For the historian," he writes, "as for the ethnologist, the goal is to make function a cultural whole, to make its laws appear, to structure a landscape."†

It is easy, now, to see how such a mechanistic seesaw of power and resistance could go on to form the backbone of Anglo- American cultural studies' celebration of ludic resistance through consumption. Here, too, there is the presumption of a fully formed commodity relation, or "real subsumption." But, already in 1977, the *Révoltes Logiques* collective, in an interview with Foucault, asked questions they and Nicos Poulantzas were alone in formu- lating at that time, questions that showed how power, in Foucault's schema, operates like full subsumption. For, in such a schema, wasn't power, presupposed to be always already there, locked in the grip of a battle with equally unchanging mass-resistance tactics—wasn't power thus rendered absolute? Wasn't it better to begin a discussion of power with the question of whom it serves, in whose interests?‡

De Certeau arrives at the same ratio of unknowingness and repetitive motion as Pierre Bourdieu, whose guiding concept of

---

* Ibid., p. 26.

† De Certeau, "La beauté du mort," *La culture au pluriel* (Paris: Christian Bourgeois, 1980), p. 69.

‡ See Michel Foucault, "Pouvoirs et strategies: Entretien avec Michel Foucault," *Révoltes Logiques* 4 (1977), pp. 89–97.

habitus houses both humans and their habitual dispositions. *Habitus* is that which allows us to practice an accumulation of collective experiences without knowing we are doing so. For Bourdieu, it goes without saying because it comes without saying. Once again, the *Révoltes Logiques* collective was alone at the time, in the early 1980s, in showing the way in which Bourdieu represented a powerful afterlife to Durkheimian sociology and its logic of social cohesion. What is eternalized and internalized—the aptly named "second nature"—becomes what is forgotten in history. And a once-lively history filled with agents and eventfulness subsides into the stable representations of the *habitus*—where no horizon other than being in perfect conformity to one's condition is visible.

I wanted to revisit these widely read thinkers whose concerns with popular culture bore at least a passing resemblance to those of Rancière in order to highlight how different, in fact, his own questions were. Beginnings, points of departure, are more important for Rancière than for most thinkers, and the gesture of throwing the engine into reverse is one way he likes to begin. What happens if you begin not with culture conceived of as one's proper allotment of symbolic capital, nor with culture conceived of as a set of consoling rituals? What happens if you don't begin with culture at all, but instead with emancipation? "The concept of culture," Rancière noted in his book on history, "whether one applies it to knowledge of the classics or to the manufacture of shoes, has the sole effect of effacing this movement of subjectivization that operates in the interval between several nominations and its constitutive fragility."* The concept of culture presupposes an identity tied to a way of speaking, being, and doing that is itself

---

* Jacques Rancière, *The Names of History: On the Poetics of History*, trans. Hassan Melehy (Minneapolis: University of Minnesota Press, 1994), p. 98.

tied to a situation, a name, a body, assigned to a place, a life station. Culture is inherently functionalist, noncontingent.

Arlette Farge has written very eloquently about the antiethnological dimension of Rancière's work on history writing, and the disquiet with which social historians initially greeted it, only to have their hostility subside into a willed forgetting.* What I take from her remarks is this: as long as space—territory or *terroir*— is the departure point for an analysis, if you begin with space, whether it be the space of the region, island, factory, or banlieue, then people's voices, their subjectivities, can be nothing more than the naturalized, homogenized expression of those spaces. Rancière's project, in this sense, could be said to be at the forefront of one kind of cultural studies—but only an anti-identitarian one: a cultural studies where the concept of culture has been banished from the outset and identitarian matters twisted into a fluid and unscheduled nonsystem of significant misrecognitions.

It was when I taught a recent seminar on the various ways eventfulness is constructed and perceived that I began to get a full sense of the untimeliness of Rancière's project. For one way of characterizing the intellectual labor of the late 1970s and early 1980s is to see it as a massive and relentless dismantling of the event or eventfulness, at the hands not only of progressives like Bourdieu and de Certeau, but of virtually everyone in the vicinity. First and foremost, of course, there was the Annales school's preoccupation with summoning up the full weight and inertia of centuries of ways of doing, with reaffirming the whole circularity of nature and function. The New Philosophers, in another corner, wielded the weapon of scale, rendering every action negligible or suspect, dwarfed or criminalized in the face

---

* See Arlette Farge, "L'histoire comme avènement," *Critique* 601–2 (June–July 1997), pp. 461–6.

of the twin catastrophes of the Gulag and the Holocaust, and the various "endisms" to which these gave rise. In a not-unrelated enterprise, François Furet set his sights on dismantling the event par excellence, anchoring his attempt to turn the French Revolution into the American Revolution squarely within the ideology of the present and the wish to provide a different genealogy for the liberalism (in the French sense) of the 1980s. An opportunistic but talented journalist, and a powerful model for followers like Tony Judt in the United States, Furet's reign as *roi des historiens* in France was no less long-lived or far-reaching than was Bourdieu's as *roi des sociologues*. It is not, I think, an exaggeration to say that these two academics—with the various associates, journals, and *équipes de travail* each presided over, and the institutional privileges each was granted—virtually controlled the production and direction of countless French intellectual careers in and beyond their respective disciplines throughout the 1980s. In the case of Bourdieu, his own trajectory took an existential turn, if not a theoretical one, after 1995, with his increasingly militant political activities. In the case of Furet, his work was enormously facilitated by the emergence of American-style think tanks in the 1980s, including the Fondation Saint-Simon, over which he presided until his death. This foundation, whose history has yet to be written, brought together for the first time in France a mix of government leaders, academics, industrialists, and media people in a kind of dinner club organized around a nebulous "modernizing project," with modernity being understood to mean conformity to the economic constraints of the neoliberal order. The goal was to bring the social sciences into direct service to the state, and the result was, clearly, a further consolidation of the intellectual's position as expert or consultant to the state, clear-eyed and cognizant of hard economic realities. The idea was that intellectuals, liberated from abstraction and engaged in pragmatic problem-solving, would encounter social problems unbiased by ideological considerations. The model here had, of course, been provided by the American "servants of power": social scientists who were early on enlisted in the service of the state. The American ideal of Weberian-Parsonian "value-free" social science found a home at the Fondation Saint-Simon, where Furet, deeply engaged in a recuperation of the American model, attempted to bring France in line with the kind of seamless integration of media, capital, and state power I evoked earlier under the figure of "perception management." Any adversaries—critical intellectuals or those engaged in social movements—could be disqualified in advance as flaming ideologues, irresponsible, hellbent on swimming against the tide of history, or, in a favorite accusation of the time, "anti-American." And to be called anti-American in France in the 1980s was tantamount to being accused of fascist tendencies, Stalinist tendencies, or both at the same time—a kind of post-Arendtian Red-Brown fusion.

Rancière's battle, in this sense, was and, I believe, continues to be a battle with strategies whose aim is the suppression of time. After the *Révoltes Logiques* experiment came to an end in 1981, he was sustained in his fight, I think, by an abiding loyalty to what is perhaps an unlikely source: to a certain reading of Benveniste, from whom he derived his insistence on the ways in which eventfulness depends upon speech. In Rancière's writing, all of the startling and expansive emancipatory power Benveniste attributed to the production of the first instance of enunciation is retained and dramatized. "Language," wrote Benveniste in a famous formulation, "is so organized that it permits each speaker to appropriate to himself an entire language by designating himself as 'I.'"* Something of the enormous potentiality of the moment of

---

*   Emile Benveniste, *Problems in General Linguistics*, trans. Mary Elizabeth Meek, vol. 1 (Coral Gables: University of Miami Press, 1971), p. 226.

subjectivity, the appropriation of an entire language—and not the crablike, sideways entry into subjectivity that Monique Wittig, in her reading of Benveniste, would later say is allotted to women*— is retained in Rancière's version of the event. And something of the conscious framing or staging, as well: subjectivization in Rancière's texts never takes on the consistency of a theory of the subject, let alone a fixed or coherent subject, just as no underlying ontology to his analyses is ever explicitly designated as such. Yet the instance of appropriation is invariably, for him, at one and the same time a moment of disidentification, the creation of an *écart* or fissure in whatever had previously secured identity. Adrian Rifkin, commenting on the recurrent thematics of the *écart* throughout Rancière's work, has suggested that *écartement* (setting aside, deflection, displacement) is deployed there in several ways: It is a way of using images or themes in his writing, moving them around so that other figures become visible or recede from view. It is a strategy he deploys in the positioning of his writing vis-à-vis the current intellectual ambiance (what I am calling here his untimeliness) on the one hand, and in deflecting his reader from any doctrinal readings of materials on the other. It is even related to the kind of thought-effect he creates in his readers.†

These delineations are extremely illuminating. Yet Rancière is

---

*   Monique Wittig, *The Lesbian Body*, trans. David Le Vay (New York: Avon, 1976).

†   Adrian Rifkin, "Il y a des mots qu'on ne souhaiterait plus lire," *Paragraph* 28, no. 1 (March 2005), p. 105. For Rifkin, the intellectual adventure implied by the title *Révoltes Logiques* (a title borrowed from Rimbaud) relocated revolt in this "setting aside," this écartement from and of the doctrinal concerns of disciplinary formations—even at the point of their most radical self-consciousness. He makes the point that it would be an error to confuse this effect with that of Derridean différance, since the process of écartement that characterizes Rancière's most compelling work is highly specific and emerges in his working through of a particular set of arguments regarding a painting, a film, or a social formation. It is not, in other words, a theoretical procedure that can be generalized as with Derrida.

a thinker whose first major work, *The Nights of Labor,* drew our attention very powerfully to the act of stealing time. His study relocated workers into another kind of time, outside the temporal regime established by Marx. Marx's "workday," he showed, was actually exceeded by night and all its possibilities. In this astonishing critique, what becomes clear for the first time is how closely aligned Marx's own perspective was: not with that of the worker, but rather with that of capital—the perspective of "the production of surplus value." Taking our lead from this early text, I think it may be useful to think of Rancière's *écartement* as first and foremost a fissure or wrinkle in time: a *décalage,* a moment of nonsynchronicity or fracture, an interval, as in "the rift or the interval through which subjects of history pass."* To this end I want to trace the temporal thematics of Rancière's work.

The first thematizing of time occurs in the atmosphere immediately after May '68, right before the launch of the *Révoltes Logiques* journal in 1975. It appears in the pages of *La leçon d'Althusser,* where Althusserian theory is construed as the enacting of so many theoretical ruptures in order that none be put into political practice. Althusserian theory, in other words, becomes in Rancière's work the first example of a temporality proper to "those who know." To those who know is granted the science of the conjuncture, the ability of determining the timing of the revolt, as well as when best to wait it out. What was revealed in the failed meeting between Althusserian theory and the insurrection of 1968 was that the antagonisms and disagreements of empirical politics will never provide philosophy with the right moment to connect with political action: it is never the moment, and it will never be the moment. The temporality proper to those who know is that of waiting, deliberating, persevering, allowing theory to take its

---

* Rancière, *The Names of History,* p. 98.

time; '68 was not the proper moment. This initial experience and its critique is, I think, at the origin of all of Rancière's subsequent concern with the relation of knowledge and the masses—with theorists who see themselves as advocates of equality but who reconstitute a hierarchy that is in large part a temporality that others are presumed not to share. By positing a relation between temporalities, Rancière's antifunctionalism is already apparent. For in the logic of functionalism, time is encapsulated in a given social system or culture: a singular, flat, unidimensional, linear, or worse, circular time. Each of these cultures can then be studied separately, ethnographically, according to a timeless theory or method. Time within cultures was worth studying, and could be, in any number of taxonomies, but time was virtually eliminated from the study of relations between cultures. It was the relation between different temporalities that, for Rancière, instead merited attention.

Jacotot, the ignorant schoolmaster, develops the theme of a temporal structure of delay, the distance in time that separates pedagogue from student. But, before we continue, we need to confront the question raised by the figure of Jacotot himself—and that has to do with the status of the example in Rancière's text. Who are these individuals, these mostly marginal characters who are also historical figures, often drawn forth from the most obscure archives? Jacotot, like Gauny, Blanqui, or the worker poets, arrives like a time traveler as if by accident, neither as spokesperson nor sociological representative, but nevertheless mobilized to do battle or at the very least to serve as a diagnostic of the contemporary situation. Such figures also appear as untimely, remnants or revenants from beyond the reach of standard time, emanating perhaps from the future. Though their ability to straddle great temporal expanses lends them a kind of science fiction–like aura, they do not resemble the characters in Philip K. Dick's *Ubik*, bloodless, or suspended in some half life. Each retains all of his individual singularity and historical contingency, as befits Rancière's obstinate insistence on staying at the level of the particular case, his insistence—against generalization, system, sometimes even against concept—on the particular, material, interlocutory situation. His concern is, first and foremost, with what specific historical actors have said and written in contingent situations. Yet the particular actions and points of view of marginal individuals, when resuscitated with care and attention, reframed and staged, can be mobilized against the dominant ideology. Provided, of course, that the right transversals are created. Historical figures, framed like literary characters, in order to refute, via philosophy, various political myths or ideologies—Rancière's peculiar and powerful version of transdisciplinarity takes this form. His response—that is, to the institution of fixed disciplinary knowledges—is not to merge or combine different knowledges but rather to use one to undermine and contest the other: to use history against philosophy, or literature against political theory. The way Jacotot is staged has the political effect of denouncing theories that invent the dominated that best suit their theoretical presuppositions. But it also has the advantage of infusing a kind of revitalized energy and potential for the new into history. History, in fact, is given much the same power Rancière grants to fiction: that of reframing, and thus expanding, perception, reconfiguring what is thinkable, scrambling perception management.

So, Jacotot is the anti-Bourdieu, whose enterprise of demystification is revealed to be yet another interlocutory situation based on explication, an activity that preserves formally the hierarchies and inherited subject positions it was intent on undermining at the level of content. And Jacotot can also be the anti-Althusser. For Jacotot, and the other autodidacts who inhabit Rancière's texts, effectively eliminates or short-circuits the very temporality of the pedagogical relation: the principle of infinite regression separating the ignorance of today from the science of the future. At the heart of the pedagogical relation is the representation of inequality as evolutionary epistemology: the people who can never catch up with the enlightened elite, or who can never be completely modern. People who are trapped, without knowing it, at one stage along the trajectory of progressive time, and who are destined to remain there, imprisoned in this other time, that of the child, or that of the primitive. But inequality can't be gradually whittled away, just as equality is not a goal to be one day attained, nor arrived at by dint of a series of concessions made by the state. Short-circuiting the temporality of pedagogy makes equality a point of departure, *the* point of departure, an axiom anterior to the constitution of a particular staging of politics and which makes such a staging possible. Rather than being the criteria that determines how long it will take for society as it is to become society as it might or should be, equality as an axiom enables thought, experiment, invention.

Jacotot, Rancière tells us, is a man of the previous century, a man of the revolutionary moment, out of sorts or out of sync with the burgeoning century of progress gradually taking shape around him. He is, in this sense, something of an anachronism—the second temporal disjuncture dear to Rancière I want to discuss. Jacotot is a time traveler in his own moment, a figure of non-contemporaneity, and like all such figures, either ahead of or behind his times, residual or emergent—or probably both at the same time. Rancière's 1996 essay on anachronism, perhaps more than the book he devoted to historicity, *The Names of History*, reveals the symptom of the whole naturalizing tendency the Annales school put into place, that immobile interlacing of thought, identity, practice, and belief to be encapsulated in the fear of anachronism.* Fear of anachronism was another name for the conception Febvre articulated but that others shared as well—the conception that existence means belonging to, coinciding with, or resembling, one's time. Rabelais could not have not believed in God, because disbelieving was inconceivable in Rabelais's era. This is really nothing more than pure Rankian historicism, an extreme version of "cultural respect"—like judging the native by his own standards or judging the period according to its own presuppositions. But Febvre is not alone in seeing the historian's task as being that of establishing what is thinkable in a given era. Foucault's notion of the episteme, which eliminates event or time as agent, does much the same. And the purpose of social history is limited to understanding ideologies and social movements within the particular economic and political contexts these secrete like a mollusk's shell—thus flattening any possibility of event or change. The presuppositions of the more recent cultural history are no different. For the new cultural historians, culture behaves in a way identical to Parsons's social system†—as fully formed, with only periodic disfunctions or deviations. Culture and social system, in turn, act like the nation-state—the authority figure behind all these categories, and one that Rancière, to my knowledge, doesn't really address. Social science in general spends its time making the people who don't resemble their moment get back into the harness, making any aberrant speech fit the context—and in so doing affirming not only the noneventfulness, but the unknowingness, even the duped nature, of the objects of history as well—making them at one with the beliefs of their era. For the only way you can belong to your era is without knowing it—which is to say, through belief. The people are people who can't think otherwise.

---

* See Rancière, "Le concept de l'anachronisme et le vérité de l'historien," *Inactuel: Psychanalyse et culture* 6 (1996), pp. 53–69.

† See Talcott Parsons, *The Social System* (Glencoe, IL: Free Press, 1951).

But in the history of social formations, there is a multiplicity of times, some of which present themselves as repetitions, while others effect tesseracts, wrinkles that join the ancient with the contemporary—different times, as Rancière puts it, "telescoping" into one another.* Thus the future appears in the present, the present repeats the past, and what some call anachronisms can inhabit an era. This is all very disturbing for those of us who learned to conceive of "era" as one of those large, homogenous blocs or signifying totalities, as in the books we read as children, books with titles like *The Baroque Period*, where you are made to understand that the baroque period was baroque because back then sculpture was baroque, legal systems were baroque, poetry and even the people who wrote it were baroque ...

Perhaps the most audacious and influential attempt to suppress time in the 1970s and 1980s took the tried-and-true form called "revisionism"—François Furet's influential rewriting of the French Revolution such that it didn't occur. Revisionism, for Rancière, is another name for what happens in the architecture of historical narration when you assemble data in such a way that it remains a pile of data, such that it does not take on the shape and consistency of a singular event. Extreme contextualization, thick description—these can show that the event really wasn't one. No new object—or rather, no new subject—appears. Furet showed the revolution to have transpired to create what was, in fact, already in place; revolutionary actors acted under "the illusion of defeating a State that had already ceased to exist."† They toppled an enemy that wasn't even there—the poor fools. They were too late, exerting themselves for no reason; it wasn't the right moment. The revolution had already happened without

---

*   Rancière, "Histoire des mots, mots de l'histoire (entretien avec Martyne Perrot et Martin de la Soudière)," *Communications* 58 (1994), p. 93.

†   François Furet, *Interpreting the French Revolution* (Cambridge: Cambridge University Press, 1981), cited in Rancière, *The Names of History*, p. 38.

them. But who was to know, until Furet told us two hundred years later?

Furet's dismantling of the grand narrative of the French Revolution heralded and enabled the arrival, more recently, of the third temporal manifestation I want to mention, the particular paralysis of history Rancière has diagnosed under the name of "endism." This was the attempt made by philosophers, with a gravitas that frequently careened into hysteria, to create a specifically new and postmodern era based on announcing the end of art, for example, or the end of ideology, the end of politics, or, ultimately, the end of meaningful time. All of these endisms were about ending time, and were in effect a repetition of Parsons's banishment of time from the social system in the earlier "end of ideology" of the American 1950s. Much of Rancière's recent work has had a double focus: that of undercutting the historical pertinence of the catastrophism that claims to account for the current postmodern situation, and that of bypassing or dismantling the postmodern paradigm in its pretension to historical newness, its claim to singularity as a new and distinct era. What appears new in the era of apocalyptic pronouncements and its "unsatisfactory mise-en-scène of the 'end' and the 'return,'" is, in fact, just a restaging.* Philosophical activity undertaken under the sign of urgency is a new version of an old phenomenon: the heroicizing of the philosopher's voice, the philosopher as prophet who can see "the end" that others cannot see. Ambulance philosophy of this kind first came into being with what Alain Badiou has called the "Thermidorean subjectivity" of the New Philosophers, who tirelessly fabricated an end to history and politics out of their own political disillusionment.†

---

*   Rancière, *The Politics of Aesthetics*, ed. and trans. Gabriel Rockhill (London: Continuum, 2004), p. 11.

†   Alain Badiou, *Metapolitics*, trans. Jason Barker (New York: Verso, 2005), p. 128.

Yet politics, for Rancière, is not a matter of illusion or disillusion, but of demonstrating or verifying equality. It is an interlocutory event. And if politics hasn't ended, it is still exceptional or scarce, appearing as an event, and then only intermittently. The temporality of politics is not progressive, nor dialectical—a word he uses only rarely—it is not continuous and it's not over. Politics is an event that cannot be predicted any more than its end can be apocalyptically announced. It is always circumstantial, local, and entirely contained in its singular manifestations. Unconcerned with duration or, for the most part, with measuring any social effects or usefulness such events might have—and supremely unconcerned with institutions—Rancière's thought has produced disappointment in readers looking for a prescription or a program for action for that matter, a celebration of time spent "in the trenches," so to speak, the temporality of militant organizing.* What connects each manifestation to the next seems to be a kind of affirmative repetition; each instance, by departing from and reaffirming equality as a principle, makes possible a new manifestation; each is, as it were, "present" for the next manifestation as it occurs. This repetition is not the transmission of lessons learned or the inheritance of a legacy, nor the fixation—be it melancholy or ecstatic—on some transcendent experience from the past. It has more to do with the attentive embrace of the present situation in all of its contingency. It is worth recalling that such a goal was already apparent in the project statement written by the *Révoltes Logiques* collective in one of the early issues. The "lesson" of history, the collective wrote, is to, at best, "recognize the moment of a choice, of the unforeseeable, to draw from history

---

* See, for example, Daniel Bensaid's critique of what he takes to be Rancière's sophisticated avoidance of politics, which in his view risks, through its emphasis on politics' rarity or intermittent temporality, an esthetic or philosophical posture in flight from contradiction. Bensaid, *Eloge de la résistance à l'air du temps* (Paris: Editions Textuel, 1999), pp. 45–6.

neither lessons, nor, exactly, explanations, but the principle of a vigilance toward what there is that is singular in each call to order and in each confrontation."* In this way, perhaps, Rancière gives a new meaning to "praxis," shifting it away from its emphasis on subjects acting on objects in order to change things along a linear, progressive temporality. Praxis might, then, entail a kind of watchfulness or attention to these intermittent manifestations, to the moments when such demonstrations are produced, the moments when, in fact, something is happening. To happen, events must be perceived and acknowledged as such. Rancière's work contributes to making the moment when such demonstrations are produced more visible.

---

* Editorial, *Révoltes Logiques* 5 (Spring–Summer 1977), p. 6.

6
Yesterday's Critique, Today's Mythologies

Reading *Mythologies* today, we encounter words on every page that are as unfamiliar to us as the contours of the Citroen *Déesse:* "bourgeois art," "proletarianization," "expropriation," "our bourgeois readers," "the proletariat and the poor," "petit bourgeois ideology." Of course, fifty years ago, when Barthes published his attempt to reflect on some of the myths of French daily life, these words were part of common parlance. Why should the intellectual landscape made up of words from the recent past, words that we are no longer accustomed to reading, matter to us today? What importance could a text like *Mythologies*—little journalistic pieces, written mostly as responses to current events and *faits divers*— have for our present? Can a work like Henri Lefebvre's *Critique de la vie quotidienne*, its three volumes published across a span stretching from 1946 to 1981, speak to the everyday of the early twenty-first century? In my own cultural history of the postwar period, *Fast Cars, Clean Bodies*, I argued that what French theorists and social critics as different from each other as Henri Lefebvre, Edgar Morin, and Roland Barthes provided in a set of magisterial analyses written in the late 1950s and early 1960s was the vision of their own time as turning point—the moment when even the most remote rural villages in France had been touched by the arrival of large-scale consumer durables. What these works registered with a startling clarity was that de Gaulle comes to power and the Fifth Republic is founded precisely at the moment when "the consumer era" begins in France in earnest. This was the moment—after electricity but before electronics—when the groundwork was laid for a full-scale disruption of older popular culture and its replacement with the rhythms and habits of an American-style capitalist or "mass" culture. Even more significant than the automobiles and laundry detergent was the discourse surrounding them: the endless background noise of advertising insinuating their advantages. As Henri Lefebvre enjoyed repeating, his moment of great philosophical discovery, the discovery of the concept of everyday life, occurred one day when a woman to whom he was then married came into the apartment where they were living, and, holding up a box of detergent, pronounced the words: "Ceci est un excellent produit" (This is an excellent product). "With just the right tone," he adds in his memoirs. "These words, in their triviality, crystallized in an instant the concept of the everyday and the project of the critique of everyday life."*

The result, then, of this simple, perhaps apocryphal encounter between the philosopher and his wife was the raising of everyday life to the status of a critical concept—a *project*, as he puts it, and one that would occupy Lefebvre from the 1950s through to the 1980s. And, even beyond, to the extent that his work on urbanism essentially represents a spatial recoding of his earlier intuitions about everyday life. But the elements of the dramatic scene of origin are striking in their banality: a domestic interior, *le bonheur conjugal*, a day like any other, the sound of a woman's voice, a voice that is her own and yet isn't, some simple words spoken in

---

* Henri Lefebvre, *Le Temps des méprises* (Paris: Stock, 1975), p. 34. See also Ross, *Fast Cars*.

a tone that mimicked perfectly, and probably unconsciously, the discourse of advertising. With just the right tone: the tone, that is, through which that great abstraction known as multinational capital enters and permeates our lives and consciences.

The publication of books like Barthes's *Mythologies*, Lefebvre's *Critique de la vie quotidienne*, or the ephemeral existence in the late 1950s of a journal like Kostas Axelos's *Arguments* registered a significant break in lived experience brought on by the accelerated state-led modernization effort after the war. But these works represented just as much the invention of an entirely new mode, a new *genre*, of analysis as well. Old lines of thought, older constellations, found themselves displaced and old and new elements were regrouped around a different set of premises and themes. Each of these works sought to provide a critical history of the present. The present, in other words, existed as an object of ideological critique, not something to be merely described or documented. These were books that foregrounded in a new way questions of culture, consciousness, and experience examined under the rubric of "everyday life." This, of course, meant abandoning macro-social history of the kind favored by the Second International. It meant taking "culture" and forms of pleasure seriously as a dimension without which historical transformations, past and present, simply could not be adequately thought. It meant recognizing that everyday life practices—the way people shop, the way they move about the city—and not abstract ideas, philosophies, or beliefs, had come to play the functional role of ideology. Practices of consumption, in other words, act to legitimate and reproduce the system, regardless of an individual or a group's particular beliefs or values.

What did not occur to me at the time I wrote my book in the early 1990s is that these formative texts bear comparison with breakthrough works being produced in England at exactly the

same moment in the late 1950s: Hoggart's *Uses of Literacy* and a
series of works by Raymond Williams, *Culture and Society*, *Culture
Is Ordinary*, and *The Idea of a Common Culture*. The British and the
French projects are alike in the following way: contemporary in
focus, they were themselves focused by, organized through, and
constituted responses to the immediate pressure of the postwar
moment and the society in which they were written. At once
analytic and political, empirical and utopian, "everyday life,"
the concept, plays much the same role in the work of Lefebvre
as does "culture" for Raymond Williams.

But, where the work of Hoggart and Williams went on to find
an institutional home in Birmingham at the Centre for Contemporary cultural studies under the direction of Stuart Hall,
the French texts made little or no dent on the academy. In that
sense their material origins bear little resemblance to the Worker's Education Association and the adult education movement,
the whole commitment to educating working-class adults that
was the impulse behind the British intellectual project. Looking
back, though, the French texts do at least represent a high point,
a virtually unique and "jewel-like" moment of interdisciplinary
work—something akin to an indigenous French cultural studies
whose novelty and threat could be gauged by the almost unani-
mous hostility with which a book like *Mythologies* was greeted by
specialists in France—be they anthropologists, literary scholars,
or sociologists. It's worth remarking that productive interdis-
ciplinarity of this kind has since been progressively eliminated
in France in the wake of ever-greater pressures toward narrow
academic specialization and an ever-more-reified division of intellectual fields and areas of expertise. Thinking about the moment
of Barthes and Lefebvre makes it clear that it was the Germans
—Simmel, Kracauer, Walter Benjamin, and later Wolfgang
Schivelbusch—who in fact *invented* French cultural studies at an

earlier moment, beginning in the 1930s. They invented it with their intricate analysis of nineteenth-century Paris: an obsession with that particular city so all-encompassing that Benjamin's entrapment by Paris, in the words of Adrian Rifkin, "has in effect left us with *its* figure as that of the lost futurity of capital in the economic sense of the word and, at the same time, as the presiding substratum of cityness in general as a mental precept."* But it was the French themselves who set out after World War II to debate the discontents and anxieties surrounding modernization ideology and the adoption of American-style consumption practices in an array of interdisciplinary experiments. Even the *Cahiers du cinéma,* in that sense, can be read as one response among many, and a very different one than that of *Mythologies,* to the rise of mass culture and a burgeoning Americanism.

What precisely was at stake, then, in the emergence of the everyday as a cluster of theoretical themes and, above all, as a *project*—what Henri Lefebvre called "the critique of everyday life from within"?†

Essentially such a critique, as John Roberts has noted, studied both the negative and positive aspects of capitalist culture as they confront each other on a daily basis.‡ I want to point to what is already assumed in such a description. First and foremost, a concept of everyday life that is specifically modern and that is primarily a category of capitalism, of capitalism's proliferation of distinct, structured, specialized activities and its intensification, especially after World War II, of the social division of labor. "Everyday life," properly speaking, first comes into being only at the moment, midway through the nineteenth century, when

---

* Adrian Rifkin, "Benjamin's Paris, Freud's Rome, Whose London?" in *The Metropolis and its Image,* ed. Dana Arnold (London: Blackwell, 1999), p. 155.

† Henri Lefebvre, *Critique of Everyday Life,* vol. 1 (London: Verso, 1991), p. 9.

‡ John Roberts, *The Art of Interruption: Realism, Photography and the Everyday* (Manchester: Manchester University Press, 1998), p. 8.

European cities begin to swell with the arrival of large numbers of newcomers, the moment—and this is crucial—when Marx conceptualized and systematized the "work day" of the wage laborer. When the lived experience of those new urban dwellers became organized, channeled, and codified into a set of repetitive and hence visible patterns, when markets became common between the provinces and the capital, when everything—work hours, money, miles, calories, minutes—became calculated and calculable, and when objects, people, and the relations between them changed under the onslaught of such quantification, then and only then and only there, in the large Western metropolises, did the world, in Lefebvre's words, "turn to prose."

But the prosaic is itself double-sided for Lefebvre, carrying within it both the possibility of the realization of human needs and desires and their frustration. In this sense his version of the everyday marks a distinct departure from the purely negative connotations of Heideggerian *alltäglichkeit:* dull, ordinary rote and inauthentic existence, the dreary unfolding of base and trivial repetition. And it marked a distinct departure from the Frankfurt School's disdain for the tainted and shared realities of popular culture as well. Lefebvre's writing on the everyday—on horoscopes, women's magazines, advertising—was some of the first to connect a dialectical analysis of the contemporary identity of the object to the idea of culture as a site of alienated struggle. The alienating forms of everyday life, its commodities and detritus, contain within them real, if unconscious and fragmented, desires, vestiges of lost totalities, vestiges whose tendencies and impulses can be drawn out. As the late Michel Trebitsch put it in his preface to the English translation of *Critique de la vie quotidienne,* "everyday life in the modern world is both a parody of lost plenitude and the last remaining vestige of that plenitude."* Alienation in

---

* Michel Trebitsch, Preface, *Critique*, vol. 1, p. xxiv.

daily life must be situated in dialectical tension with forces of critique and emancipation.

And, as for Lefebvre's "method," that too was dialectical in that he sought to provide what was at once a philosophical concept of the everyday with a historical analysis of its evolving forms. The philosophical and the historical acted on each other in a kind of reciprocal critique: "The limitations of philosophy—truth without reality—always and ever counterbalance the limitations of everyday life—reality without truth."* Everyday life as such was, in the words of Peter Osborne, both empirical and utopian: empirical in the multiplicity of its concrete forms and utopian in its promise of universality or fullness.†

But to what extent can we call the highly interdisciplinary project of developing a critique of everyday life a historical project? To do so we must recognize the way in which the project rewrote historical time to now include the present—the present no longer conceived of as a teleological end point of past events, nor as a static anthropological, structural field. If the present is to emerge as a set of possibilities, as open-ended, changeable, and contradictory, then it must be *de-naturalized*. Sometime after *Mythologies* was published, Barthes commented that his own book had been written under the triple aegis of Sartre, Marx, and Brecht. These intellectual affinities make sense if we consider the short journalistic essays that make up the first part of the book to be an exercise in *historic realism*. The Sartrean concept of "situation" dominated the postwar intellectual scene, and the analysis of gestures, acts, objects, and texts in *Mythologies* can be read as a related attempt at "situated" knowledge, a construction of a common social and historical situation. Later Barthes would add another guiding

---

*   Henri Lefebvre, *Everyday Life in the Modern World*, trans. Sacha Rabinowitz (New York: Harper, 1971), p. 14.

†   Peter Osborne, *The Politics of Time* (London: Verso, 1995), p. 192.

precursor to his work: that of Michelet. "What pleased him in Michelet is ... the desire and the skill of questioning historically —i.e., *relatively*—those objects supposedly the most natural: face, food, clothes, complexion."* For Lefebvre too the present is the starting point—the present as objectively similar "situation" in the Sartrean sense. Images of a past integrity retrospectively constructed can then be compared or used as criteria for a critique of the present, again with the purpose of destabilizing the present, making it open to change:

> Knowledge of daily life is necessary but not sufficient or self-sufficient; for its objective and stake are not to ratify the existing state of affairs, but to move towards what is possible. Knowledge of daily life is not cumulative, conforming to the usual schema and project of the so-called social sciences, because it transforms itself along with its object.†

I'd like to work through each of these propositions about knowledge systematically, since the passage I've just cited gives a particularly rich sense of Lefebvre's thinking about the everyday. First: "What is at stake is not to ratify the existing state of affairs but to move towards what is possible." This, then, is not a neutral philosophical investigation, an ethical "art de vivre," nor an exercise in pure thought. To formulate the quotidian as a concept, to wrench it from the continuum in which it is embedded (or better yet, the continuum that it *is*), to expose it, examine it, give it a history, is *already* to critique it. And to critique it is to wish for and work toward change, transformation—a revolution in the very nature of advanced capitalist society in the second half of the twentieth century.

---

* Roland Barthes, *Roland Barthes* (New York: Hill and Wang, 1977), p. 84.

† Henri Lefebvre, *Critique of Everyday Life*, trans. Gregory Elliott, vol. 3 (London: Verso, 2005), p. 6.

Second: knowledge of the quotidian is not cumulative. Knowledge of the quotidian does not work through accretion or simple reproduction, nor does it aspire, as do the social sciences, to any form of "scientific" description. That kind of pragmatic or positivist approach would imply acceptance of the status quo (an acceptance, by the way, then flourishing in the United States of the 1950s in the form of "value-free" Parsonian social science). The everyday can be taken as an "object," but not as a statistical object or as the pretext for the construction of a model. It can be taken as an object only as the point of departure for action. It does not represent some level of life inferior to the intellectual or spiritual level. It thus cannot become an object in the epistemological sense—it cannot be constituted or grasped as a "field." The alienating forms of everyday life, its commodities and its trash, contain within them real, if unconscious and fragmented, desires. Were there no continuing "mystery" or ambiguity, were there no continuing unevenness produced by the ongoing reproduction of capitalist market relations, then the appropriate approach to the everyday might very well be sociological, just as the literary figures by which we could approximate the everyday might well be strictly mimetic, and most likely realist or, better, naturalist in kind. Yet, from the outset, Lefebvre's earliest attempts to provide a figuration of the everyday veered away from sociology and toward literature. The everyday, it seems, must first be fictionalized in order to be thought. The capacity of consciousness to register the everyday, he suggests, takes place through fiction; it is only through the medium of a literary text, a novel—Joyce's *Ulysses*—that we are made aware of everyday life. The choice of Joyce is at first surprising. This is a novel, after all, that, in Lefebvre's words, "lies *at the farthest reaches* from the traditional novel, the novel that recounts the formation of an individual, the rise and fall of a family, the destiny of a

group."* Instead of Zola (the "understood" example of the traditional novel), Joyce. Instead of the sociological, the tropic and
the sociological inextricably merged, the tropic, if anything, in
the ascendancy. Lefebvre's choice of Joyce over Zola is in this
sense prefigured by the relentlessness of Walter Benjamin's quest
to make Charles Baudelaire *the* figure of his nineteenth century:
Baudelaire, that is, and not Emile Zola. Zola, as Adrian Rifkin
points out, emerges nowhere as a source for Benjamin's nineteenth
century, despite Zola's unusually comprehensive depictions of
the sociology of commerce in Second Empire Paris—depictions
whose circumstantial detail went well beyond contemporaries who
exploited the same material.† All of Zola's skill in collecting the
minutiae of everyday life—the lists of fabrics, the actual lunch
menus eaten by shop girls, the methods of remuneration, all the
statistical and topographical information one could possibly desire
to recognize the emergence of the great department stores—all
this is displayed in full force in *Au Bonheur des Dames,* the novel
that well deserves its reputation as being the novel of modern
consumerism. From Zola it is but a short step to the full-blown
commodity panic of a Guy Debord or a Jean Baudrillard, the
whole post-situationist melancholic world where every activity,
every aspect of lived experience has been given over to the seamless, naturalized logic of the commodity form. Shouldn't Zola
be the logical choice to prefigure the everyday life of the 1960s?

Yet, for the purposes of Benjamin, writing about the mid-
nineteenth century, or Lefebvre, writing about the mid-twentieth,
Zola, it seems, suffers from the disease diagnosed in him by
Lukács: a view of inherited characteristics fetishized to the point of
mythology. Zola is bad, complacent, naturalist totality, drowning

---

*   Lefebvre, *Everyday Life in the Modern World,* p. 3.
†   Adrian Rifkin, "Total Ellipsis: Zola, Benjamin, and the Dialectics of Kitsch,"
Parallax 2 (1996), pp. 101–13.

in description, totality through accretion, the will to full or saturated coverage, to a complete filling in of the picture such that
nothing is missing, and nothing exceeds. For the purpose of "denaturalizing," Barthes chooses Rimbaud's *Drunken Boat* and not
the naturalist coziness of Jules Verne's *Nautilus*.

Now, back to the third point: "Knowledge of the quotidian
transforms itself along with its object." Throughout his career,
Barthes returned to the project of *Mythologies*, examining and
reconsidering the concerns that had preoccupied him at the time
he wrote the little essays. In so doing, he was pondering the
longevity or duration of the genre of popular culture analysis he
had invented. Could it continue unchanged, as its author aged, as
semiology became widespread, as France and much of the world
erupted in the massive political upheavals of the 1960s, then lived
through their aftermath? "Those pieces were the result of some
very strong feelings," wrote Barthes in 1970, looking back on
Mythologies:

> I was annoyed, at the time, by a certain tone in the press, in the
> publicity of what is called mass communications ... What I didn't
> agree with was the presentation of an event in terms of a kind of
> implicit natural psychology. As if what was said about the event
> were obvious, as if the event and its meaning coincided naturally.*

By the 1970s, Barthes had come to distance himself from
the stance of the "mythologist," the enunciatory position that
"unveils," or "denounces," a position that risks what he would
later call arrogance. Yet his reasons for this distancing are somewhat contradictory. On the one hand, he seems to feel that the
mythological project could not continue because ideological

---

* Roland Barthes, "*L'Express* Talks with Roland Barthes," *The Grain of the
Voice: Interviews 1962–1980* (New York: Hill and Wang, 1985), pp. 94–5.

criticism itself had become more subtle, more intricate than the simple gesture of reversal or unmasking he had performed in the essays in *Mythologies*. It had become more subtle, or at least it should be *becoming* more subtle. But, on the other hand, it seems, there was no longer any need for a mythologist because everyone was doing it, everyone had become a mythologist for himself or herself. "There is not a student who doesn't denounce the bourgeois or petit bourgeois character of a form (of life, of thought, of consumption),"[*] he wrote. Demystification itself, a genre Barthes had more or less invented, had become massified. Philippe Roger has argued that beginning with *L'Empire des signes*, Barthes began to substitute a form of affirmation for criticism, writerliness for critique—as in "These Are a Few of My Favorite Things."[†] But if so, the substitution was troubled and never complete; the ghost of the old mythologist was still there, for Barthes retained an allegiance to the earlier project of denaturalization or critique. In 1978, he was asked to write a regular chronicle for the *Nouvel Observateur*—short essays, signs of the time in the form of "weekly notes." Barthes seems to have used these exercises as an experiment in producing something like "affirmative" writing, writing that was not primarily concerned, as were the essays in *Mythologies*, with showing how the dominant relations of power work. The *Nouvel Observateur* pieces have no demonstrative energy, none of the momentum that careers to the bomb-like blast of the final sentence, the trigger-sharp mechanism with which so many of the essays in *Mythologies* conclude. They do not build to the moment of critique or revelation of an opening onto a world elsewhere; otherness, that is, or unevenness in what had previously seemed a seamless or saturated environment: the

---

[*]   Roland Barthes, "La Mythologie Aujourd'hui," *Le Bruissement de la langue* (Paris: Seuil, 1984), p. 80.

[†]   Phillipe Roger, *Roland Barthes, roman* (Paris: Grasset, 1986), p. 115.

Drunken Boat instead of the *Nautilus*. The journalistic chronicles of the late 1970s offer instead what I would call a "phenomenology of the everyday": a kind of neutral inscription of an echo or a reverberation in the subject's daily life; occasionally, Barthes includes social sketches, "moralities," tiny moments of fulfillment in lived experience. These, then, were to be the new *Mythologies* appropriate to a new historical moment and a new writerly aspiration. Yet readers didn't like them, and Barthes himself, it seems, didn't like them either. He quickly quit the assignment. It was his only failure in thirty years of writing.

Lefebvre, for his part, did not set out to write three different volumes on *la vie quotidienne*. After publishing the first volume in 1946, he felt obliged to return to the question again in 1962 and then again in 1981 because of what he took to be the changing nature of the object. Between the first and second volumes, for example, or between the second and third, he made no substantial correction of any conceptual or methodological error. It was rather reality itself that was transformed. The moment of the first volume, the Liberation and the end of the war, had unleashed in France a euphoria and a sense of unlimited possibilities; for a brief time, life was being lived differently, and the hope prevailed that it might continue to do so. But the promise of social transformation gave way to a gradual submersion in old daily patterns and routines. As the trappings of the everyday reemerged, they appeared for a brief moment as alien, unnatural—not inevitable. Thrown into question by the utopian optimism of the Liberation, old routines were suddenly all the more palpable and visible—and thus all the more difficult to bear. Between the first volume and the second in 1962, after fifteen years of the reconstitution of capitalism, dailiness appeared in all its impoverishment, alienation, and passivity. During this period, Lefebvre, whose earliest studies had focused on the rural village of his youth in the Pyrenees, was particularly attuned to the ways in which capitalism had conquered new sectors, chief among these agriculture, up until that point pre-capitalist to a large degree, and the historic city, in the midst of exploding and imploding simultaneously.

The second volume of the *Critique* was written during a period of close friendship between Barthes and Lefebvre; like *Mythologies*, it is clearly the result of the world of the commodity, whose chains of real and fictive equivalencies conjure up a vast swamp of uniformity beneath the apparent difference of things. This was a dailiness organized by the state and capitalism: the management of leisure, of urban space, programmed by the media, advertising, and the press—a growing dominance of state power on economic and social reality, and the insinuation of American ways, not via ideology, but via everyday life. The second volume makes a daring and extreme argument—that, during the 1950s and '60s, the everyday, in effect, "replaces" the colonies. With the waning of its empire, France turned to a form of interior colonialism; rational administrative techniques developed in the colonies were brought home and put to use side by side with new technological innovations such as advertising in reordering metropolitan domestic society, the "everyday life" of its citizens. Speculative capital, no longer drawn to foraging abroad, was increasingly directed toward investment in the built environment: Paris, the city itself, became the new site for a generalized exploitation of its inhabitants through the management of space. It was capitalism's ability to sustain and reproduce itself by producing a space that would preoccupy Lefebvre through the rest of his career. In a series of books written in the 1970s, Lefebvre takes up his initial concept of everyday life and reworks it in spatial terms under the rubric of what he calls "the urban." The everyday, the urban, the production of social space become in his work a constellation of concepts recoding the same basic idea: that the reproduction of the social relations of production is the central and hidden process of capitalist society, and that this process is inherently spatial. The conflictual, lived contradictions of space, and not the economic in general, constitute the level at which neo-capitalism is established. It was these ideas that dominated the third volume of the *Critique de la vie quotidienne,* written in 1981. The distance separating the temporal optimism of the first volume from the spatialization of the quotidian in the third is significant. The third volume is written only at the dawning of the decade dominated by Reagan, Thatcher, and Mitterrand, the moment when "consensus" first emerges as the optimal political gesture or goal. Yet Lefebvre speaks in Volume 3 already of a palpably new level of acceptance of the quotidian *tel quel*—a degree of acceptance he describes as being much more than consenting to banal acts of consumption, but that instead implies what he already calls a "consensus"—an acceptance of society, of the mode of production, in a word, of the totality.

What might a denaturalizing project, a critique of everyday life, look like today? Let's consider a recent book by Jacques Rancière, entitled *Chronique d'un temps consensuel,* published in 2005.* This is not one of Rancière's major books. I chose it because of its resemblance to Barthes's project of the late 1950s. Like *Mythologies,* it consists of brief journalistic essays, written by Rancière over the past ten years, in this case for a Brazilian newspaper; its themes are chosen, like Barthes's, among various contemporary *faits divers:* expositions, political events, films, crime scandals, bestsellers. The title of the book, "Chroniques" and not "Critique," suggests a neutral inventory of the signs of the times. But this is not, in fact, the case. Rancière's book is not a documentation or a description. It is every bit as much as *Mythologies* or the *Critique de la vie quotidienne* a critical history of the present. But the present itself has changed.

---

*   Jacques Rancière, *Chronique d'un temps consensual* (Paris: Le Seuil, 2005).

What separates our own moment from the early 1980s when the final volume of Lefebvre's critique appeared? In France, the great reactive current of the 1980s turned against what it deemed to be the errors of 1968 and shepherded in the return to good philosophy, healthy democracy, and an unbroken reign of elites. Philosophers, many of them former *gauchistes,* proclaimed a specifically new, postmodern era characterized by the end of art, for example, or the end of politics—a definitive rupture with the "illusions" of the 1960s. In the aftermath of the political upheavals of the '68 period, many soon-to-be-well-placed intellectuals felt the need to mask their reconciliation with the laws of economic fatality under a new idiom. Human rights, or humanitarianism, with its obligatory reference to the twinned catastrophes of Gulag and Holocaust, provided a kind of moral or spiritual supplement to the rearmament of capitalism that transpired in France during that decade.* The discourse of totalitarianism popularized by writers like André Glucksmann—who would go on to champion the candidacy of the most recent president of the Fifth Republic, Nicolas Sarkozy—announced that an irreparable crime had occurred, the work of a pure force of evil, exceeding any political, even thinkable, measure. After the fall of the Berlin Wall in 1989, strong passions, master narratives, and the desire for systemic change had definitively subsided into a postmodern landscape of market uniformity and rational management. The main terms of the discourse—a frantic anti-statism and a glorification of individual sovereignty—could merge rather seamlessly with the rise in France during the 1980s of a neoliberal championing of private enterprise and the minimalist state. Since any attempt to change society leads straight to the Gulag, best to let the market construct

---

*   See Kristin Ross, "Ethics and the Rearmament of Imperialism: The French Case," *Human Rights and Revolutions,* 2nd ed., ed. Jeffrey Wasserstrom (Lanham, MD: Rowman and Littlefield, 2007), pp. 155–68.

society all by itself. For a left no longer defining itself in terms of anti-capitalism, values of liberty and human rights, through their "transcendence" of older social divisions now seen as outdated, were powerful humanist alibis. Dissidence and human rights rapidly became little more than slogans that enabled a significant number of French intellectuals to disengage from politics in the name of a spiritualized or ethical "revolt," a revolt that offered the important guarantee of keeping existing structures in place. Ethos, as Rancière reminds us, first meant "lifestyle" rather than a set of moral values.* Much of what counts as ethical reflection today serves mostly to protect the status quo of a certain lifestyle and strengthen the identity of the speaker (the West, for example, as the place of the good).

How then can the present re-emerge as an object of critique? Let's recall the "strong feelings" that motivated Barthes to write *Mythologies*—an anger against what he called "an implicit naturalizing psychology, as though event and meaning coincided naturally." For Rancière, consensus is simply that: an agreement on what is available to the senses, and an agreement as to the interpretation of the sensory given. Consensus is not about people getting along with one another, it is much more an agreement on the perceptual givens and on the meaning to be assigned to that perception; agreement on what can be seen or heard, on *who* can be seen or heard, on what's old, what's new, what's important, what's accessory, what's possible, what's impossible. Rancière's motivation to denaturalize that consensus is, I would say, the same as Barthes's. What is different is his method.

Much of that method derives from the reluctance (which we saw in Barthes as well) to occupy the position of master demystifier and unveiler of the truth. For Rancière, the stance of maintaining

---

* See Jacques Rancière's "Le 11 septembre et après: une rupture de l'ordre symbolique?," *Lignes* 8 (May 2002), pp. 35–46.

a distinction between the world of mere appearances and the truth those appearances conceal mostly serves to benefit the demystifier —he who alone perceives what others cannot. The pleasure of demystifying, in other words, lies mostly in bolstering one's authority. But where Barthes discarded the role of ideological unveiler by essentially abandoning critique for "writerliness," Rancière has spent the last thirty years constructing, little by little, what he calls an egalitarian or anarchist theoretical position. This is a position, or better, a practice, that avoids the symptomatic reading invented by his old teacher, Louis Althusser, as much as it does any number of hermeneutical, vertical depth models that rely on unveiling the truth hidden behind an obscure surface of appearances. But as a practice it nevertheless succeeds in performing what Foucault was fond of calling "a cleansing operation"—disrupting, through reframing, notions which are simply taken as given, or even set in stone. This is a simple, and a limited operation, but it is one that is nevertheless materialist.

For, in fact, it's all there on the surface, where anyone can see it—and this has everything to do with Rancière's particularly disruptive understanding of democracy. Rancière thinks in terms of horizontal distributions and their reconfigurations, destabilizing commonsense understandings by reframing what is available to be seen, reworking the conceptual networks that cause the everyday to appear inalterable and given over to endless repetition, such that it appears open to change, replete with possibilities. The idea is not to get behind it or beneath it, as Barthes might have done, but to rearrange, dislodge, reframe, reconfigure it—to create a topography of the configuration of possibilities. Like Lefebvre, and against the catastrophism of the dominant strain of contemporary philosophy, Rancière's concern is with reaching the possible. Just a slight shift of the frame, it seems, can reconfigure what is thinkable about the present moment.

7

Democracy for Sale

Cuchulain vs. Kouchner

Am I a democrat? "Democrat," at least for Auguste Blanqui writing in 1852, was a word, as he put it, "without definition": "What is a democrat, I ask you. This is a vague and banal word, without any precise meaning, a rubbery word."*

Is "democrat" an any less rubbery name to embrace in our own time?

In June 2008, Ireland, the only country to hold a popular referendum on the European constitution, voted to reject it. One of the principal authors of the treaty, Valéry Giscard d'Estaing, was the first to admit that the text of the treaty (which ran over 312 pages in the English-language version) was little revised from the version the French and the Dutch had rejected three years earlier, when they too held a referendum by popular vote. "The tools were exactly the same. They just had been rearranged in the tool box."† The same treaty, in other words, was being revoted,

---

* Auguste Blanqui, letter to Maillard, June 6, 1852, in *Maintenant, il faut des armes* (Paris: La Fabrique, 2006), pp. 172–86.
† Valéry Giscard d'Estaing blog, October 26, 2007.

after having been rejected by the French and the Dutch. This time around it was a "quirk," as the mainstream media regularly called it, in the Irish constitution, which gave the Irish the right to approve or disapprove the treaty by popular vote when all the other countries, including now France and Holland, were to be represented by deputies. A mounting mood of suspicion toward the Irish vote was palpable in the European press, which viewed "the quirk" as a potential occasion for irrational and destructive behavior on the part of the public. The Irish, after all, like the Third World, might lack the political sophistication to make the right choice; they might not be ready for democracy. The suspicion boiled over in the days immediately preceding the election when French foreign minister Bernard Kouchner took it upon himself to make clear to the Irish that they were, in effect, *obliged* to vote yes out of gratitude to a Europe that had dragged them out of the bogs. It would be, he stated, "very, very annoying for the right-thinking people ["la pensée honnête"] if we couldn't count on the Irish, who themselves have counted heavily on Europe's money."* The division he established between the Irish, cast now as brigands who had absconded with Brussels's cash, and *la pensée honnête*, presumably all other Europeans who have learned to regard politics as a giant intercountry game of treaties, summits, and committees, had been suggested a few days earlier by Daniel Cohn-Bendit: "The Irish have gotten everything from Europe, and they aren't conscious of it."†

The language of a "new" and technocratic Europe barely masked the repetition of colonialist tropes of older empires: the Irish figured as the latest rendition of the uneducated and unteachable people, whose appropriate response could only be gratitude to its leaders. But there was a new twist. Irish support

---

* Bernard Kouchner, interview, *RTL*, June 9, 2008.

† Daniel Cohn-Bendit, cited in *Le Monde*, June 7, 2008.

for the constitution was viewed as an obligation of *repayment*; an investment, it seems, had been made, and the EU wanted a return on the investment. As President Sarkozy reportedly told his aides, "They [the Irish] are bloody fools. They have been stuffing their faces at European expense for years and now they dump us in the shit."*

The referendum was supposed to be nothing more than an exercise in rubber-stamping the experts' text. But the Irish decided to treat the vote as a real vote. In their decision to reject the treaty and their refusal to align themselves with the powerful nations, some heard an echo of Bandung. The Irish were constituting themselves not only as a minority, but as a different kind of minority: those whose recent history had been a colonial one. Others, after the election, expressed what they took to be a general explanation for the treaty's defeat: the reluctance of voters to approve something they had been told in advance they were incapable of understanding and should leave to their betters to administer. As one "No" voter put it, "The reason that the treaty went down to defeat is that we Irish voters found it to be an impenetrable read and an impossible thing to get our collective heads around. The treaty was *purposefully drafted* to defy our understanding."†
It was purposefully drafted, in other words, to communicate to voters through its very form that it was best to leave such complex matters of governance up to the experts, the technocracy.

EU officials were quick to blame "populism" for the defeat. The Irish, they insisted, must be made to *revote*, presumably until the correct result could be reached. Valéry Giscard d'Estaing and Nicolas Sarkozy immediately called for a new vote. Giscard went on the airways:

---

* Nicholas Sarkozy, as reported by the *Canard Enchainé* and quoted in the *Irish Times*, June 20, 2008.
† Bosco, Bantry County Cork Eire, my.telegraph.co.uk.

GISCARD: The Irish must be allowed to express themselves again.

NICOLAS DEMORAND (the radio interviewer): Don't you find it deeply shocking to make people who have already expressed themselves take the vote over?

GISCARD: We spend our time revoting. If we didn't, the president of the Republic would be elected for all eternity.*

Sometimes there is all the time in the world to vote again. After all, the Lisbon Treaty was itself a revote, after the French and Dutch had defeated it. Other times, as in the contested Bush/ Gore US election in 2000, there is no time to revote or even to recount existing votes. In the impoverished rural area in the Hudson Valley where I live, we indeed pass our time revoting. Our county ranks near the bottom—which is to say with counties in Mississippi and Alabama—in the mediocrity of its school system, a mediocrity measured in terms of the ratio of money spent per student and uniform test results. Our county spends the highest amount of money for the worst results. But, on the rare occasions when voters manage to vote "No" on yet another inflated school budget proposal in an attempt to hold bureaucrats and administrators accountable, the same exact proposal, accompanied by a renewed chorus of warnings against "abandoning our kids," is put up for a vote month after month until it succeeds.

"Revoting," then, in today's actually existing representative democracies, is nothing unusual. "No," apparently, doesn't really mean no. What was striking about the aftermath of the Irish vote was not only that a treaty pronounced dead by popular vote was still very much alive, but that through exercising their democratic right to vote, by taking the election seriously, the Irish, in the view of the EU oligarchy, had struck a blow not against the powers of the Parliament, but *against democracy itself*. Here

---

* *France Inter,* June 24, 2008.

is Hans-Gert Pöttering, president of the European Parliament: "It is of course a great disappointment, for all those who wanted to achieve greater democracy, greater political effectiveness and greater clarity and transparency in decision-making in the EU, that the majority of the Irish could not be convinced of the need for these reforms of the EU."*

The proof, it seems, was in the numbers. Five hundred million Europeans had been taken hostage by fewer than nine hundred thousand Irish—less than 0.2 percent of the European population. The leaders of the large nations, France and Germany, reacted:

> AXEL SCHÄEFER (SPD leader in the German Bundestag): "We cannot allow the huge majority of Europe to be duped by a minority of a minority of a minority."†
>
> WOLFGANG SCHAUBLE (German interior minister): "A few million Irish cannot decide on behalf of 495 million Europeans."‡
>
> JEAN DANIEL: "A country of four or five million inhabitants can't hold countries made up of 490 million citizens hostage."§

Now, presumably among the 500 million Europeans held hostage by Irish banditry could be counted the French and Dutch who had themselves voted "No" on the constitution earlier. But we won't quibble over numbers. What is more interesting is to see the reappearance of a discursive figure, a familiar character, that made its debut during the most recent historic moment of high panic among the elites, the 1960s, and has been strategically conjured up at subsequent crisis moments: the "silent majority." When "the silent majority" appears, the world has been divided

* *Institutions,* June 13, 2008.
† *Irish Times,* June 14, 2008.
‡ *Deutsche Welle,* June 15, 2008.
§ Cited in Dominique Guillemin and Laurent Daure, "L'Introuvable souveraineté de l'Union européenne," *L'Action Républicaine,* July 3, 2008.

into two according to a quantitative logic whereby forces are presented in both numerical and moral terms: the "law" that a silent, reproachful, and now purportedly "oppressed" majority must defend against a stigmatized and vocal minority, a civic and majoritarian Europe hijacked by a subversive and destructive minority. The "silent majority" appears when the largest number is *spoken for* rather than speaks and when the voice of the minority is increasingly voided of authority and rendered illegitimate.

Frédéric Bas has traced the invention of the term "the silent majority" back to the moment it originated in the mouths of Richard Nixon and Spiro Agnew as they attempted to counteract the noisy opposition to the Vietnam War out in the streets. In France the first use of the term, in the context of the passage of the *loi anticasseurs* in 1970, was, as Bas points out, inscribed in the framework of a general reflection on democracy: "In our democracy it is the duty of each citizen to prevent minorities from imposing their law on the silent majority of the country. If that majority acts like sheep, it will awaken to the reign of the colonels or that of majority agitators who, without taking account of existing laws, will impose their own."*

But it was none other than Valéry Giscard d'Estaing who Bas credits with introducing (in latent form) the figure in the midst of the May-June insurrections, on May 19,1968, back when he was a deputy from Puy-de-Dôme:

> In the grave national circumstances our country is undergoing, I want merely to express the point of view that I know to be that of the greatest number of students, workers, but also of French men

---

* Eugène Claudius-Petit, oral report before the National Assembly, April 30, 1970, cited by Frédéric Bas, "La 'majorité silencieuse' ou la bataille de l'opinion en mai-juin 1968," in Philippe Artières and Michelle Zancarini-Fournel, *68: une histoire collective* (Paris: La Découverte, 2008).

and women everywhere. This majority wishes that order be restored
and liberties be protected … Up until now, the greatest number of
French people, who love order, liberty, and progress, and who accept
neither arbitrariness nor anarchy, have remained silent. If necessary,
they must be ready to express themselves.*

In the 1960s, the indeterminate silence of "the greatest number"
could be confidently translated or ventriloquized by government
officials as expressing a bastion of good sense against anarchy or
arbitrariness. The minority had "seized speech" in the streets,
but the *highly valorized* silence of the majority could function as
a vast reserve army, a force held back until the moment when it
would be called upon to express itself, in the legitimate way, that
is: by voting. In 2008 the silent majority, the "greatest number"
of Europeans, finds its silence just as confidently translated by
the ruling elite, but its silence is now constrained to be eternal—
democracy as voiceless assent. The situation is one in which those
who are deprived of their political say function comfortably in
the belief that "governability"—a concept massively promoted
in the 1990s—benefits everyone, despite the fact that "governability" actually consists of the most unlimited wielding of power
by the most powerful and wealthy classes. Indeed, another way
of looking at the Irish referendum is that the Irish, invested with
the specter of democracy as lawless or violent, were being asked
to vote away their right, as well as everyone else's, to ever vote
again, by helping force through a ruling bureaucracy insulated to
a virtually impermeable degree against democratic accountability.
The EU had made an investment in Ireland and the interest they
required as a return on their investment was either the abroga-
tion of the right to vote or what amounted to the same thing: the

* Valéry Giscard d'Estaing, cited in Bas, p. 363.

obligation to keep voting until the correct vote—assent—was obtained. Governability—the creation of faraway supranational European bureaucratic bodies against which no worker's organization can fight directly—is designed to prevent radical minorities in wealthy or overdeveloped societies from upsetting the system in any way.

In 1968, many of the minority engaged in direct democracy out on the streets viewed elections, the tired, ritualized exercise of representative democracy, as, in the famous words of Sartre, "a trap for fools." What the gap between our own time and the 1960s indicates is first of all a progressive dismantling of universal suffrage—the attempt to deprive even "representative" democracy of its validity in the effort to offset the unpleasant effects of universal suffrage and in favor of "rationalizing" people's will and the expression of that will. The term "consensus" is no longer adequate to describe what is in fact a kind of socializing of people into silence—silence as consent. But it also says something about the creative, bricolage-like capacity of the demos, when even a ballot box can become a weapon. It suggests that democracy can reassert itself via the most diverse of political forms. By taking an outmoded ritual seriously when, as Giscard's cynicism makes patently clear, no one else does, even voting, in this instance, can become an instantiation of "fugitive democracy": the political potentialities of ordinary citizens.* The vote could be treated as a weapon to be used in the antidemocratic assault on popular sovereignty by a Europe that presents itself as the reign of democracy on earth, a brand name sold by evoking peace, justice, and above all, democracy.

---

* See Sheldon Wolin, "Fugitive Democracy," in *Constellations* I (1994), pp. 11–25.

Democracy for Sale

The modern, received understanding of democracy is rule by voting, the authority to decide matters by majority rule, the rule of "the greatest number." But another understanding of the term, familiar to readers of Jacques Rancière's *Le Maître ignorant*, conveys a sense of power that is neither quantitative nor concerned with control. It is rather one of potentiality or enablement: the capacity of ordinary people to discover modes of action for realizing common concerns. Rancière's encounter with Joseph Jacotot, and his continuing reworking of that encounter, have helped make available what was in fact the original, more expansive and suggestive, meaning of the word "democracy": namely the capacity to do things. Democracy is not a form of government. And it is not concerned with number—neither with a tyrannical majority nor a minority of agitators. In ancient Greece, as Josiah Ober points out, of the three major terms designating political power—*monarchia*, *oligarchia*, and *demokratia*—only *demokratia* is unconcerned with number. The *monos* of *monarchia* indicates solitary rule; the *hoi oligoi* of oligarchy indicates the power of a few. Only *demokratia* does not provide an answer to the question "How many?"* The power of the *demos* is neither the power of the population nor its majority but rather the power of anybody. Anybody is as entitled to govern as he or she is to be governed.

Yet, if democracy as "the capacity to do things" is free from the law of number, it does presuppose an existing division of the world into two, a division between those who are defined as having the capacity to participate in collective decision making

---

* See Jacques Rancière, *The Ignorant Schoolmaster*; see also Josiah Ober, "'The Original Meaning of 'Democracy': Capacity to Do Things, Not Majority Rule," *Constellations* 15 (2008), pp. 1–9.

(the "best people") and those said to be without that capacity. Democracy refuses this division as the basis of organizing political life; it is a call for equality on the part of the people defined as not being among the best people. "The best" have been defined in different ways throughout history, as those who possess noble birth, the right race, those who exhibit military power, as the wealthy, or those who possess complex knowledge or managerial skills. And, as Immanuel Wallerstein reminds us, the modes of defining who count among "the best" have always been accompanied by assumptions about the ethos or lifestyle of "the best people"—assumptions, for example, that a "civilized" nature is their particular endowment.*

When Blanqui, in 1852, complained about the rubbery nature of the name "democrat," he was already registering the profound modification the term was beginning to undergo—a modification that would last throughout the Second Empire and beyond. Up until then the word had largely retained its revolutionary 1789 heritage; "democrat" was the label, for example, of many far-left organizations in the 1830s and 1840s. But, during the Second Empire, the imperial regime had effectively appropriated the term for itself, for the most part successfully, by opposing what it called real "democracy" to the bourgeois "party of order."[†] The emperor, in other words, claimed to have given sovereignty back to the people by the "plebiscite" or the *appel au peuple*. Monarchists in the 1850s and 1860s embraced the word, equating it favorably with Empire; the minister of the interior, an impassioned Bonapartist, was able to call himself "the defender of democracy." By 1869, a partial enumeration of the kinds of "democrats"

---

* Immanuel Wallerstein, "Democracy, Capitalism and Transformation," lecture at Documenta 11, Vienna, March 16, 2001.

† See Jean Dubois, *Le Vocabulaire politique et sociale en France de 1869 à 1872* (Paris: Larousse, 1962).

flourishing in French political life included *démocrates socialistes*, *démocrates révolutionnaires*, *démocrates bourgeois*, *démocrates impérialistes*, *démocrates progressistes*, and *démocrates autoritaires*. The list reflects both the point Blanqui was making—that the term was entirely up for grabs—as well as the effort made by some socialists to affirm the revolutionary heritage of the word by lending precision to their position with an appropriate qualifier. But the word on its own—then as today—conveyed virtually no information. Blanqui was not the only Republican or socialist to hesitate to use a word his adversaries used to describe themselves. As he writes to Maillard:

> You say to me: "I am neither bourgeois, nor proletarian. I am a democrat. Beware of words without definition, they are the preferred instrument of schemers ... It is they who invented the beautiful aphorism: neither proletarian nor bourgeois, but democrat! ... What opinion couldn't manage to find a home under that roof? Everyone claims to be a democrat, even aristocrats.

"Democrat" no longer named the division to be overcome between those judged capable of governing and those judged incapable: it was too rubbery, it did no labor, it created consensus rather than division. Even the Communards of 1871, engaged in their short-lived experiment in taking control of the administrative and institutional functions normally reserved for traditional elites, did not call themselves democrats. The declaration of the communal form of government in Paris in the wake of the French capitulation to the Prussians signified nothing if not the most renewed commitment to democratic politics in modern times. In their brief existence, the Communards replaced long-entrenched hierarchic and bureaucratic structures with democratic forms and processes at every level. Yet these agents of democracy preferred other words—*républicains, peuple*—to describe themselves. But I think it is significant that they did not entirely abandon the word *démocratie*. Even though it had been derailed from its true meaning and had fallen into the hands of the enemy, it still retained the heritage of 1789.

When Arthur Rimbaud entitled one of his last prose poems "Démocratie," a poem written soon after the demise of the Commune, the title is nothing more than a banner under which a mobile and imperialistic bourgeois class expands out from the metropolis to the "languid scented lands," feeding, as the poem says, "the most cynical whoring," "destroying all logical revolt":

Democracy
"Toward that intolerable country
The flag floats along
And the beating drums are stifled
By our rough backcountry shouting …"
"In the metropolis we will feed the most cynical whoring. We will
    destroy all logical revolt."
"On to the languid scented lands! In the service of the most
    monstrous industrial or military exploitations."
"Goodbye to all this, and never mind where."
Conscripts of good intention,
We will have savage philosophy;
Knowing nothing of science, depraved in our pleasures,
To hell with the world around us …
"This is the real advance! Forward. March!"*

---

* Translations of Rimbaud are taken from Paul Schmidt's *Arthur Rimbaud: Complete Works* (New York: Harper and Row, 1976) and have been in some cases slightly modified.

What if it were Rimbaud, and not Baudelaire, whom we read as the poet that best compiled the central tropes and figures of the nineteenth century? With images courtesy of Edgar Allan Poe and Jules Verne, with prophecies drawn from political pamphlets, with figures taken from children's novels and popular science texts, Rimbaud assembles the emblems and possible futures of his moment. And the colonial soldier is very much one of those figures, producing as many, if not more, of the principal postures, orientations, stereotypes, and directions, as does the ragpicker or *flaneur* for the future of the twentieth and twenty-first centuries. "Démocratie" the poem, and Rimbaud's collection of prose poems, *Illuminations,* taken as a group, stand on the brink, so to speak, of a mutating world system: their moment is the inauguration of a world drawn together by colonialism, the moment when a genuinely bourgeois regime begins to install itself definitively.* Just as significant, though, is what occurs immediately before the writing of these poems: the class massacre, the mass shootings of tens of thousands of Communards, that occurred in the heart of "civilized Europe" in May 1871. This attempt on the part of the bourgeois-republican government to physically exterminate one by one and *en bloc* its class enemy, to kill all those who had engaged in the brief attempt to change the political and social order, is quite extraordinary:

> The executions were not just happening in the Luxembourg. They were shooting people down on the street corners, in the passageways between houses, against doors. Wherever they could find a wall to push victims up against.

---

* See Kristin Ross, *The Emergence of Social Space: Rimbaud and the Paris Commune* (Minneapolis: University of Minnesota Press, 1988; rpt. Verso, 2008); see also Fredric Jameson, "Rimbaud and the Spatial Text," in Tak-Wai Wong and M. A. Abbas, eds., *Rewriting Literary History* (Hong Kong: Hong Kong University Press, 1984).

The banks of the Seine were witness to ferocious massacres. Underneath the Pont Neuf they were executing people for eight days straight. In the afternoon, gentlemen and their ladies would come out to watch the prisoners being killed. Elegant couples attended the butchery as they would a play.

In a corner of the Left Bank that surrounds the neighborhood of the Pantheon, a half dozen courts-martial were functioning. The mass killings took place at the Luxembourg. But they were shooting people at the Monnaie, at l'Observatoire, at the law school, at the Ecole polytechnique, at the Panthéon. They were executing people at the Collège de France, based on condemnations pronounced by a provost seated in the room on the left of the main entrance. There were continuous executions in the Maubert market.

Six courts-martial for this one neighborhood. For each of them, more and more deaths. The Luxembourg alone counted more than a thousand. As they advanced, the Versaillais installed sinister military magistrates, one by one in each square, whose only task was to organize the killing. Judgment didn't matter.

Around the large slaughterhouses—the Luxembourg, the Ecole Militaire, the parc Monceau, La Roquette, the Père Lachaisé, the Buttes Chaumont, and still others—countless massacres were conducted in a more muffled fashion, with less ostentatious display and less glory.*

I have quoted at length from this eyewitness account of the *semaine sanglante* because I think we should linger on the sheer magnitude of the hatred exhibited by the bourgeois-republican government, on what Luciano Canfora calls "the furious hostility of the *majority*."† For it was this class massacre, he reminds us, that

---

* Maxime Vuillaume, *Mes Cahiers rouges au temps de la commune* (Arles: Actes Sud, 1998), pp. 68–9.

† Luciano Canfora, *Democracy in Europe* (Malden, MA: Blackwell, 2006), p. 120.

was the defeat of democracy that gave birth to the Third Republic. In November of that year, Rimbaud and his friend Delahaye walked the streets of Paris, examining the traces of bullet holes left in the walls of houses and of the Pantheon; the months and, in fact, years after the massacre left a political atmosphere infused, as Rimbaud remarked to his friend, with "annihilation, chaos … all the possible and even probable *reactions*."* The *Illuminations* open onto the movement of late nineteenth-century expansionism and the wholesale creation of a consciousness conducive to reproducing a colonialist expeditionary class this entailed. In certain of his more futuristic poems, Rimbaud foresees that movement culminating in a bland and homogeneous universe: "a little world, pale and flat" as he puts it in one poem, or in "the same bourgeois magic wherever your baggage sets you down." In others—I'm thinking here of "Métropolitain," "Barbare," and "Soir historique"—he shows us some of the ways the bourgeois imagination intoxicates itself with apocalyptic images of its own death. In this second cluster of poems, Rimbaud presents the canceled future of a now-vanished imperial destiny: a panoramic vision where crystalline and fantastic cityscapes rejoin ancient prefigurations of the end of the world in geological cataclysms of exploding ice and snow, intertwining bridges and highways lie flanked by barbarian tribes, a recurring planetary conflagration, at once polar and fiery, chaotic yet eerily still.

How can the future be imagined after the demise of the Commune? Having lived the eruption, evolution, and liquidation of that unusual experiment in democracy, faced now with the "swamp," as he called it, of the French middle classes consolidating the colonial impetus that would propel them through the next several decades, Rimbaud chooses to prefigure both the triumph

---

*   Rimbaud, cited by Ernest Delahaye in Arthur Rimbaud, *Oeuvres completes*, ed. Rolland de Renéville and Jules Mouquet (Paris: Gallimard, 1965), p. 745.

and the death of that class in a series of futuristic and fantastic prose poems—the triumph of that class in a progressive homogenization of the planet, its death in an exploded earth.

Rimbaud's "Démocratie," then, marks the precise moment when the term "democracy" is no longer being used to express the demands of the *peuple* in a national class struggle, but is rather being used to *justify* the colonial policies of the "civilized lands" in a struggle on an international scale between the West and the rest, the civilized and the noncivilized. Rimbaud recounts that saga in the "Mauvais Sang" section of *Une Saison en enfer* and provides an additional class portrait of the civilizing missionaries in a poem called "Movement":

> These are the conquerors of the world,
> Seeking their personal chemical fortune:
> Sport and comfort accompany them;
> They bring education for races, for classes, for animals
> Within this vessel, rest and vertigo
> In diluvian light,
> In terrible evenings of study.

The resonance of democracy registered by Rimbaud was definitively changed, not merely diluted but filled with an alien content, as the very groups who feared it at the beginning of the century begin to embrace it at the century's end. As in Rimbaud's poem, democracy becomes a banner, a slogan, a proof of being civilized as well as the vital spiritual supplement, the ideal fig leaf to the civilized and civilizing West. The state, in the name of representative democracy, inaugurates a history of class massacre, within Europe in the form of the Commune and beyond, in the colonial domains, a violence whose echoes can be heard in the language of threat and contempt directed at the Irish at the time of the 2008 vote. The West, as democratic, can become the world's moral leader, since its hegemony is the basis of progress throughout the world. From these "conquerors of the world" to Woodrow Wilson's "making the world safe for democracy" and on to Harry Truman's recoding of "democracy" into the language and project of development economics requires no leap at all.[*]

But, before we leave Rimbaud's prefiguration of world history, we must consider, in the context of "Democracy" and "Movement," a poem that may have much to say to our own historical moment, the poem structured as one long advertising spiel entitled "Sale." In an atmosphere made up of equally modern and magical installations, the poem presents the revolutionary cry and the advertising slogan as indistinguishable from each other in a generalized onslaught of consumer goods and services: "For sale—Priceless bodies, beyond race or world or sex or lineage!" Both "Sale" and "Democracy" relate changes in consciousness to the relative penetration of market relationships into everyday life—whether these be in the *outremer* colonies or in the heart of the European metropolis. (A sonnet written around this time, entitled "Paris," consists entirely of advertising pitches lifted off of Parisian storefronts.) What might be called the prophetic or extraordinarily contemporary feel of these poems—read together, they amount to the title of this essay, "Democracy for Sale"—has something to do with the way the twentieth century solidified the equation between democracy (in its inverted form) and consumption begun in Rimbaud's time: democracy as the right to buy. Today's Western liberal democracies are all the more assured in their well-being in that they are more perfectly depoliticized, lived as a kind of falsely timeless ambience, a milieu or style of

---

[*]   Harry Truman, January 20, 1949: "We must embark on a bold new program for making the benefits of our scientific advances and industrial progress available for the improvement and growth of underdeveloped areas."

existence. And this is the atmosphere envisioned by Rimbaud in "Sale," the free exchange of merchandise, bodies, candidates, lifestyles, and possible futures. "For sale—Homesteads and migrations, sports, enchantments and perfect comfort, and the noise, the movement and the future they entail!"

Today, democracy is the slogan of almost all of the leaders on the planet (and the rest, sooner or later, will be brought forcibly into the fold). What separates our own time from the extraordinary moment of Rimbaud is something called the Cold War and its ending. In terms of the development of "democracy," it is difficult to overestimate the enormous gain Western governments managed to consolidate when they successfully advanced *democracy* as the opposing counterweight to *communism*. They had actually gained control of the entire word for themselves, leaving nary a trace of its former emancipatory resonance. Indeed, democracy had become a class ideology justifying systems that allowed a very small number of people to govern—and to govern without the people, so to speak; systems that seem to exclude any other possibility than the infinite reproduction of their own functioning. To be able to call an unchecked and deregulated free market economy, a ruthless, no-holds-barred opposition to communism, a right to intervene, militarily and otherwise, in countless sovereign nations and their internal affairs—to succeed in calling all this democracy was an incredible feat. To successfully present the market as an evident condition of democracy and to have democracy viewed as inexorably calling forth the market, is an astounding accomplishment. It was considerably helped along, in France, at least, in the reaction against the '68 years, as the French Revolution, under the profoundly antidemocratic tutelage of François Furet, was submitted to a patient labor of inconsideration, denigrated in comparison to the acceptable revolution of 1776 and ultimately affiliated to Stalinism and the crimes of Pol Pot. And, with the end of "actually existing socialism," we at last, it seemed, finished definitively with moments of rupture or conflict, and society could be from now on the place for uninterrupted "democratic" deliberation, dialogue, debate, and a perpetual regulation of social relations. Rimbaud's moment, as we have seen in "Democracy," initiated the age of "democratic empire": a natural, inevitable project designed to bring about a predestined future of the peoples or entities being developed. But "democracy" is just as much at work, as we saw in "Sale," on the home front: where the main system of rule in a society is the economy, a vast historic force beyond human power, and where a silent consensus informs us that the equilibrium produced by the economy defines the best of all possible worlds.

Is this a permanent contamination of the language of politics? Can I call myself a democrat?

It's certainly not enough to criticize, in an incrementalist way, the "failed" or "insufficient" democracy of this or that law, party, or state. To do so is to remain enclosed in a system that is perfectly happy to critique, say, the blatant seizure of electoral procedures by Robert Mugabe in Zimbabwe, but remains powerless before the same process when it is accomplished by economic phenomena that respect democratic rituals—like the exactions of the IMF, for example. In fact, the understanding of democracy as having to do with elections or with the will of the majority is a very recent historical understanding. What is called representational democracy—in our own time said to consist of free elections, free political parties, a free press, and, of course, the free market —is in fact an oligarchic form, representation by a minority granted the title of stewards or trustees of common affairs. All today's "advanced industrial democracies" are in fact oligarchic democracies: they represent the victory of a dynamic oligarchy, a world government centered on great wealth and the worship of wealth, but capable of building consensus and legitimacy through elections that, by limiting the range of options, effectively protect the ascendancy of the middle and upper classes.[*]

I think we must both recognize this to be the case, that is, recognize the nonexistence of democracy or its inversion in reality, at the same time that we acknowledge how vitally necessary it is to retain the original, expansive sense of the term. If we remain enclosed in an understanding of democracy as a form of government, then we have no choice but to abandon the word to the enemy who has appropriated it. But precisely because it is not a form of government, because it is not a type of constitution or institution, democracy, as the power of anybody to concern himself or herself with common affairs, becomes another name for the specificity of politics itself. It may exist or not exist at all, and it may reassert itself in the most varied of manifestations. It is a moment, at best a project rather than a form. As the name of the struggle against the perpetual privatization of public life, democracy, like love in one of Rimbaud's many slogans, must be reinvented.

---

[*] See Canfora, *Democracy in Europe*, pp. 214–52.

Part II. Everyday Life: Cultural Interventions

8
Shopping: An Introduction to Emile Zola's *The Ladies' Paradise*

Au bonheur des dames, Zola's phantasmagoric hymn to the marvels of modern commerce, was the first of his novels to be translated into English. When *The Ladies' Paradise* appeared in England in 1883, it received the critical acclaim and wide readership that had greeted its appearance in serial form a year earlier in Paris; the novel was also translated, almost instantaneously, into Portuguese, Spanish, German, Russian, and Swedish. But, although translations of Zola's *L'Assomoir* and *Germinal* have remained in print in an assortment of readily accessible editions in the United States and in England, an English translation of *Au bonheur* has been virtually unavailable throughout this century. In recent years, however, with the convergence of a wide variety of theoretical interests—those of Marxists, postmodernists and feminists, cultural theorists and social historians—intent on charting the transition from an economy based on production to one based on consumption, Zola's novel has again come to the forefront as an indispensable document in the history of what Guy Debord in the 1960s called "the society of the spectacle." Of the twenty volumes that make up Zola's vast Rougon-Macquart series, only perhaps *Nana*, the story of woman as commodity, can compete for the attention of contemporary readers with *The Ladies' Paradise*, the story of women shopping.

The Ladies' Paradise is the eleventh volume of the series that represents Zola's attempt to chart, as its subtitle proclaims, "the natural and social history of a family during the Second Empire." Deemed by some to be a transitional novel in the series, *The Ladies' Paradise* opens the way to the more contemporary social and economic studies of *Germinal* and *L'Argent*. It is the first and most important of Zola's novels to allow capitalist mechanisms to play the leading role, and it is the only late nineteenth-century French novel to treat in detail the social environment surrounding the emergence of the modern commercial techniques of retailing and advertising pioneered, above all, by France during the Second Empire (1851–1870). In *La maison du Chat-qui-pelote* (1829) and *Grandeur et décadence de César Birotteau* (1837), Balzac chronicled those predecessors to the modern department store, the *magasins de nouveauté* of the 1830s, that appeared, almost prematurely, in the cramped, provincial Paris of the Restoration. But the stores that provided the models for Balzac did not survive the economic and social upheavals of 1848, and the models for Zola's store, the Bon Marché (founded in 1852) and the Louvre (founded in 1855), were built, in a sense, on the ruins of those first forms of the new commerce.

Much of the melodramatic energy of Zola's novel derives from the fact that a social and economic evolution that, in reality, extended through half a century is here made to transpire in five short years. *The Ladies' Paradise* takes place between 1864 and 1869, but the conditions that enabled the rise of the department store in the latter part of the century were decades in the making. These included the slow and steady growth of the textile industry in France throughout the nineteenth century, a development that favored—indeed spurred the growth of—the clientele attracted by the department stores. The great public works of the Baron Haussmann transformed Paris, opening up a network of boulevards and avenues to vehicles and carving out sidewalks for pedestrian traffic; Haussmann's changes enabled this city, uniquely among world capitals, to become what Rosalind Williams called "the pilot plant of mass consumption."* Developments in iron and glass technology allowed the increases in window size that became essential to modern display of merchandise, while improvements in artificial lighting enhanced the theatricality of that display.

The electrification of Zola's store provides a telling instance of how Zola's historical foreshortening creates the impression of accelerated mutation in everyday life. Electric lighting comes to the Ladies' Paradise in 1864, although the first Parisian department store was lit electrically in 1883. This store was, in fact, the Printemps, which was under construction during the writing of the novel in 1882. The architecture of Zola's store is more like that of the Printemps than that of the stores of the Second Empire; indeed, many of the architectural innovations of Zola's fictional store prophetically announce the Samaritaine that designer Frantz Jourdain, who provided Zola with an imaginary layout for a department store, would build a few years later.

Perhaps the most important factor was the consolidation of a sufficiently wealthy and numerous clientele. A massive influx of those potential consumers called tourists, both foreigners and French provincials, poured into the capital, drawn by the International Expositions of 1855 and 1867, while permanent emigration from the countryside to the capital increased dramatically

---

* Rosalind Williams, *Dream Worlds: Mass Consumption in Late Nineteenth-Century France* (Berkeley: University of California Press, 1982), p. 11.

throughout the second half of the century. Paris gained 121,000 inhabitants between the years of 1851 and 1856 alone.

All the founders of the Second Empire *grands magasins* were, like Zola's protagonist Octave Mouret, of provincial origin. When the most innovative of these newly transplanted Parisian entrepreneurs, Aristide Boucicaut, took over the small retail store Bon Marché in 1852, he initiated a number of startling practices designed to accelerate sales that would soon become the virtual commandments of commerce in Second Empire department stores. Boucicaut was the first to bring an enormous variety of goods under the same roof, and he was the first to apply fixed prices to the merchandise. (Laws passed in the last decades of the *ancien régime* had forbidden retailers from displaying fixed prices.) He could also be called the inventor of "browsing": passersby could, for the first time, feel free to enter a store without sensing an obligation to buy something. Goods were rotated frequently, with a low markup in price; high volume and frequent rotation created the illusion of a scarcity in supply among what were in fact mass-produced and plentiful goods. Departments within the store increased dramatically in number; the illogical design of their layout served to increase customers' disorientation—a disoriented or dazzled customer was more prone to impulse buying. The opportunity to return goods after purchase was also initiated by Boucicaut. In the novel, this innovation, and others, is credited to Mouret:

> He had penetrated still further into the heart of woman, and had just thought of the "returns," a masterpiece of Jesuitical seduction. "Take what you like, madame; you can return the article if you don't like it." And the woman who hesitated was provided with the last excuse, the possibility of repairing an extravagant folly, she took the article with an easy conscience.*

---

* Emile Zola, *The Ladies' Paradise* (Berkeley: University of California Press, 1992), p. 206.

Salesclerks were given commissions, variable percentages on the sales they performed.

In *The Fall of Public Man* Richard Sennett analyzed the effect of these new commercial techniques in terms of a "detheatricalizing" of public life.* Gone, for instance, was the stylized interplay, the obligatory performance enacted by merchant and customer under the old commercial regime; the haggling, jockeying for position, the melodrama and posturing that characterized the urban theater of everyday bargaining. Before the onset of fixed prices and free entrance, both buyer and seller were obliged to perform a role—to bargain—or they would lose money. From the perspective of commercial entrepreneurs like Boucicaut, such ancient and quotidian theater took too much time: it interfered with the volume of rapid sales. Besides, the number of salesclerks required by the sheer size of the new operation made it difficult for the entrepreneur to trust that uniformly successful bargaining would take place throughout the store. Under the new system, goaded on by the commission incentive, salesclerks no longer presented themselves as worthy opponents to potential customers but instead took it upon themselves to cater to or even stimulate the desires of a comparatively passive brand of customer. Shopping began to take shape as a leisure activity for the urbanized middle class, a distinctive pursuit bearing as little resemblance to the activity of procuring absolute necessities as the colossal, phantasmagoric dream factories, the department stores, bore to the older, merely reliable, boutiques and shops—those dark, dank, and decaying establishments the tale of whose demise takes up much of Zola's novel.

In his customary fashion, Zola researched the lives and habits of the inhabitants and habitués of the department stores, writing three preparatory articles between 1878 and 1881 on the

---

* See Richard Sennett, *The Fall of Public Man* (New York: Vintage, 1974).

psychology and sociology of department store employees. Zola spent four to five hours a day for a month at the Bon Marché and the Louvre before he began his novel, compiling over 380 pages of notes on the demoiselles of the stores and their environs; their rooms, overheard conversations, love life, clothing, hours, and salaries. (The menu for a meal that appears in Chapter 10 was actually served in 1881 to the clerks of the Louvre.) The tragic lives of shopgirls, frequently locked into their attic rooms above the stores, had come to the forefront of public attention when a fire consumed the Printemps on March 10, 1881, causing 25 million francs worth of damage and leaving 2,400 people unemployed; this news item seems to have spurred Zola to work on the novel he had been considering since at least 1864. But the hundreds of pages of notes and the early sketches, the correspondence between the author and architect Jourdain, and such things as the descriptions of floor layouts indicate that Zola was at least as interested, if not more so, in the physical circumstances of the lives of his *calicots*, as the clerks were called, than in those lives themselves. And this fact alone encourages us to take Sennett's argument about the loss of theatricality in public life a step farther.

Theatricality, in *The Ladies' Paradise*, as well as in the new commerce, is not, properly speaking, erased—it is displaced: from the actors (the buyers and sellers) onto the set. By creating a spectacle out of the store itself, early commercial pioneers like Boucicaut discovered that they could endow metonymically what were essentially nondescript goods with the fascination that was lacking in the merchandise. Window displays became more fantastic and elaborate, highlighting the most unusual objects in the store. The technique of "unexpected juxtaposition"—the accumulation of widely disparate kinds of things, placed side by side—became commonplace. Then again, the opposite tactic, namely sheer hyperbolic repetition of the same item, proved equally effective; Mouret adopts this strategy in one of his sales when he fills an entire hall with umbrellas. Whether by metonymy or by exaggerated repetition, the goal was to free the paraphernalia of domestic life from banality. Exotic goods, mostly garnered from the colonies, were highly coveted by Parisian department store managers, not only as articles of trade but more importantly for their usefulness in being, simply, unexpected: buyers accustomed to the idea of finding in the store what they didn't expect to find would become accustomed to leaving the store with something they weren't looking for. The manipulation of exotic colonial objects and Orientalist backdrops (like the Arabian Nights extravaganza executed by Octave Mouret in Chapter 4 of *The Ladies' Paradise* that simulates "the decor of a harem") certainly contributed to the department stores taking on the aspect, as Rachel Bowlby argued, of a fantasy world of escape, a "second home" for a mostly female clientele, who were eager to flee for an afternoon the drab routines of domesticity to enter into a whole phantasmagoria.* The democratization of luxury enticed these women: the carefully orchestrated spectacle of other worlds and other lives appeared available to everyone. And even if the goods themselves were not equally available to all, the *vision* of their profusion was not only available, but virtually unavoidable.

Thus, readers should not be surprised to find the store itself dominating the novel, dwarfing in importance the love story between Mouret and the shopgirl Denise Baudu, the description of the daily lives of the clerks, and the torturous demise of the small boutiquiers in the neighborhood. The store is the novel's main character, and it is in this sense that *The Ladies' Paradise* can be viewed as the crucial formal precursor to certain mass-market paperbacks of the twentieth century, those catastrophe

---

* See Rachel Bowlby, *Just Looking: Consumer Culture in Dreiser, Gissing and Zola* (New York: Methuen, 1985).

melodramas which, like *Hotel* or *The Towering Inferno*, lend dramatic agency to a complex central setting. Many readers have noticed that Zola excelled throughout his oeuvre in documenting the excesses and abuses of some highly representative institutions: Georg Lukács noted Zola's deployment of mines and markets, theaters and battlefields, and his focus on institutions as the "outer trappings of modern life" against which the haphazard movements of tiny human characters appear dwarfed and insignificant.* Henry James considered this aspect of Zola's work to be his most important achievement:

> To make his characters swarm, and to make the great central thing they swarm about as large as life, portentously, historically big, that was the task he set himself very nearly from the first, that was the secret he triumphantly mastered.†

Zola himself indicated the narrative centrality of the store in his early sketches and descriptions of the project. In a letter from October 1882, he writes:

> *The Ladies' Paradise* is the story of the creation of one of those big department stores, like the *Bon Marché* or the *Louvre*, that have so shaken up and reinvigorated commerce in France. I show it at war with small commerce, which is little by little devoured by it. To do so I introduce a rival house, an old store that incarnates old-fashioned customs, that is killed off by the department store—which gives me a family drama.‡

---

* Georg Lukács, *Studies in European Realism*, trans. Edith Bone (New York: Grosset and Dunlap, 1964), pp. 92–3.

† Henry James, "Emile Zola," in George Becker ed., *Documents of Modern Literary Realism* (Princeton: Princeton University Press, 1963), p. 518.

‡ Emile Zola, *Correspondances 1880–1883*, ed. B. H. Bakker (Montreal: Presses de l'Université de Montréal, 1983), p. 329.

A store that was larger than life would, according to Zola, serve as an allegory for "the whole materialist and phalansterian century" and would encompass the forward momentum of the age: the bold new forms of capitalism. "My first idea," he writes in his notes, "[is] of a department store absorbing, smashing all the small commerce of a neighborhood ... but I would not weep for them, *on the contrary*: for I want to show the triumph of modern activity; they are no longer of their age, too bad for them! They are smashed by the giant."*

Readers are treated to a first view of the giant from the uplifted eyes of the novel's virginal heroine, Denise Baudu, freshly arrived from the provinces:

> Denise began to feel as if she were watching a machine working at full pressure, communicating its movement even as far as the windows. They were no longer the cold windows she had seen in the early morning; they seemed to be warm and vibrating from the activity within. There was a crowd before them, groups of women pushing and squeezing, devouring the finery with longing, covetous eyes. And the stuffs became animated in this passionate atmosphere: the laces fluttered, drooped, and concealed the depths of the shop with a troubling air of mystery; even the lengths of cloth, thick and heavy, exhaled a tempting odour, while the cloaks threw out their folds over the dummies, which assumed a soul, and the great velvet mantle, particularly, expanded, supple and warm, as if on real fleshly shoulders, with a heaving of the bosom and a trembling of the hips. But the furnace-like glow which the house exhaled came above all from the sale, the crush at the counters, that could be felt behind the walls. There was the continual roaring of the machine at work, the marshalling of the customers, bewildered amidst the piles of

---

* Zola, cited in Lewis Kamm, *The Object in Zola's Rougon-Macquart* (Madrid: José Porrua Turanzas, 1978), p. 21.

goods, and finally pushed along to the pay-desk. And all that went on in an orderly manner, with mechanical regularity, quite a nation of women passing through the force and logic of this wonderful commercial machine.*

Here, in the first of many lengthy descriptions, the store emerges as a huge combustion machine. Its moving parts, the laces, linens, and mannequins are seen to gain in life and vitality only in proportion to the reification of its clientele and personnel. What facilitates this transfer of animation can be traced in the metaphors: throughout the novel Zola uses words traditionally associated with the means of production and applies them to the means of consumption. The store is described as a factory ("furnace-like" here is actually *usine*, or factory, in the French)— that is, the world of commerce borrows the energy of production or industry, and selling becomes akin to making. The erotic heat that emerges from the depths of the store ("the laces ... concealed the depths of the shop with a troubling air of mystery") is ultimately agitated by the "longing, covetous eyes" of the female customers, a longing gaze that, mirrored by Denise's from afar, virtually brings the products to life. The female crowd provides the motor or fuel for the machine as its members pass, helplessly and inevitably, between its churning gears.

Jean Richepin, writing in 1881, succinctly outlined the problem facing Zola in his project of depicting the sudden crushing profusion of consumer goods in the capital, arrayed for the first time under one roof. It is a problem curiously akin to that experienced by Zola's fictional hero, Octave Mouret, as he seeks to enhance desire for nondescript mass-produced goods:

---

*   Zola, *The Ladies' Paradise*, pp. 12–13.

The danger will be that of drowning in the Flemish silks, the satin, the velvet, the lace, the rugs, the suits, the falbalas, the lighting, the colors, just as *Le Ventre de Paris* [the third volume in the Rougon-Macquart series, which dealt with Les Halles, the central Parisian food market] got sunk in the vegetables and the cheeses. The danger will be that of treating the department stores like a still life, instead of seeking out their portrait, instead of seizing their soul.*

By skimming rapidly over the erotic surface of the commodity, by diffusing the atmosphere of the store's interior with the signs of a fleeting eroticism, Zola avoids the still life. Readers are presented with a flux of rapidly described part-objects: both goods and body parts. In the great "sale" sequences that structure the novel (Chapters 4, 9, and 14), Zola's phrases and clauses crowd together, eclipsing the verb, creating the impression of syntactic blocks as movable or interchangeable as any of the counter displays in Mouret's store. And the store itself, variously described throughout the novel as a "lighthouse," a "cathedral," a "devouring monster," a "ship," a "battlefield," and finally, as an entirely self-sufficient "city" complete with barbershops, reading rooms, and cafes, takes on vampiric dimensions in the plot: the store is ready to devour indiscriminately not only the sexual and emotional lives of its employees, but any economic establishment, any neighboring building, and any individual or small group that stands in its path. Much of the novel's plot thus follows a horizontal development that explores the store's spatial expansion, its conquest of the surrounding real estate, and its feeding on the blood of the *quartier*, which is represented by the symbolic deaths of Geneviève Baudu and her mother in the final chapter, Robineau's accident, even the "baptismal" blood of Mouret's

---

* Jean Richepin, "Le Calicot," *Gil Blas*, November 21, 1881, p. 8.

dead wife that supposedly fertilized the store's foundation before the novel begins.

This tale of urban empire clearly mirrors the more global historical movement of Western bourgeois expansion that lies outside the novel's frame. Traces of the colonial narrative are, however, perceptible in the Orientalist fantasy and the whole eroticized display of Asian products, as well as in the diffusion of the store's catalogs throughout the French provinces and beyond. The horizontal expansion of the store, which Zola thought of as the principal plot mechanism ("The fight between two stores must be the true drama, very vibrant. The old commerce defeated in one shop, then in other less important ones scattered around the neighborhood")* is counterbalanced by an equally exhilarating vertical momentum: the rise of shopgirl Denise Baudu to a position in upper management; her emotional conquest of Mouret, granted the spiritual intensity of a vengeance performed on behalf of the entire female sex; the furious rising and ebbing of the tide of shoppers in the "sale" sequences; the gradual proliferation and piling up of goods, sales devices, customers, and new services in each of the sales so that each exceeds the last in density, volume, and in the fever pitch and frenzy of the customers; the mounting cash receipts that conclude each sale.

But, if the store is described initially as a vast combustion machine, it is likened most consistently during the course of the novel to a cathedral—a temple where woman is both goddess and worshipper. Zola's novel shows the department store in the midst of becoming the permissible public space for women's social interchange, replacing in a sense both church and salon. The same women characters who meet in Madame Desforges's

---

*   Zola, sketch, in *Les Rougon-Macquart: Histoire naturelle et sociale d'une famille sous le second Empire*, ed. Henri Mitterand, Vol. 3 (Paris: Gallimard, 1964), p. 1681.

late afternoon salon in an early chapter of the novel meet again
in the store in the final chapter; Madame Desforges herself joins
them. The store, Zola writes in his sketches for the novel, must
be on the one hand, "a vast feminine enterprise, woman must be
queen in the store, she must feel it a temple elevated to her glory,
for her pleasure (*jouissance*) and for her triumph."* And, on the
other, Zola saw it as the place where middle-class women may
go as supplicants to a dream, to relieve their *ennui*, to pass time,
to escape domestic confines:

> The cult of woman, woman-queen in her domain. The days of
> exposition, the great sale-days, she reigns in crowd form, as if in a
> conquered country, willful, arrogant ... The great department store
> tends to replace the church. This derives from the religion of the
> body, of beauty, of flirtation and of fashion. They go there to pass
> the time as they would in a church: an occupation, a place where they
> become excited, where they struggle with their passion for clothes
> and their husband's budget, and finally with the whole drama of
> existence, the above and beyond of beauty.†

Middle-class men, of course, took flight from the confines of
domesticity in their own way: into real estate speculation, playing
the stock market, and walking the tightrope of overextended
credit. Zola's novel situates shopping, the female flight from
domestic routine, in a parasitic and parodic relation to the masculine dream-world of Second Empire high finance. Woman is both
goddess and worshipper at the altar of fashion, and the department store elevates her at the same time that it manipulates and
captivates her. "The all-powerfulness of woman," Zola writes in
his notes, "dominates the entire store—And Octave's commercial

---

*   Ibid., p. 1681.
†   Zola, sketch, cited in Kamm, p. 11.

idea is there, more or less consciously and overtly."* The illusion of female omnipotence in the store, in other words, is the result of a deliberate strategy of masculine seduction of women as consumers, a strategy consummately deployed in the novel by Mouret, whose simultaneous contempt for and dependence on the "nation of women" makes him, like Baudelaire's *homme de la foule*, a palpable male modernist type. Mouret is the slave of the new cult, and also, as Zola deems him, its high priest; he is promiscuous and sensuous in his relation with the female crowd ("He lost his breath deliciously, he felt against his limbs a sort of caress from all his customers"[†]), and at the same time, curiously removed, detached, given to surveying the frenzied bargain-seekers from a great height. The relation of the modern entrepreneur to the (female) crowd for Zola is, like that of the modernist poet for Baudelaire, one of both promiscuity and erotic ascesis.

And what of the female crowd? Early in the first chapter, Zola provides a telling prelude to his later, less allegorical representations. Standing before the display windows, Denise observes:

> There was something for all tastes, from the opera cloaks at twenty-nine francs to the velvet mantle marked up at eighteen hundred. The well-rounded neck and graceful figures of the dummies exaggerated the slimness of the waist, the absent head being replaced by a large price-ticket pinned on the neck; whilst the mirrors, cleverly arranged on each side of the windows, reflected and multiplied the forms without end, peopling the street with these beautiful women for sale, each bearing a price in big figures in the place of a head.[‡]

* Zola, sketch, in *Les Rougon-Macquart*, p. 1680.
† Zola, *The Ladies' Paradise*, p. 94.
‡ Ibid., p. 4.

In this admirably "economic" image, Zola evokes both the condition of the woman consumer and the image she is called upon to purchase: herself as commodity, as superior commodity in the masculine traffic in women. As the image of the mannequins is refracted out onto the streets, consumers and female passersby become indistinguishable from the mannequins; all are soulless but beautiful replicants, "women for sale." The female image that peoples the street is headless and, by extension, credulous, irrational, lacking in critical judgment and decisiveness. This image bears the characteristics of the new generation of woman consumer as she was then being constructed within capitalist society (disoriented and distracted) and more generally, the characteristics traditionally attributed to women in a crowd, or to the crowd itself as woman. Historians like Zola's contemporary Hippolyte Taine, writing in the 1870s and 1880s, and early social psychologists like Gustave Le Bon and Gabriel Tarde in the 1890s, did much to disseminate the idea of crowds as womanish hordes: impulsive, delirious, and prone to violence. Throughout his work, Zola's female masses tend to reinforce this representation. There is no great distance separating Zola's depiction of women revolutionaries in *Germinal*, his story of striking mine workers, and the middle-class shoppers of *The Ladies' Paradise*. Whether seduced by Etienne's persuasive rhetoric in *Germinal* or by Mouret's advertising in *The Ladies' Paradise*, women, it seems, are particularly susceptible, given over to contagion and delirium. Their excitability, particularly when in large public gatherings, leads to violence, destruction, and general pillage. In *Germinal* it is the women, positioned by Zola at the forefront of the crowd, who are the instigators and perpetrators of violence. The great "sale" sequences of *The Ladies' Paradise*, fueled by momentous energy, the "brutal gaiety" of female desire, are indistinguishable from battle scenes: "Everything appeared like a field of battle still warm with the massacre of the various goods."* In *Germinal*, La Mouquette bares her buttocks as a mark of disdain for the bourgeoisie and the military; in *The Ladies' Paradise* the image of the silk department after the shoppers have departed retains traces of a similarly aggressive and threatening female sexuality.

> The furs were scattered over the flooring, the readymade clothes were heaped up like the great-coats of wounded soldiers, the lace and the underlinen, unfolded, crumpled, thrown about everywhere, made one think of an army of women who had disrobed there in the disorder of some sudden desire.†

Once they have assembled themselves into a crowd, women, whether strikers or shoppers, revert to a primitive state: "public" woman is woman preyed upon by savage and violent impulses.

In *Distorting Mirrors*, Susanna Barrows argued that, behind the female hordes evoked by Zola, Tarde, and Taine, lurks the shadow of another, more ominous crowd of women: French feminists.‡ In the early 1880s, the moment when Zola was writing his novel, feminists had made some advances: divorce, for example, abolished since 1816, would be reinstated in 1884. Before 1880, women in France had practically no access to secondary education; in December of that year laws were passed that allowed the establishment of independent *lycées* for girls, which the state promised to support. But the longer history of feminist struggle in France, from the late eighteenth century onward, documents an intimate association between periods of feminist action and the onset of violent revolution. Beginning with Olympe de Gouge's

---

* Ibid., p. 100.

† Ibid., pp. 100–1.

‡ See Susanna Barrows, *Distorting Mirrors: Visions of the Crowd in Late Nineteenth-Century France* (New Haven: Yale University Press, 1981).

La Déclaration des droits de la femme et de la citoyenne (1791),
feminists came forward in each successive revolution to demand
their rights and to press for a public voice. In 1848, women's
clubs and associations again formed in Paris and the provinces;
these, however, were unable to ensure women's inclusion in the
platform for "universal suffrage" enacted that year. But it was
undoubtedly the 1871 Paris Commune, the last revolution of
the nineteenth century, that cemented the connection between
feminist struggle and violent revolution in the popular imaginary.
The "female" character of the events of the Commune was the
stuff of both right-wing legend (the violent "new woman" of the
cartoons and engravings, the Pétroleuses setting Paris aflame) and
of first-person accounts by Communards: "Women started first, as
they did during the revolution. Those of March 18, hardened by
the war in which they had a double share of misery, did not wait
for their men."* If memories and images of the violent women
insurgents had receded somewhat during the repressive decade
following the Commune, they would be newly awakened by the
1880 amnesty that allowed thousands of deported Communards
to return to France.

Although three French film versions were made of *Au Bonheur
des dames* between 1913 and 1943, perhaps the most ambitious film
rendering of the novel was a 1929 Russian production entitled
New Babylon. In this film, the two great late nineteenth-century
female crowds, the insurgents and the shoppers, are united in
a single narrative, and Marx's writings on the Paris Commune
collapse onto the love story between Denise Baudu and Octave
Mouret. (In one particularly memorable scene, grand pianos
are pushed out of the department store windows to be used for
barricades.) Certain twentieth-century Marxist interpretations

---

* Prosper-Olivier Lissagaray, *Histoire de la commune de 1871* (Paris: La
Découverte, 1990), p. 110.

of the Commune, notably that of Henri Lefebvre, enacted a similar *theoretical* collapse—or perhaps I should say expansion. Instead of focusing on the insurgents' struggle as one of merely or primarily gaining control over the means of production, the factory, Lefebvre interpreted the Commune as an intervention into the area of the reproduction of the social relations of production, or, as he called it, everyday life. Such an interpretation must necessarily focus on women: as the primary victims and arbiters of social reproduction, the subjects of everydayness and the victims of everyday life, the class of people most responsible for consumption, and those responsible for the complex movement whereby the social existence of human beings is produced and reproduced. Lefebvre's book on the Commune and the extensive analyses of everyday life and modernity he conducted through the 1950s, 1960s, and 1970s, helped mark a theoretical shift in France that was itself occasioned by a new wave of economic changes. For, if France in the late nineteenth century pioneered the twin pillars of modern commerce, retailing and advertising, France, from the 1950s on, was experiencing the sudden and abrupt onslaught of high technological advances and durable consumer goods, a process which in America had been a slow and gradual accumulation. Lefebvre's isolation of the concept of everyday life was predicated in part on his recognizing a qualitative change in post-1960 France, its transformation into what he called a bureaucratic consumer society, or what Guy Debord and the Situationists, writing at the same time, called the "society of the spectacle," and what others have theorized more globally as postmodernism. Advertising that, in the world of *The Ladies' Paradise*, was designed to promote the consumption of goods has become, Lefebvre argued, the primary good being currently consumed. Lefebvre, the Situationists, the early Baudrillard, and others began to chart the contemporary shift from a conception of ideology based on inner belief or value systems, to one whereby everyday life practices—ways of moving about a city, for instance, or shopping—come to play the functional role of ideology. This contemporary turn in the analysis of ideology, along with recent feminist work, primarily in the United States and Britain, on the specific and ambiguous position of women in everyday life as the primary buyers and the consumers of merchandise as well as the symbols of that merchandise, has made the reissue of an English translation of *Au Bonheur des dames* particularly timely.

A Note on the Translation

Au Bonheur des dames, the first of Zola's novels to be translated into English, was also the first to be subjected to expurgation and revision. In the triple-decker three-volume version that appeared in November 1883 from Tinsley Brothers, specific references to sexual matters had been altered, changed into vague generalizations or euphemisms, or simply deleted. The fact that Tinsley Brothers chose to translate *Au Bonheur des dames* over more popular Zola novels suggests the company's desire to cash in on the notoriety of the author's name, which was a major motivation in the marketing of Zola in England, where the subtitle, "A Realistic Novel," was invariably interpreted to mean pornographic and was invariably blazoned on the cover. A more accurate retranslation of *Au Bonheur* was published in 1886 by a young firm headed by Henry Vizetelly that specialized in sensational fiction; it is this version that is reprinted here. (Whether the translation was by Vizetelly himself or a staff member of the firm is unknown.) In the wake of a relentless campaign by self-proclaimed watchdogs of moral standards, most notably an institution called the National Vigilance Association and an individual member of the House of Commons who proclaimed Zola novels responsible for the moral decay of France, Vizetelly was charged in October 1888 with publishing an obscene libel (his firm's translation of Zola's *La Terre*). He was tried, convicted, and imprisoned for three months, managing, however, to capitalize on the notoriety of his trial to sell other "revised" and newly expurgated versions of Zola. A comparison between the 1883 Tinsley version and the 1886 Vizetelly version gives us some indication of what was deemed, at the time, to be offensive in England; any passing reference to Denise's brother Jean's affairs with married women, for instance, or to the sexual arrangements of the shopgirls, is softened or eliminated:

> *Certainement, une pauvre fille ne pouvait soutenir ses deux frères, payer la pension du petit et régaler les maitresses du grand.*
> Certainly a poor girl could not support her two brothers, and pay their board and lodging. (1883)
> Certainly a poor girl could not support her two brothers, pay the little one's board and lodging, and regale the big one's mistresses. (1886)

> *Il la suivit dans la pièce voisine. Clare ne fut pas dupe de la manceuvre: elle murmura qu'on ferait mieux d'aller chercher un lit tout de suite.*
> He followed her into the next room. Clare was furious and said, "If girls will cry so, they ought to be sent to bed at once." (1883)
> He followed her into the next room. Clara was not duped by this manoeuver, and said they had better go and fetch a bed at once. (1886)

The early English publishers of Zola, concerned with expurgating traces of sexuality from *The Ladies' Paradise*, might well have looked elsewhere. Jean's mistresses or Clare's affairs constitute tiny, literal instances of sexuality in a novel where very little lovemaking actually takes place or is even intimated. The erotic energy of the novel is everywhere apparent, but it is displaced onto the fetishes of retailing, the fluttering linens, the beckoning advertisements and fragrances, and the yearning gazes, onto the surging orgasmic crescendo and waning tide of the shoppers and Mouret's whole prolonged embrace with his clientele. No surgical incision could remove the traces of a sexuality diffused among signs and accoutrements, or of a seduction that is, above all else, commercial.

This aspect of the book's appeal (or obscenity, depending on one's point of view) was perhaps better understood by Alton F. Doody, president of the American consulting firm of Management Horizons, Inc., than it was by editors like Tinsley. Doody's firm, it seems, made the only attempt in this century to keep *The Ladies' Paradise* in print, reissuing in 1976 a very limited edition of the 1886 Vizetelly translation. It did so, Doody noted in his preface, because of the book's status as an outstanding documentary on the spectacular development of the first large-scale retail institution. More importantly, he added:

> The book remains a truly unique and distinctive work on how to create store excitement. The principles and techniques described in *The Ladies' Paradise* are as pertinent to retailing today as they were one hundred years ago.
>
> *The Ladies' Paradise*, therefore, is a pragmatic guide which can be used in our time to increase the merchandising effectiveness of almost any retail store … We predict that it will help you create stores which are more exciting places to shop for your customers, assuring the continued prosperity of your enterprise.

9

Jacques Tati, Historian

It makes me sound old-fashioned, but I think I am an anarchist.

—Jacques Tati

Comedians are often our best historians of the present because they are at once intensely invested in and poorly adapted to their moment, at one and yet out of sync with their surroundings and situation. Unlike professional historians, who feel compelled to try to explain why the present had to evolve in exactly the way it did from what came before it, comics trade in making the lived elements of the present appear to be as unnatural, as unexplainable as possible. Commenting upon the strikingly memorable soundtracks that he designed to accompany all of his important films from *Mon oncle* (1958) to *Parade* (1974), Jacques Tati remarked, "Well, when people are in strange surroundings, natural sounds always sound louder." Each of Tati's films works to turn the most familiar lived landscapes of postwar French society into *strange surroundings*.

Tati's first feature-length film, *Jour de fête*, appeared in 1949; his last, *Parade*, twenty-five years later. His work in the cinema spans roughly the three-decade-long period that has come to be known in France as les Trente Glorieuses—the thirty glorious years—evoking the happy effects of continual economic growth. The term was coined in 1979 by Jean Fourastié, one of the many avid promoters of the state-led postwar modernization effort, and its ubiquity as the name for the years between the end of World War II and the oil crisis of the mid-1970s has gone mostly unquestioned, then and now. Historians still refer to the postwar period that way as though it were natural, a periodization and not a value judgment, as though that span of years were uniformly glorious and not interrupted by violent political disruptions surrounding the end of the French empire in Indochina and Algeria (as well as the insurrections of May '68), or as if those decades were uniformly "glorious" for all French alike, the country's economic well-being visited bountifully and evenly upon farmers and bureaucrats, immigrants and developers, bankers and small-shop keepers. Proponents of capitalist modernization in France used the phrase (and continue to do so) without a second thought to summon up the image of a French society surging forward in consensual lockstep, marching to the cadence of increased productivity, higher salaries, and the rewards of privatized consumption into a dazzling future of all-electric kitchens—with an American-made lifestyle to match. Anyone who has caught a glimpse of the peculiar gait of Tati's recurring character, Monsieur Hulot, cannot help but see in it an indication of how Tati viewed the vision of the world forged by postwar modernizing technocrats. Hulot's walk, his way of moving through the world, contains within it a certain built-in aesthetic reflex against that image of uniformity, against the rationality to which the postwar economic surge aspired. "Our world becomes every day more anonymous," Tati once remarked. "In other times, the butcher was a man with a colored shirt. Now he puts on white overalls like a male nurse. The world is in the process of becoming an enormous clinic."

Tati borrowed the physical elements, the governing tropes, and the urgency of the modernization program and made them strange; he denaturalized its sounds and textures at the same moment that advertising and Hollywood movies were busy making them appear natural. He arranged the automobiles and domestic trappings, the new social types and transformations in the built environment into an elaborate choreography designed to show the psychotechnics of exhilaration and fatigue that occur whenever groups or individuals, obliged to adjust to abrupt changes to home and transport, leisure and labor, find themselves leading two, and sometimes more, lives at once. Parisians of the postwar period lived in one Paris intersecting with and colliding into another in a process of demolition and reconstruction on a scale equivalent to the one Haussmann had overseen one hundred years earlier. And, as in the earlier moment, the transformations Tati was to make the subject of his filmmaking were completely given over to traffic.

A still from Jacques Tati's *Playtime* (1967)

Already in *Jour de fête*, the new watchwords of "speed," "efficiency," and "mobility" coming from America are seen to have
penetrated into the farthest reaches of French village life. A provincial postman named François goes to see a promotional film
about the postal service in the United States; daring Yankee mail-
men are seen diving out of helicopters to deliver the mail. François
takes the lesson to heart, and soon the whole village has become a
spectator to François's "doing things American-style!" But it is not
until the three major films—*Mon oncle* (1958), *Play Time* (1967),
and *Trafic* (1971)—that the central vehicle of twentieth-century
capitalist modernization, the automobile, receives its full due for
starring in the creation of a modernity mediated by objects. In
Mon oncle, the arrival of the enormous pink-and-green Chevro-
let ("Everything is automatic!") is treated by the camera as an
outlandish, even alien visitation. But that moment of singularity
lasts only an instant; turn the corner and the car has joined an
endless row of similar vehicles, creeping forward at a snail's pace.
At the conclusion of *Play Time*, pinwheels made of cars filmed
from an aerial view bring to mind Siegfried Kracauer's analysis of the Tiller Girls as ornament, each dancing girl no longer
individual but part of indissoluble girl clusters whose movements
are demonstrations of mathematics. Here the car becomes a fatal
element in a geometrically precise ballet of seriality and repetition. The aptly titled *Trafic* opens with footage taken of an auto
assembly line and ends with acres and acres of stalled vehicles.
In between, the film recounts the story of an ill-fated journey
to bring the model "camping car" from France to Amsterdam,
a trip beset with breakdowns and mishaps—even the car, being
transported inside a truck, has an accident! In the final sequence,
the windshield wipers of the hundreds of stalled cars take over the
aesthetic task of rhythmic synchronized movement at the point
when driving and parking have become, in the final analysis,

virtually indistinguishable. The traffic jam emerges as Tati's most effective figure for conveying how cumbersome any movement has become in a new environment that demands that absolutely everyone comply with higher levels of speed and mobility.

Tati's films make palpable a daily life that appears to unfold in a space where objects dictate to people their gestures and movements—gestures as yet unlearned. Such a world conjures up whole new professions and career opportunities in middle management, like the American "public relations" woman in *Trafic*—go-betweens who exist to mediate the new technologies and their hapless users. What, after all, is "public relations"? Often broadly referred to as "communications," PR is a set of vague practices designed to promote products and people, practices that themselves intersect with or, like the ultramodern layout of Madame Arpel's domestic interior in *Mon oncle*, "communicate with" nearly every other industry. Job definition in such a world is always in flux. ("That's not my job!" "You're doing my job!"—these phrases punctuate the dialogue of *Trafic*.) But newer incarnations like the public relations woman have an easier time than most negotiating what in Tati's world is, more than anything else, just a new relationship of bodies in space. "Actors like to have their legs showing" was one of Tati's favorite rules of thumb, and we see it best put to use in the elongated physique and leggy stride of the PR woman, in the gymnastic ease with which she changes clothes in a tiny car and emerges, transformed, on the sidewalk, utterly chic, more than Parisian, and ready to take on the world. Physical flexibility—having the elastic body of the clown—is the visual translation of the mental and psychological adaptability needed to survive and even flourish in the ambiguous positions of the new corporate structure.

Those in older or more traditional professions adapt less easily. The character of the architect who built the restaurant in *Play Time* whose chaotic opening night takes up much of the film's second half is kept busy all evening rearranging tables and chairs to facilitate the flow of dinners, dancers, and diners—exhausted, he balks at adjusting the furniture one more time and barks: "Bring me waiters who know how to move around tables!" Unemployable in *Mon oncle*, Hulot in *Trafic* has now become one of the masterminds of the new built environment, and can even occasionally be seen directing traffic. He is the designer and inventor of the most advanced of commodities, the camping car, a truly wondrous item, an automobile whose every working part doubles as a household appliance: barbecue, soap dispenser, coffeemaker, electric shaver. It is a commonplace that all of twentieth-century capitalist modernization flows along the horizontal plane from the countryside to the city, and Tati's films follow that progression: from the provincial village of *Jour de fête*, to the family beach of *Monsieur Hulot's Holiday* (1953), to the quaint old neighborhood of *Mon oncle*, to the city as airport of *PlayTime*. But, in *Trafic*, we have come full circle: the camping car unites and synthesizes not only interior and exterior space but also the lost countryside and the most sophisticated of urban gadgetry. Carrying atop its vehicles enormous tree limbs needed to build the bucolic decor they will use to frame their fabulous creation at the International Automobile Show in Amsterdam, the small caravan tries to make its way from Paris. But a final irony awaits the car's designer at the end of their journey: though the camping car has brought joy to all those along the way who experienced it, the entry arrives too late to compete in the automobile show, and Hulot is unceremoniously fired.

Fired, but not, in the end, fallen. There is never a moral dimension to Hulot's adventures, and there is no moral lesson for us to learn. As Serge Daney has pointed out, Tati's comedy contains none of the verticality of the catastrophe, or even of the *felix*

culpa, the fortunate fall that allows the protagonist to redeem
the fallen world or become a hero through losing everything, à
la Chaplin. Despite the enormous vulnerability of Hulot's over-
exposed and childlike ankles, falling is not a part of his comic
repertoire. But wobbling, maneuvering, sidestepping, teetering,
beetling, reversing direction, retracing his steps, attempting to
stay on his feet, propping himself up with an umbrella—all of
these are. This is why it would be wrong to say that Hulot moves
more slowly than the world around him, or that Tati is turned
fatally to the past, longing nostalgically for a Vichy-infused model
of *la vieille France*. For one thing, the image of an immobile Third
Republic village mentality was itself an invention of the postwar
promoters of capitalist modernization, an idea promulgated to
increase the urgency with which the French of the 1950s and
1960s were supposed to fling themselves into American-style
consumption habits. Hulot may well be out of step, but his step
is often brisker than other people's. His body leans forward—
purposefully—into the future. He rarely drags his feet.

10
Schoolteachers, Maids, and Other Paranoid Histories

I. With effort, the small woman manages to turn the large metal crank that controls the flood slough, unleashing a torrent of water to gush down the stream below her. She is wearing a high-necked formal dress, fingerless fishnet gloves, and shiny high-heeled shoes that make her lose her footing from time to time on the rough terrain. Later we will learn that she is the village schoolteacher, and that the flood she has unleashed is designed to drown the livestock belonging to the villagers below while they are attending a funeral. We will also see Mademoiselle—for this is what she is called, the only name the film gives her—donning again and again before the mirror, with ritualized precision, the same dress, patent leather shoes, and net gloves in a ceremony of her own design. But for now, as the film opens, the woman's appearance in the still country landscape, her hair elaborately swept up, her stiletto heels sinking into the mud as she walks, is merely incongruous, out of place. Why is she there?

Mademoiselle, Jean Genet's first significant encounter with cinema, was directed by Tony Richardson in a Franco-British coproduction and released in 1966. Genet provided the original screenplay. The film starred Jeanne Moreau as a pyromaniacal provincial schoolteacher who perpetrates a series of catastrophes on the village where she lives and works: fires, floods, poisonings. The assaults are blamed by the peasants on a handy scapegoat, an itinerant Italian woodcutter called Manou who is the focus of a great deal of sexual attention on the part of the village women (including Mademoiselle, who will consummate her passion in an extended night of love with the woodcutter), and sexual rivalry on the part of the men. As Mademoiselle's destructive ceremonies increase in number, the village builds to a xenophobic frenzy, and when Mademoiselle announces she has been raped by the Italian, the villagers execute the foreigner in a ritual killing. Its fury spent, the village subsides once again into a timeless, provincial calm; Mademoiselle herself moves on to a new job in the next village.

The film opened in 1966 in Paris and London to nearly uniform bad reviews. Its screening at Cannes that year was interrupted by booings and catcalls which erupted, in particular, during the long sex scenes between Mademoiselle and Manou—scenes in which Moreau, on her hands and knees, barks like a dog. Critics labeled the long-awaited encounter between the three "enfants terribles," Richardson, Genet, and Moreau, as the "greatest deception of the festival."* "A strange masochism," wrote the reviewer in *Le Monde*, "has pushed *Mademoiselle*'s screenwriter, director, and leading actress to give themselves over, each in his own way, to a bad parody of their talent."† The feeling of parody expressed in more than a few of the film's reviews seemed to arise from the way in which the film's elements—subject matter, style, casting— refused to mesh. (Today's viewers have a different name for the set of aesthetic responses brought on by these incongruities: they would, I think, experience the film as full-fledged kitsch.) Jeanne

---

*   *Paris Presse*, May 14, 1966.
†   *Le Monde*, May 14, 1966.

Moreau was simply too serious an actress to crawl through the mud barking like a dog. The French, it seemed, were too serious about social issues like xenophobia to see them treated by a perverse Jeanne Moreau in fingerless gloves. The English, on the other hand, were far too serious about perversion to tolerate having it mixed together with a social issue like xenophobia. Eager to make a film with Moreau, Richardson had given her free choice of the material for their collaboration; she chose the screenplay by her then neighbor, Genet. Was Genet's script ill served by the heavy-handed naturalism of Richardson's directorial style? Richardson wanted, as he put it, to make "an above all *realist* film;"* he shot the film entirely in stills (people and animals move, the landscape doesn't) and refused to provide a musical soundtrack. Several French reviewers, obviously responding to the film's desired realistic effect, protested vigorously against having the daily life of a remote French village be represented, "naturalistically," by a remote Englishman who had never before set foot in the countryside, let alone the French countryside, let alone the Corrèze department, in his life. Was this xenophobia on the part of the reviewers? Perhaps, though more than one reviewer concluded that the film might have been salvaged had it been directed not by a Frenchman, but by a different foreigner, one with a lighter touch: Luis Buñuel.

Two years earlier, Buñuel had proven himself adept at bringing to the screen a similar mix of rural France, fetishism, and xenophobia in his remake of Jean Renoir's 1941 *Journal d'une femme de chambre*, based on Octave Mirbeau's 1900 novel by the same name. (In the novel and the film the crime that shatters the village calm—the rape and murder of a little girl—is blamed on Jews.) Buñuel's film also cast the leading French actress of the day, Jeanne

---

* Tony Richardson, quoted in *Arts*, May 22, 1965.

Moreau, in the starring role of Célestine, the prototypical "bonne à tout faire" (maid). The maid and the schoolteacher: in both films the quintessentially elegant and urbane actress—Moreau was voted by Americans the best-dressed woman in the world in 1966—was called upon to play an improbably "deglamorized" role, rural chambermaid or humble schoolteacher. Her roles in these films were those of stock female characters from a long, middlebrow literary tradition devoted to *faits divers*, sensational crimes, and the illumination of obscure lives.

But Moreau the Parisian was in fact an inspired choice to play this particular maid and schoolteacher. Célestine, after all, in Mirbeau's novel and Buñuel's film, does not follow the usual geographic destiny of "the maid." History and fiction alike show the maid arriving bewildered in the capital in waves of immigration from Brittany first, or the Morvan, or other destitute French regions at the turn of the century, then from Spain or Portugal later, and later still from North Africa. Most maids move from the countryside to the city to work, or, like the Papin sisters, historical models for Genet's *Les Bonnes,* work for the wealthy of their own small towns. Célestine moves in an unexpected direction: born and bred in Paris where she has worked all of her life, she is obliged to quit the city and accept a position in a rural bourgeois household. In the film's credit sequences she is seen alighting from the train from Paris, suitcase in hand, wearing the high heels that connote urbanity, to be met by a sullen peasant coachman. In this she resembles not so much the maid as the prototypical schoolteacher, that missionary of laicization sent forth to enlighten obscure corners of the hexagon, who, following a long literary and cinematic tradition, is always from Paris. Disembarking from a train from the capital, "a young girl, foreign to the area": this is how Léon Frapié in his *locus classicus, L'Institutrice de province*—written, like Mirbeau's novel, at the dawning of the new century—introduces his heroine, Louise Chardon. Louise is a tidily dressed and high-minded young woman raised in Paris who with great difficulty has won a position as *institutrice* and will shortly find herself making her way gamely amid "a race of thin peasants, shrunken in stature, taciturn and cunning … the mobility of [whose] lowered faces, elongated into the muzzle of a dog, made them look as though they were constantly looking for something on the ground."* Or consider, more recently, the more mature Mademoiselle Hélène in Claude Chabrol's 1969 film, *Le Boucher.* Played by Stéphane Audran, this provincial schoolteacher has been wounded in love, and has come from Paris to a village in the Dordogne to recover. She lives, like all schoolteachers, in a room adjoining the schoolhouse; her window, like that of Genet's Mademoiselle, overlooks the small, somewhat desolate school courtyard lined with plane trees.

> II. From her window Mademoiselle can see the frantic villagers organize themselves into a makeshift bucket brigade in an attempt to save the burning barn. Manou, the shirtless Italian woodcutter, is among them—a hero, ("the god of the catastrophe," writes Genet) rescuing livestock from the barn. Quickly she changes out of her ceremonial costume and runs down to join the fight against the fire she herself has set only minutes before. As she takes her place in line, she is politely brushed aside by a villager: "This is no place for you, Mademoiselle, go back home."

The profession that most represented social mobility for women throughout the first half of this century in France was by most accounts a lesson in stifling claustrophobia and disturbing rootlessness. Firsthand testimonies from turn-of-the-century *institutrices* evoke a psychological misery that is socially produced,

---

* Léon Frapié, *L'Institutrice de province* (Paris: Bibliotech Charpentier, 1897), p. 9.

a misery distinct from the material difficulties and the physical fatigue that accompanied a wearing and badly paid *métier*. Mademoiselle's rooms above the classroom are exactly like those of Stéphane Audran in *Le Boucher*: the same chest of drawers, the small kitchen table that doubles as a desk for grading papers. Sparse, bare objects that testify to a life lived outside sociability, almost outside history—a life of repetition, embedded in the slack, drab time of everyday life: lessons to prepare, recitations and *dictées* to correct, meals to prepare and eat alone. In Mademoiselle's case, that repetitive time will suddenly be shot through with "the event": her ritual violence, her transfigurative acting out. But the violent exceptionality of her attacks on the village is predicated on the solitary, isolated space of her room. Testimonials from early French *institutrices* frequently begin with a description of their rooms:

> The director showed me the room set aside for me where I had to live. I can still see that room, a place where air and light never entered ... The humidity was such that the wallpaper was damp, and I developed all the aches and pains I still suffer from in that room.*

In a rare—perhaps the lone—scenic instruction in his screenplay, Genet underlines the chalk-dust-ridden and stagnant air of a claustrophobia from which the peasants, happily self-contained and autarchic, do not seem to suffer:

> The night was beautiful. And yet despite the beauty of the night, all the village was asleep; the doors and the shutters were closed; peasants do not suffer from claustrophobia! If possible, it's essential *to show* the odor of [Mademoiselle's] rooms.†

---

*   Danielle Delhome, Nicole Gault, Josiane Gonthier, eds., *Les premières institutrices laïques* (Paris: Mercure de France, 1980), p. 91.

†   Jean Genet, *Les rêves interdits* or *L'autre versant du rêve* (screenplay for

In Genet paranoiac, stifling intimacy, exclusion from the social, has an odor, and that odor must be shown: for Mademoiselle, the odor becomes the space of the room where she lives alone, dressing for her secret ceremonies with methodical gestures in front of the mirror, telling herself stories. (The town mayor in the film remarks: "She's young, all alone, she has no one; she tells herself stories.") For Claire and Solange in *Les Bonnes*, trapped in what Jacques Lacan called "le mal d'être deux" (the illness of being two) or what Sartre, in a wonderful phrase, called "a solitude that has mated," the odor is each other. Claire to Solange: "I've had enough of this terrifying mirror that reflects my own image back to me like a bad odor. You are my bad odor."*

Mademoiselle has a room, but she has no place in the sociability of the village: "This is no place for you, Mademoiselle." The solicitous "hands-off" isolation with which the villagers treat her is a pedestal which cordons her off from the social workings of the town. The room, for any itinerant worker, is a series of rooms, and schoolteaching is a migratory job: Frapié's schoolteacher heroine, Louise Chardon, has five different positions, and thus rooms, in five different villages during her brief career, and all of her displacements are dictated against her will, from above, by the Ministry in Paris. "The most aggravating effect of these

---

Mademoiselle). Unpublished text; Editions Gallimard is currently editing Genet's scenario for publication as an annex to his complete works. Laurent Boyer, in charge of the edition, notes that he is not completely certain if the text of the screenplay, in the collection of IMEC, is entirely by Genet, or if it is in fact a later version that had been reworked by Michel Cournot in view of the film on the request of the film's producer. Thanks to Albert Dichy at IMEC for allowing me to consult the screenplay, and to Laurent Boyer for allowing me to quote from it.

* Jean Genet, *Les Bonnes* (Paris: L'Arbalète, 1963), p. 48. Genet's screenplay contains a flashback that has not been incorporated into Richardson's film. In this sequence, Mademoiselle, in the village for a year and completely isolated, splits, like Claire and Solange, into two characters. A schoolteacher double, Martha, appears—a flirt, where Mademoiselle is demure and repressed in her high-necked dress. The two women commiserate, again like Claire and Solange, on how best to escape from "ce trou" (this hole).

frequent moves," she comments, "is that one doesn't have time to make oneself liked: foreigner when you arrive, foreigner when you leave."* The schoolteacher is as much an alien in the village as is Manou in Genet's screenplay, the seasonal, non-French immigrant worker. Revered and rejected by the villagers, both grand and abject: in Frapié's grim naturalistic bestseller—the novel was dedicated to Mme Zola—the woman teacher's lot is that of never fitting in. One of the few people to ever befriend Louise Chardon, an elderly doctor, explains her situation to her: "You represent the intellectual work that manual labor hates; you bring with you an odious critique of vulgar language and common manners; you don't eat or drink like everyone else; people feel ill at ease around you; you're not from the area."†
For Genet, of course, that very isolation, exclusion, or alienation contains the seeds for exaltation, Genet's familiar "transcendence downward." By virtue of a solitude which is first undergone, then chosen, Mademoiselle becomes *an example*; she unites within herself what Genet called in *Les Bonnes,* "the eternal couple of the criminal and the saint." Just as Manou, the Italian woodcutter is "le plus beau," "the hero of the catastrophe," Mademoiselle is "a goddess." The gendarme and the brigadier called in to investigate the string of floods and fires plaguing the village survey Mademoiselle approvingly: "In Paris she'd be nothing special; here, she's a goddess." "In Paris," the other replies, "there are no goddesses." Early in the film a brief interchange underlines the way in which Mademoiselle is considered a goddess, untouchable and above other women:

Brigadier: Manou is accused of being too handsome and of having had all the women.

---

* Frapié, *L'Institutrice de province*, p. 249.
† Ibid., p. 279.

Mademoiselle: That's false!

Gendarme: Of course, not … you, Mademoiselle.[*]

Even Frapié in his 1897 novel is driven to admit a kind of sanctification or exaltation of the suffering of the schoolteacher. The resentment directed against Louise Chardon is, the friendly doctor maintains, identical to that directed against the artist:

> You are contaminated with most of the execrable qualities that people abhor in the *artist*. How? There you are, a woman earning her living all alone, who gets by without anyone's help, through a proper vocation, a job where you don't get your hands dirty, a thinking job, a job of the head. A woman who is allowed to be generous and to think about things that men, despite their muscles and their sex, and that other women, despite their dowries, cannot think, who allows herself to have noble ideas, to perform actions … who allows herself to haunt regions inaccessible to the vulgar masses.[†]

Schoolteachers, then, by daring to dream, performed a kind of successful (as in remunerated) Bovarysme. They reached regions inaccessible to the vulgar masses, or what Genet once called "the land of the Chimeras"—the only one, according to him, worth inhabiting.[‡]

III. Walking through the forest, Mademoiselle stops to pick a flower. An elderly peasant whom she hasn't noticed nearby tells her the name of the flower, a "couronne de mariée" (bride's crown). Ignoring him, Mademoiselle continues on, spots a nest on the ground full of tiny, delicate bird's eggs, and smashes them with her heel.

---

[*] Genet, *Les Rêves interdits*.

[†] Frapié, *L'Institutrice de province*, pp. 280–1.

[‡] Genet, cited in Jean-Paul Sartre, *Saint Genet: Actor and Martyr*, trans. Bernard Frechtman (New York: Pantheon, 1963), p. 13.

The mere allusion to marriage produces a violent act on the part of Mademoiselle. Genet made a present of his screenplay to actress Anouk Aimée on the occasion of her marriage to his friend Nikos Papatakis in the summer of 1951. (Apparently he forgot he had given her the gift, for he subsequently sold and resold the screenplay several times, once to Louis Malle and his brother.)* The scene which shows Mademoiselle smashing the bird's eggs after hearing marriage mentioned occurs in the first few minutes of the film. Claude Chabrol's film, *Le Boucher,* also opens with a commentary on marriage. Mademoiselle Hélène attends the wedding of her male colleague, the *instituteur,* a wedding that Hélène is perhaps secretly dreaming of for herself. The close-up of the figurine of the wedding couple, dominating the set piece at the end of the meal, underlines the force and unreality of this desire. Chabrol also lets slip into the representation of the marriage several discordant notes: a malicious look, a clumsy gesture, a cake that falls. Both Chabrol and Richardson rely on a chain of "heat" metaphors—notably a fetishized cigarette lighter hidden in the schoolteacher's drawer in both films—to denote thwarted sexual desire.

The model schoolteacher: the phrase is redundant for the schoolteacher is always a model; it is this aspect of her as a social type that intrigues Genet. Women, according to Sartre, appear in Genet's work only as mothers: "Genet disregards girls, except to turn them over to his handsome murderers who casually slaughter them … [Just] mothers, incestuous and sacrilegious mothers."† But what about the maids, Claire and Solange? Just disguised male homosexuals, Sartre replies—Genet wanted to write about homosexuals, but "the necessities of public performance" forced him to substitute maids instead:

* See Edmund White, *Genet: A Biography* (New York: Vintage, 1994), p. 455.
† Sartre, *Saint Genet,* p. 8.

We know that neither women nor the psychology of women interests him. And if he has chosen to show us maids and their mistress and feminine hatreds, it is only because the necessities of public performance oblige him to disguise his thought.[*]

And yet what if it is the condition of the woman schoolteacher, the *institutrice*, or that of the chambermaid, what if it is that very condition, a condition only women can occupy, that made each a model, a fitting example, for Genet? What if it is the confluence of gender and occupation in these particular instances that enables Genet to identify with the role? In part, what makes both figures, maids and schoolteachers, so ideal for Genet is their semi-mythic qualities—qualities that derive perhaps first and foremost from the erotic position each plays for the young child. Like the maid, the schoolteacher is likely to play for the child the role of the first woman *other than the mother*: a kind of shadow mother, tinged for the child with maternal eroticism—in France primary school is called "la maternelle"—and yet not the mother: new, alien, exciting. The semi-mythic qualities that both Chabrol and Richardson, following Genet, grant their Mademoiselles suggest a veering toward the alien side: not a magnified or impoverished image of the mother, but rather the foreign, the non-mother.

But maids and schoolteachers share another condition that renders them abject and grand, and that is the analogous way that each is, almost by definition, deprived of subjectivity. Genet's character is known only by her title, "Mademoiselle"—behind the title of honor, the invariable sobriquet, lurks a stripping away of the schoolteacher's subjectivity in view of function. Some villages successfully rid themselves of several interchangeable *institutrices* in a single year, through concerted campaigns of anonymous

---

[*]   Ibid., p. 614.

denunciatory letters; the schoolteachers' serialized replacements prevented each from becoming fully human, individualized, in the eyes of the villagers. The maid's interchangeability is put to great comic effect by both Mirbeau and Buñuel in the scene in which the fetishist asks the maid to don not just the little boots he requires for his pleasure, but also the requisite first name:

> Monsieur Rabour ... bowed to me and, with the greatest politeness, asked: "What is your name, my dear?"
>
> "Célestine, sir."
>
> "Célestine?" he repeated. "Célestine? Bless me! A pretty name and no mistake ... But too long, my child, much too long. If you have no objection I shall call you Marie. That's also a very nice name, and shorter. Besides, I always call the maids who work here Marie."*

Why must the schoolteacher for Genet be a woman? Why not an *instituteur*? The *instituteur* is not excluded in the same way from the village; he may become part of its hierarchical functioning, befriended by the mayor, the gendarme, integrated into the town's social life. He is a more accepted representative of the laicization dreaded by the peasants. Frequently, as a way of hedging their bets or serving two masters, peasants in the early days of compulsory public education adopted a compromise formation: sons would be sent with good grace to the newly arrived *instituteur* while daughters continued to be sent to the *bonnes soeurs*—and not the

---

*   Octave Mirbeau, *Diary of a Chambermaid*, trans. Douglas Jarman (Sawtry: Dedalus Ltd., 1991), pp.12–13. Another, unintentionally funny, representation of the annihilation of the maid's personal being occurs in Douglas Sirk's film, *Imitation of Life*, when the dying black maid asks her distraught mistress to alert certain members of the black community to her funeral wishes. Not only had the two women shared the same house for all their adult life, they had shared, affectionately, it seemed, the trials and tribulations of raising a daughter each as well. The mistress, a surprised look on her face, exclaims: "Why Annie, I didn't know you had any friends!"

feared *institutrice*. "As for the *instituteur*, secretary to the mayor, he has the best of all situations: with a little cunning, a little skill, he can muzzle the town council. He helps cook their accounts; his services render him indispensable to the illiterate mayor."* The woman schoolteacher, composite of abnegation and devotion, has, in most cases, no husband, child, or lover: "How and with whom would the *institutrice* marry?" asks a woman schoolteacher at the turn of the century.

> Not with a peasant; what would he do with such a doll, for that's how the villagers treat us; not with a shopkeeper, for he would require a dowry; not with a landowner, for he would require double or triple his income ... [and] because of her education, her spiritual culture, her refined tastes, the *institutrice* can't ally herself with a worker whose financial situation is the only one that matches her own.†

Her male colleague, on the other hand, was likely to marry: "Most frequently the *institutrice* is unmarried while the *instituteur* is the happy possessor of a fat peasant woman whom he married for the acres of land she spread out in the sun."‡ A male schoolteacher in 1897 writes that "male schoolteachers succeed rather well in marriage when it comes to fortune. Young girls in the countryside who have a few coins stuffed in an old stocking even seek out such marriages."§ Married, and frequently implicated in the management of town functions, the *instituteur* was enmeshed in village life. Genet the welfare child, on the other hand, learned very young, as he put it, that he was "not a Frenchman," and that he didn't "belong to the village":

---

* Frapié, *L'Institutrice de province*, p. 280.

† Cited in Francine Muel-Dreyfus, *Le métier de l'éducateur* (Paris: Minuit, 1983), pp. 69–70.

‡ A. Dezouche, cited in Danielle Delhome et al., eds., *Les premières institutrices laïques*, p.171.

§ Mittet Victor, cited in ibid., p. 167.

I grew up on public welfare. I learned when I was very young that I am not a Frenchman, that I don't belong to the village. I grew up in the Massif Central. I learned it in a very stupid, ridiculous manner: the teacher told us to write a short composition. Every pupil was supposed to describe his home. The teacher thought that mine was the prettiest description. He read it out loud, and they all made fun of me. They said: But that's not his home. He is a foundling. And at that moment such a void appeared. I immediately felt totally a stranger. Oh, the word "hating" France is not strong enough, it is nothing, there should be more than "hating," "spewing out France."*

In this perhaps apocryphal anecdote, the *instituteur* provides the occasion for potential rescue from the village of the young Genet via writing, but he does nothing to combat the sadism of the village students: the scene of pedagogy cements the young Genet's isolation. But Mademoiselle, the woman schoolteacher, is, unlike her male counterpart, excluded from the workings of the village—and this *by virtue of* her function, her role at the head of the classroom. Like the young Genet, ward of public welfare growing up in an Alligny-en-Morvan that resembled closely the village in his screenplay, Mademoiselle has only the trees or herself to talk to. The *institutrice* is sufficiently excluded from the sociability of the village to provide grounds for an identification with her situation on the part of Genet. Public welfare child and schoolteacher, one from below and one from above, the one its beneficiary, the other its missionary, are both creatures of the Third Republic, and thus of the faith that the world could be remade through state functions and policies. Mademoiselle, the character, would become a vehicle for Genet to find the dark

---

* Genet, cited in Hubert Fichte, "I Allow Myself to Revolt: Interview with Jean Genet," trans. Christa Dove, in P. Brook and J. Halpern, eds., *Critical Essays* (Englewood Cliffs: Prentice Hall, 1979), p. 180.

underlining of that Third Republic optimism and pervert it. In his biography of Genet, Edmund White quotes another public welfare boy who grew up in Genet's village:

> What it really was to be a public welfare child no one else can tell you. Other people don't understand. They think we were all raised the same way, but it's not true. We were kept separate … We weren't like other children. When they referred to us they didn't ever say *pupilles* (wards) … they said *culs de Paris*. That was the common expression … As soon as there was a problem in the district, right away we were blamed for it. For instance, if there was a fire—and they occurred frequently—straight away it was our fault. In the Morvan *patois* we were called "fire-starters."*

The young Genet, whose persecution mania was predicated, for Sartre, on the "simplistic and puerile ethics" of the village framework, is given names by the village: *cul de Paris* and "fire-starter." It is these childhood names that provide the associations and crimes—arson and an obscene urban origin—which he would later displace and transfigure in the character of Mademoiselle.

Solitude and surveillance—the schoolteacher lives under constant inspection: that of students, parents, colleagues, state inspectors, all of whom expect the maintenance of a chaste appearance. She is surrounded by a ceaseless conversation which concerns her but in which she cannot participate, a conversation that may include anonymous denunciations, rumors, sudden silences when she walks by. She is watched by the villagers and the children; authorities sweep into town unannounced "to inspect her." In Frapié's novel, it is the public nature of the schoolteacher's *métier* (like the all-too-public status of the public welfare ward) that makes her "*une créature à part*":

---

* Edmund White, *Genet*, p. 19.

A public creature who has no home, no fixed address, a foreigner wherever she is found, separated from her family, teased by her peers, hated by the children, suspected by the parents, menaced rather than supported by the local authorities.[*]

He concludes, "The *institutrice* has nothing but enemies." Frapié's plucky heroine, Louise Chardon, undergoes horrendous isolation and unjust persecution, not to mention constant uprooting and readjustment, before succumbing to that "worried mind and fearful soul" that for Frapié is the inevitable lot of the schoolteacher:

Among people responsible for teaching, second thoughts begin to accompany all their actions … their way of looking at things in life isn't the same as that of other individuals … [theirs is] a combination of fears and preoccupations: the continual fear of a visit from the authorities, of students failing their exams, a feeling of inferiority in relation to one's colleagues, the fear of gossip (the "*on-dits*"), of seeing one's most simple acts or gestures incriminated.[†]

What Louise Chardon's mental deterioration and melodramatic demise were designed to illustrate—she is found one morning dead at her desk, facedown in an overturned ink bottle—is that the schoolteacher's *métier* had an occupational hazard: the mental illness or condition known as paranoia.

IV. "Much solitude had forced me to become my own companion."[‡]

Jacques Lacan shared Genet's interest in the dramatic social situation of those middlebrow social types, the maid and the

---

[*]   Frapié, *L'Institutrice de province*, p. 37–8.
[†]   Ibid., pp. 218–19.
[‡]   Genet, cited in Sartre, ibid., p. 145.

provincial schoolteacher. His first patient, Marcelle, was a paranoid schoolteacher who took herself for Joan of Arc, and whose antisocial activities included a litigious *"passage à l'acte"*: she sued the French government for 20 million francs on the grounds of deprivation of intellectual and sexual satisfaction. Aimée, the patient who would become the subject of Lacan's doctoral dissertation on paranoia, and who would, in his words, take him "to the threshold of psychoanalysis," was an autodidact clerk in a railway station whose parents had dreamed she would become an *institutrice*. What Lacan would discover in Aimée's crime (she stabbed a well-known actress outside the theater's stage door) and in the murderous rage of the provincial sisters, the Papins, maids who butchered their mistresses, was not only the mirror stage, but a distinctly new figure of modernity as well.*

In 1977, when Lacan posed the question, "What has become of the hysterics of the past, of those marvellous women like Anna O. and Emmy von N.?" his question was undoubtedly facetious.† For Lacan more than any other figure in the analytic community had been responsible for relegating women like Anna O. and Emmy von N. to a definitive past, for locking them up in a hazy tableau entitled the nineteenth century. Gone were the catatonics of Charcot's Salpêtrière theater, those women of the interior who suffered from a domestic disease, women in loose-fitting robes frozen into attitudes, captured in photographic stills. Instead of Anna O., a whole new pantheon of criminal women had come into focus: Violette Nozière and the Papin sisters, Marcelle, Aimée, and—

---

*   The early history of Lacan's career has been beautifully rendered in four books: Catherine Clément's *Vies et légendes de Jacques Lacan* (Paris: Grasset, 1981); Elisabeth Roudinesco's *La Bataille de cent ans: Histoire de la psychanalyse en France*, vol. II (Paris: Seuil, 1986) and *Jacques Lacan. Esquisse d'une vie, histoire d'un système de pensée* (Paris: Fayard, 1993); and David Macey's *Lacan in Contexts* (London: Verso, 1988). The discussion that follows owes much to these accounts.

†   Jacques Lacan, cited in Macey, *Lacan in Contexts*, p. 72.

were we to continue the lineage forward to the post–World War II era—Mademoiselle, and even beyond to the recent maid-and-postal-clerk duo in Chabrol's 1996 *La Cérémonie*. The hysteric's theatrical acting out of highly charged emotional scenes on the dais of the Salpêtrière would be replaced by what Lacan and the surrealists called the *"passage à l'acte."* Not theater but action, not somatics but crime: the Papin sisters' murderous rage, and, in fiction, Mademoiselle's floods and fires.

What Freud did for hysteria Lacan did for paranoia. By focusing on paranoia, Lacan claimed a distinct pathology to be the definitive field of investigation for French psychoanalysis. He also brought together three of his own most compelling interests: women, language, and social place or position. For, while he would devote much of his 1955–56 seminar on psychosis to revisiting the case of the German judge, Daniel Schreber, his earliest paranoid patients were women, frequently literary women who helped bridge the gap between his own medical training and the world of his friendships: Breton, Dalí, the surrealists.* Women, too, whose disease revealed a preoccupation with social position or status—their own and those of the women around them. Aimée strikes out at an idealized "liberated" woman, an actress who enjoys privileges and social mobility Aimée does not possess; Marcelle holds the State responsible for her own intellectual and sexual deprivations; the Papins butcher their middle-class mistresses. To be interested in paranoia was to bring another kind of patient and another kind of woman to the forefront: women who suffered from what Lacan called "social tensions," women

---

* Indeed, Breton seemed to share Lacan's interest in the figure or social type of the psychopathological schoolteacher: his *Nadja* contains a long excursus on his "unbounded admiration" for the only dramatic work he chooses to recall, a play entitled *Les Détraquées*, which concerns the murderous behavior of two women: a teacher and the director of a girl's school. See *Nadja* (Paris: Gallimard, 1964), pp. 45–55.

for whom a role in society was a question, women who had lived during early twentieth-century feminist and anarchist movements, women turned, as much as they were able, toward the future. Paranoia retained the figure of the woman as emblem of modernity but changed her characteristic gestures: from catatonia to crime, from paralysis to act.

Among those acts, for the schoolteachers if not for the maids, was the act of writing. Lacan's initial attraction to paranoid women seems to have been, as Catherine Clément suggests, a stylistic or literary one. In his seminar on the Schreber case Lacan would later note the propensity of paranoid patients to produce literary works, and it is Aimée the would-be novelist and Marcelle, the troubled, incoherent stylist, who drew Lacan's interest:

> One can conceive of the paranoid lived experience and the concep-
> tion of the world it engenders, as an original syntax that contributes
> in affirming, through links of comprehension that are its alone, the
> human community. The knowledge of that syntax seems to me to be
> an indispensable introduction to the comprehension of the symbolic
> values of art, and especially to the problems of style.*

It is as though Lacan had located a new poetic discovery capable of rivaling hysteria's role as the great poetic discovery of the nineteenth century: a paranoiac syntax, specific to our era. With Lacan paranoia passes from being a timeless psychic category into being a social practice, a historical activity—not, that is, an eternally abstract condition but a key symptom of twentieth-century culture. Many of the attempts to historicize a "paranoid"

---

* Jacques Lacan, "Le Problème du style et la conception psychiatrique des formes paranoïaques de l'expérience," *Minotaure* 1 (June 1931), pp. 68–9; reprinted in *De la Psychose paranoïaque dans ses rapports avec la personnalité, suivi de Premiers écrits sur la paranoïa* (Paris: Seuil, 1975); pp. 387–8.

twentieth century (one that accelerates, particularly, after World War II) concentrate on a masculine lineage. These include the trajectory mapped by Elias Canetti from Schreber to Hitler or to the dictator figure in general, and the whole, largely American, novelistic tradition of ever-broadening webs of bureaucratic and corporate control in atmospheres marked by political conspiracy on the one hand, and new degrees of commodification on the other. (The key figures here are Thomas Pynchon, Philip K. Dick, William Burroughs, and J. G. Ballard.)* Still other partial histories are yet to be written: a narrative that would highlight, for instance, the role played by the iconic paranoid figures of Nixon and the later Elvis in the United States of the 1970s; or, more importantly, the story of the Cold War as Lacanian mirror-stage, a tale replete with spies, intelligence agents, and the paranoid violence of narcissistic miscognition, of the United States propping up the Soviet Union that it might better resemble us. A complete history of paranoia as historical topos in the twentieth century would certainly include these landscapes of misinformation, new levels of reification and social control, and key male figures and social types. But Lacan and Genet point to another no less relevant way to historicize paranoia—a more shadowy history, one that threads its way through the obscure desires and lived claustrophobia of maids and schoolteachers, individuals who suffer, no less than dictators, crises of "social investiture."

Christine and Léa Papin, maids in the town of Le Mans who murdered their mistresses in 1933, whose lives spawned a host

---

* See, for example, Elias Canetti, *Crowds and Power* (New York: Farrar Straus Giroux, 1962); Dana Polan, *Paranoia and Power: History, Narrative and the American Cinema 1940–1950* (New York: Columbia, 1986), or Carl Freedman, "Towards a Theory of Paranoia: The Science Fiction of Philip K. Dick," in *Science Fiction Studies* II, no. 32 (March 1984), pp. 15–24. See also Fredric Jameson, *The Geopolitical Imagination: Cinema and Space in the World System* (Bloomington: University of Indiana Press, 1992), for a stimulating discussion of 1970s post-assassination films.

of literary, journalistic, dramatic, and cinematic representations, were themselves no stylists. Yet Lacan's attention to the formal dimensions of language allows him to interpret their crime in a new way. For the paranoid crime to be committed, he writes, a metaphor must pass into the real. In the case of the Papins, "the most worn-out metaphor of rage,"* "*Je lui arracherais les yeux,*" (I will tear out her eyes) is "accomplished," literalized, in the savage gesture with which the maids clawed the faces of their mistresses and pulled out their eyes—eyes which had surveyed them and inspected their work, seeking out deficiencies or lapses, in a largely silent household.

If the metaphor is shopworn, it is perhaps because of scenes like the one that occurs in Mirbeau's 1900 *Journal d'une femme de chambre,* when two servants, a maid and a footman, are preparing for the wedding party of their employer's daughter:

> Just for a joke, I asked Baptiste, the footman:
>
> "Where's yours, then? Aren't you giving them a present?"
>
> "Mine?" said Baptiste, shrugging his shoulders.
>
> "Go on, what is it?"
>
> "The only present I'd give them would be a can of lighted petrol under their bed."
>
> It was a jolly good answer. But Baptiste was always one for politics.
>
> "And what about yours, Célestine?" he asked me.
>
> "Me? Why this ..." I replied, holding up my hands, with the fingers curved like claws, and pretending to scratch someone's face
>
> ...
>
> "My nails in her eyes."†

---

* Jacques Lacan, "Motifs du crime paranoïaque: le crime des soeurs Papin," in *Minotaure* 3–4 (December 1933); reprinted in *De la psychose,* pp. 399–406.

† Octave Mirbeau, *Diary of a Chambermaid,* p. 213.

The specific class dimension of the rage apparent in Mirbeau's staging of the expression is kept at bay in Lacan's rhetorical interpretation; for Lacan the condition that enables the Papin sisters' crime is less their situation as domestics than their relation to each other, that "mal d'être deux," that would later provide him with the means of theorizing the mirror stage. The two sisters were for each other, in the words of Catherine Clément, "the only universe":

> True Siamese twins, they form a world closed forever, to read their depositions after the crime, writes Doctor Logre, "you would think you are reading double." With the only means available on their little island, they must resolve the enigma, the human enigma of sexuality.*

The impossibility of each sister distinguishing herself from the other constituted their madness; it also meant that Christine was too close to Léa to project her hatred onto her sister. Instead, together, acting as one, the pair found another solution: they projected their hatred onto another pair of women.

In an article entitled "L'Affaire des soeurs Papin" which appeared in 1963 in *Les Temps modernes*, psychiatrist Louis Le Guillant acknowledged the brilliance of Lacan's analysis, but took him to task for barely alluding to the sisters' situation as domestics.[†] As such, Lacan provides an analysis that, in Le

---

*   Lacan, "Motifs du crime paranoïaque," p. 397.

†   See Louis le Guillant, "L'Affaire des soeurs Papin," in *Les Temps modernes* (November 1963), pp. 868–913. The Papin sisters' crime had been newly publicized by the 1962 release of a highly expressionistic film on their case by Nico Papatakis, entitled *Les Abysses*. Papatakis had originally wanted to shoot a film version of *Les Bonnes*, but Genet withdrew the rights from his friend when Papatakis staged a publicity stunt involving Jeanne Moreau and Annie Girardot, the actresses he wanted to play Claire and Solange, dressed in maids' costumes! Genet, however, defended his friend's film when it generated enormous controversy; Sartre, Breton, and Beauvoir joined in defending the film. See White, *Jean Genet*, p. 459.

Guillant's critique, is viable for any pair of sisters or even for a lone paranoiac; he sees no role played by their social condition in the genesis of their crime. But the social condition *is* alluded to in Lacan's account both when he underlines the importance of the social isolation of the sisters and when he refers to a linguistic phenomenon, namely the silence that reigned within the household between its two sets of inhabitants, maids and masters. The banal instigating cause of the maids' attack was an electrical failure that delayed them in completing their tasks. In a striking, perhaps overly poetic, passage in Lacan's article, the power shortage materializes the silence between the two camps, the current doesn't flow because the words don't flow:

> From one group to another "no one spoke to each other." This silence could not have been empty, even if it was obscure in the eyes of the actors.
>
> One evening, on February 2nd, the obscurity becomes material through the fact of a banal electricity blackout.[*]

The young Lacan, as both Macey and Roudinesco make clear, adopted a slogan from Georges Politzer to guide his work: "Towards the concrete." (Politzer is also the intellectual model for Louis Le Guillant in his more explicitly social analyses of the psycho-social conditions of maids in the first half of the twentieth century in France.)[†] Politzer's influence is perhaps most clear in Lacan's dissertation, where elements from a Freudian psychoanalysis are woven together with a "concrete" psychology which takes as its object the specific life of a specific individual, a life with

---

[*] Lacan, "Motifs du crime paranoïaque," p. 389.

[†] See, in addition to his article on the Papin sisters, his more extended study entitled "Incidences psycho-pathologiques de la condition de 'bonne à tout faire,'" in *L'Evolution psychiatrique* 1 (1963), pp. 1–64.

histories and reactions to social environments. Or life, as Politzer would put it, in the "dramatic" sense of the word:

> Besides biological life, there is a properly human life … Human life constitutes a *drama*. That we situate our daily existence first and foremost within drama cannot be refuted. The vision that we have of ourselves is a *dramatic vision*. Dramatic as well, the *comprehension* that we first have of each other.*

Both Lacan and Le Guillant, in quite different ways, devise a methodology that involves applying to psychopathology Politzer's notion of drama, which is essentially the situation of the individual as the center of events, events which only take on meaning when they have been brought into relation with a "first person." In an attack on all behaviorist or "objectivist" psychologies, Politzer argued the tie between meaning and the "first person" to be that which distinguished psychological facts from every other kind of fact. For Lacan, then, Aimée's case must be analyzed by looking at the entire personality as the center of a confrontation between a personal drama and a social milieu. Within the personal drama could be found the figures of persecutory women characters, a mother, an older sister; the social environment was a cell of utmost claustrophobia from which Aimée gazed out onto a world of writers, actresses, and society women, women who enjoyed the liberty and social power she lacked. In striking the actress Aimée struck her own exteriorized ideal; as in a mirror, she struck herself.

Paranoia is a disease of social position. In the Aimée case and in Lacan's early writings on paranoia in general, what emerges quite

---

* Georges Politzer, *La Crise de la psychologie contemporaine* (Paris: Editions sociales, 1947), pp. 36–7, Politzer's emphasis.

clearly is the inherently social dimension of a disease brought on by failed sociality:

> The symptom does not manifest itself in relation to random percep-
> tions, inanimate objects lacking in affective significance, for example,
> but especially with regard to *relations of a social nature*: relations with
> the family, colleagues, neighbors ... The delirium of interpretation
> ... is a delirium of the stairway, the street, the marketplace.*

And within the context of discussing a general formula provided by Kretschmer for the eclosion of the disease, "a tension of self-love in an oppressive situation," Lacan goes on to list the typical social constellations which favor paranoiac pathology, the situations of ambiguous social status or symbolic investiture conducive to the illness. These include the situations of unmarried young women who are professionally active, for example, old-fashioned provincial spinsters, or "ambitious autodidacts of working-class origin." But the most typical of all is that of "the highly ambiguous social and spiritual situation of the schoolteacher, fertile in pretentions who nonetheless receives no consecration, placed at a superior level and yet insecure because of an incomplete spiritual formation."†

Occupying an allegedly esteemed position at the head of the classroom, the schoolteacher holds little or no prestige in the eyes of the middle class, a fallen prestige in the eyes of workers; and she is a target of both awe and contempt in the eyes of peasants: Mademoiselle's lot is one of simultaneous grandeur and abjection, and an unabated solitude. As director Tony Richardson summed up his view of the character of Mademoiselle in his film, "She is

---

* Lacan, *De la psychose paranoïaque dans ses rapports avec la personnalité* (Paris: Seuil Points, 1980), p. 211–12, emphasis Lacan's.

† Kretschmer, cited in Lacan, ibid., p. 93.

closed off in a universe of mirrors; she never tries to enter into contact with others."*

V. Solange: *"Loving each other in servitude is not loving each other."*
Claire: *"It's loving each other too much."*†

The schoolteacher, like the ward of public welfare, is *too public*: associated with and tainted by the state, a functionary or reject from the capital, distrusted and spied upon by the villagers, moved from village to village; each has no private life. The maid, on the contrary, is deprived of a private life precisely by having her entire life circumscribed by the interior; she is *too private*. Genet, however, points out that the two can overlap: "Here in the Morvan, a lot of people take on welfare children in order to have servants and make them work. The kids," he adds, "should rob them if they have the chance."‡ Louis Le Guillant was also concerned with a possible proximity between the situation of the maid and that of the welfare child: in his article on the psychopathology of the condition of the maid, he analyzes a set of behaviors determined by psychological conditions which are, in the end, of a social order, conditions defined by domination and servitude, which, at their broadest, he writes, would include that of being "a Muslim Algerian in Paris today, or, just about anywhere, a ward of Public Welfare, or a *bonne à tout faire*."§ On an empirical level, many welfare children later became maids. But what concerns Le Guillant is isolating and analyzing the pathogenic aspects of the maid's or (he promises, in a forthcoming study), the welfare child's "condition." Le Guillant pauses over that word, noting the

---

*   Tony Richardson, *Nouvel Observateur*, May 17, 1966.
†   Genet, *Les Bonnes*, p. 48.
‡   Genet, cited in White, *Jean Genet*, p. 29.
§   Le Guillant, "Incidences Psychopathologiques," pp. 2–3.

familiar phrase used by girls who refer to becoming a maid as "se mettre en condition." "Condition" is defined by the *Littré* as "the class to which a person belongs in society, through his fortune, his quality, his occupations, his profession." Thus, "condition," it seems, shares some ground with "class" or "métier," without being quite synonymous. Marguerite Duras, in her novella *Le Square*, allows her main character, a maid, to elaborate on the condition of the *bonne* à *tout faire:* "It isn't a profession [*métier*] what I do. It's called that in order to simplify it, but it isn't one. It's a kind of state, a whole state unto itself, you understand, like being a child, for example, or being ill."* Or, in the words of Célestine in *Le Journal d'une femme de chambre*:

> Maids are not normal social beings, not part of society. The lives they lead are disjointed, and they themselves are made up of bits and pieces that do not fit together. They are worse than that, they are monstrous hybrids. They have ceased to be part of the common people from whom they spring and they will never become part of the bourgeoisie whom they live amongst and wait on.†

The "state," or condition, then, is one of social ambiguity in an oppressive situation. Cut off from her own family, she leads a frequently asexual existence (if she is not prey to the sexual demands of her employers), isolated in another social class all of her work life, neither integrated into nor rejected by the dominant class. And like the schoolteacher in her room above the schoolhouse, the maid in her *chambre de bonne* lives no separation between her space of work and her private life.

She occupies, as her space, the most private and familial of spaces, and yet a space that is not one's own. Geneviève Fraisse,

---

* Marguerite Duras, *Le Square* (Paris: Gallimard Folio, 1955), pp. 18–19.
† Mirbeau, *Diary*, p. 129.

in her illuminating book on the status of maids, isolates the key economic peculiarity underlying their condition.* All other workers sell their services to a person or people who do not consume them: the miner, for example, is paid by the company who sells the coal to clients. The maid, on the other hand, contracts her services to one person, and that person is precisely the one who consumes the services. The consequences of such a contract are enormous, for they set up, in effect, an unmediated relation between mistress and maid, an entirely closed system of the type that appealed so much to Genet and Lacan. Nothing intrudes, no third term, no corporation or union, no structural mediation of any kind intervenes to break the dyad of dominance and submission. Unlike other work contracts, the mistress/maid contract contains no opening out onto the social world or the Symbolic; in and of itself it constitutes a psychopathological condition, the locked dance-steps of the imaginary.

It is a condition, Fraisse continues, predicated on the closing off of the social world to create an unbearable claustrophobic intimacy within the space of intimacy. And it is a condition whose labor consists of the domestic activities that are the most private of the private: washing the dirty linen of family life.

The maid's situation in the household is thus one of extreme hierarchical domination (she is not only an object, but a "bad object" in the household, present and alien to it, necessary and rejected, like the schoolteacher in the village) but it is also more complex than mere subordination. For to be the caretaker of the house and the children is to be the mistress's shadow—and this is what distinguishes her situation from that of the manservant or the valet. The maid must "take the place of" the mistress, vis-à-vis the children especially, and yet at any moment fade back into

---

*   See Geneviève Fraisse, *Femmes toutes mains: Essai sur le service domestique* (Paris: Seuil, 1979).

the décor; the maid slips uneasily into the place of the "femme du foyer" and yet does not replace her: her condition comprises both an intolerable mirroring/merging and an intolerable subordination. She leads, vis-à-vis the mistress, a kind of parallel life—with important distinctions; she is, for example, completely exposed to the corporeal dimensions of the mistress—her body, her sexuality, her confidences—while her own body and sexuality are foreclosed. Abject in its preoccupation with the most sordid and banal details of unpaid labor, the maid's position is grand in the exaggerated sentimental value assigned to the maternal devotion that is hers by proxy.

Genet, writes Sartre, had no interest in the psychology of women; in his preface to *Les Bonnes,* Genet writes that his play should in no way be read as a plea for the amelioration of the social condition of maids. And yet the psychosocial existence of the maid and the schoolteacher, both social anomalies and emblems of a new modernity as well, both "jeunes filles seules," (young girls alone) each a shadow mother with no space of her own, the one defined by being all hands, the other all head—their drama, in Politzer's sense of the term, became, for a moment at least, Genet's own, and his comprehension of their drama became, in turn, a dramatic one.

11

Watching the Detectives

|

The literature which concerned itself with the disquieting and threatening
aspects of urban life was to have a great future.

—Walter Benjamin

In his last work, *The Politics of Modernism* (1989), Raymond
Williams proposes a history of modernism constructed through
different experiences of exile and emigration. By concentrating on
the social formations of modernist artists, their lived experience of
isolation and *dépaysement* in the transnational capitals of the new
imperialism, he locates the decisive factor of modernism in the
experience of the metropolis on form and language: "Their self-
referentiality, their propinquity and mutual isolation all served
to represent the artist as necessarily estranged, and to ratify as
canonical the works of radical estrangement."* The political and
cultural scope modernist artists set for themselves was clearly a
universal one—in his most concise formulation, Williams defines

---

* Raymond Williams, *The Politics of Modernism* (London: Verso, 1989),
p. 35.

modernism as "the metropolitan interpretation of its own processes as universals."[*]

If we take Williams's definition of modernism as our own, what then has changed, if anything, in the move to postmodernism? To what extent is postmodernism a continuation of, rather than a significant break with, "the metropolitan interpretation of its own processes as universals?" Or do postmodern urban intellectuals and artists no longer interpret their own processes as universals? Has the nature of the metropolis changed, so that the city is no longer central, no longer a point of origin? Or is the shift rather one in the international balance of cultural power, a shift in dominant cities—Los Angeles, say, taking the place of Paris—but still continuing a modernist, universalizing project? To what extent is postmodernism (including the *theorizing* of postmodernism) synonymous with Americanization, its particularity based on the difference in urban "structures of feeling" experienced in North American versus European cities?

Williams and Rimbaud are not the first to analyze the privileged temporal language of modernism in terms of world realignment, nor to show that the nineteenth-century European middle-class discovery of—and obsession with—time and history, was at one and the same time its production of space as colonial space. Williams is not the first to approach modernism spatially—that is, to use the analytic tools and coordinates we have learned to associate with postmodernism. Walter Benjamin provided the most influential version of French modernism by meditating on the role of lyric poetry and the emergence of the detective story—a genre which takes as one of its principal tasks the representation of the ordinary, everyday entanglement of people with their surroundings—in the modernist capital of Paris.

---

[*] Ibid., p. 47.

Commenting on Williams's affinity to Benjamin, Tony Pinkney writes that "Modernism can now be located, not on the 'inside' of its self-validating ideologies nor in the 'outside' of a political trauma of the order of 1848, but in the *intermediate zone of urban experience* ... in a 'structure of feeling' that has not yet assumed the relatively formalised shape of aesthetic doctrine or political act."* It was precisely by raising to the status of a concept such an "intermediate zone of urban experience"—or "everyday life" as he called it—that Henri Lefebvre arrived at his own conception of the modernist period.

My interest in writers and theorists who approach modernism through a primarily spatial perspective has its counterpart in a preference for contemporary writers who confront, engage directly with the problem of history, whose work, in some sense, tries to "save the narrative." I think it is important at this point to work towards recasting the productive but now-hardened-into-stone opposition that has resulted from the periodizing of postmodernism—an opposition variously conceived as the present moment's general substitution of spatial coordinates for the privileged temporal coordinates (the lags and anticipations, the deferrals, the promise of future reconciliations) of modernism; or, the society of consumption (production organized for a market) replacing a society of production; with its concomitant replacement of the political figure of the citizen by today's figure of the quotidian: the consumer. We must begin to determine the ways in which such a periodization may in fact obscure, not illuminate reality. For such a reified opposition in fact takes the point of view of consumption, thereby masking the relations of production that have by no means disappeared in contemporary society. It ignores the fact that industrialization remains the primary propulsive

---

*   Tony Pinkney, "Editor's Introduction: Modernism and Cultural Theory," in Williams, *Politics of Modernism*, p. 11.

force in development everywhere in the world, and it often denies the contradictions that arise from an increasingly international division of labor. "From time to time events of the moment," Jacques Rancière points out, "make it all too clear that nine-tenths of humanity, or a little more, suffer from what postmodernism has long since moved beyond: archaic stories of hunger, of faith, and of the people."*

The overemphasis on consumption issues has also had baleful effects on much of recent cultural studies intent on charting the "dominant cultural logic of postmodernism" within an ever-more-narrowly-conceived present moment. Often taking the form of a kind of catalog or "shopping list" of current cultural and consumer practices or images, these studies have rapidly become symptomatic of the very practices they seek to analyze—precisely, some would argue, the postmodernism effect (or trap) itself. For postmodernism, as writers like J. G. Ballard began to inform us in the early 1970s, is about the effacement of history, the loss of the past, the inability to conceive of a before or beyond to the vast condominium or shopping mall of Being:

> Just as the past itself, in social and psychological terms, became a casualty of Hiroshima and the nuclear age (almost by definition a period where we were all forced to think prospectively), so in its turn the future is ceasing to exist, devoured by an all-voracious present. We have annexed the future into our own present, as merely one of those manifold alternatives open to us. Options multiply around us, we live in an almost infantile world where any demand, any possibility, whether for lifestyles, travel, sexual roles and identities, can be satisfied instantly.†

---

*   Jacques Rancière, "Après quoi," *Confrontation* 20 (Winter 1989), p. 191.

†   J. G. Ballard, "Some Words about *Crash!*" *Foundation: The Review of Science Fiction* 9 (November 1975), p. 48.

Postmodernism is a conceptualization of the present that seeks to historicize the effacement of the historical—thus, in some ways, eternalizing itself, freezing the movement of time. An enormous sense of "period" competition or envy must be at work here— generated, no doubt, by the extraordinary success of modernism. For modernism was a period so powerful that it was able to make all of the rest of history nothing but its own precedent or antecedent. The least postmodernism can do is become eternal.

II

You cannot have art without a public taste and you cannot have a public taste without a sense of style and quality throughout the whole structure. Curiously enough this sense of style seems to have very little to do with refinement or even humanity. It can exist in a savage and dirty age, but it cannot exist in the Coca-Cola age ... the age of the Book-of-the-Month and the Hearst press.

—Raymond Chandler, *Raymond Chandler Speaking*

In 1970, while living and teaching in southern California, Fredric Jameson published an essay—his first about American literature—on detective novelist and Hollywood screenwriter Raymond Chandler. I want to consider "On Raymond Chandler" at some length, for it contains many elements—a fascination with Los Angeles, a reflection on nostalgia, a concern with periodization, a centrality given to the category of reification and to the figure of Andy Warhol—that would resurface in what remains the most important and influential theorization of postmodernism, Jameson's widely-read 1984 essay, "Postmodernism, or the Cultural Logic of Late Capitalism."* In fact, Chandler, in the

---

*   In what follows I will refer to this essay, "Postmodernism, or the Cultural Logic of Late Capitalism," *New Left Review* 146 (1984), pp. 53–92, rather than to

first essay, becomes the vehicle for Jameson to talk about what he really wants to talk about: a set of cultural phenomena that had not yet been theorized as the postmodern.

At a moment in the history of literary studies when allusion to biographical data about an author was singularly unfashionable, Jameson begins the essay by underscoring two facts about Chandler's life: that he worked for fifteen years as an oil company executive in Los Angeles before beginning writing, and that he spent his childhood and adolescence in England. The essay in its entirety builds on the opposition suggested by the two phases of Chandler's life: European art, writes Jameson, is "metaphysical and formalistic," while "any picture of America is bound to be wrapped up in a question and a presupposition about the nature of American reality."* America, then, is situated on the side of realism, and, moreover, on the side of a reflection about the nation, a particularly *American* reality.

To situate America on the side of realism is firmly in keeping with the object of Jameson's study, for it was Chandler's well-known essay, "The Simple Art of Murder," first published in 1949, that definitively established the opposition between the formal, game-playing ratiocination of the classical, generally British detective story, its "mechanical," "artificial," "superficial" aspects, versus the "authenticity," "reality," and "life" of the American product, which strives for "the authentic flavor of life as it is lived."† In this essay, and throughout his letters, Chandler

---

any of Jameson's subsequent more lengthy meditations on postmodernism. This essay, along with Laura Mulvey's 1975 "Visual Pleasure and Narrative Cinema," are perhaps the most widely read and cited essays in cultural studies of the last twenty years.

* Fredric Jameson, "On Raymond Chandler," *Southern Review* 6 (1970); rpt. in Glenn Most and William Stowe, eds., *The Poetics of Murder* (San Diego: Harcourt, Brace, Jovanovich, 1983), p. 126.

† Raymond Chandler, "The Simple Art of Murder: An Essay," in *The Simple Art of Murder* (New York: Vintage, 1988), p. 11.

delights in the national stereotype: "The English may not always be the best writers in the world, but they are incomparably the best dull writers."* Because the English formula still, according to Chandler, "dominates the trade," much of the energy of the essay is spent asserting the generic superiority of Dashiell Hammett, and in establishing for him a national genealogy passing through Theodore Dreiser, Ring Lardner, Sherwood Anderson, and Walt Whitman.

Jameson is less concerned with evaluative judgment. Rather, he uses Europe and European literature to provide a backdrop of social cohesion against which the atomized and fragmentary nature of American society can emerge. The well-known vertical social organization of Parisian apartment houses in Zola's *Pot bouille* provides the contrast for Los Angeles's horizontal urban sprawl. The episodic, "picaresque" form taken by the detective's quest (duplicated, to a certain extent, by Jameson's own form in "On Raymond Chandler" and to a much greater extent by his form in the postmodernism essay), is explained by the center-less, fragmented city he moves through:

> In European countries people no matter how solitary are still somehow engaged in the social substance; their very solitude is social … But the form of Chandler's books reflects an initial American separation of people from each other, their need to be linked by some external force (in this case the detective) if they are ever to be fitted together as part of the same picture puzzle.†

Chandler's Los Angeles—its seedy rooming houses and luxurious dry-out spas in the desert, its off-shore gambling yachts, dingy hotel lobbies, and elegant private mansions, the juxtaposition of

---

*   Ibid., p. 11.
†   Jameson, "On Raymond Chandler," p. 131.

its clearly demarcated dreary and luxurious zones—all this is no mere background scenery to some more crucial drama unfolded on its stage: for Jameson the very *content* of Chandler's novels is a scenic one. The divided scenic content conjures up the figure of the detective, Marlowe, who alone can unite the disparate parts of the city into a social whole.

Many of Chandler's readers have described his Los Angeles as already "dated"; his novels, set in the 1940s and 1950s, seem to unfold in an early 1930s Los Angeles of crime and power and money. Leigh Brackett, for example, author of the screenplay of *The Long Goodbye*, writes in 1969: "The Los Angeles Chandler wrote about was already long gone."[*] Jameson, however, writing at the same time, sees a more futuristic, prophetic Los Angeles in Chandler's books, one whose paradigmatic status of the country as a whole was already certain:

> But already the Los Angeles of Chandler was an unstructured city … His social content anticipates the realities of the fifties and sixties. For Los Angeles is already a kind of microcosm and forecast of the country as a whole: a new centerless city, in which the various classes have lost touch with each other because each is isolated in his own geographical compartment.[†]

By a kind of accident, then, Chandler's modernist detective finds himself in a postmodern city, one which forecasts the social organization of the country as a whole. By the 1980s, Jameson's Los Angeles would have an even greater paradigmatic power; its downtown, crowned by the Bonaventure Hotel, would prophesy

---

* Brackett, cited in Peter Wolfe, *Something More than Night: The Case of Raymond Chandler* (Bowling Green, OH: Bowling Green State University Popular Press, 1985), p. 39.

† Jameson, "On Raymond Chandler," pp. 133, 127.

the vast new multinational hyperspace of postmodernism.* While Marlowe moved horizontally between the isolated class compartments, Jameson as postmodern critic stands above, high atop the Bonaventure tower, adopting a panoramic perspective that excludes the intricacies or conflicts of social relations surrounding the hotel: the communities of Central American immigrants nearby, the potentially *conflictual* urban geography of a post-Fordist political economy. The hotel, for Jameson, denuded of its historical and geographic context, stands as symbolic icon of postmodernism: "It [the elevator] gives us the chance at a radically different, but complementary, spatial experience, that of rapidly shooting up through the ceiling and outside, along one of the four symmetrical towers with the referent, Los Angeles itself, spread out breathtakingly and even alarmingly before us."† But,

---

* Jameson is certainly not alone in putting Los Angeles and Southern California at the center of postmodern culture. The most important precursor to the flood of 1980s writing about Los Angeles is Reyner Banham's *Los Angeles: The Architecture of Four Ecologies* (London: Allen Lane, 1971). Most recently, Edward Soja's *Postmodern Geographies* (New York: Verso, 1989) concludes its theoretical argument with a culminating chapter entitled "It All Comes Together in Los Angeles." Soja and Manuel Castells, both students of Henri Lefebvre, live and work in California; indeed it was a visit to the Bonaventure by the trio of Lefebvre, Soja, and Jameson that provided the "fieldwork" for Jameson's essay. We must also note the importance of the Californian landscape both in the texts and travel itineraries of European theorists of postmodernism such as Eco, Marin, and Baudrillard. Even an early text like Michael Herr's *Dispatches* (New York: Knopf, 1977), which Jameson reads as the paradigmatic evocation of the space of postmodern warfare, has as a central theme something like the Americanization—read Californianization—of the rest of the world: "You'd stand there nailed in your tracks sometimes, no bearings and none in sight, thinking, Where the fuck am I?, fallen into some unnatural East-West interface, a California corridor cut and bought and burned deep into Asia, and once we'd done it we couldn't remember what for" (p. 45). Herr also reminds us that Los Angeles declared Saigon to be its "sister city" during the war, in order to provide photo opportunities for then LA mayor, Sam Yorty. For a critical history of the place of Los Angeles in twentieth-century intellectual and political life, see Mike Davis, *City of Quartz* (New York: Random House, 1990).

† Jameson, "Postmodernism," p. 83.

by adopting at once a more "horizontal" and a more historical perspective, Mike Davis (1985, 1987) offers an important corrective to Jameson's iconic reading of the Bonaventure. Davis's analysis highlights the dialectical and contradictory urban geography resulting from *two* separate macroprocesses: the multinational accumulation of bank and real estate capital (Jameson's unique concern) and another, equally important: the reflux of low-wage manufacturing and labor-intensive services provided by unprecedented Central American mass immigration. Taking the latter into account undermines the cultural dominance of Jameson's postmodernism: "The great Latino shopping streets—Broadway in Downtown and Brooklyn in Boyle Heights—have more in common with the early twentieth century city, with the culture of Ragtime than they do with a death-wish postmodernity."*

Another point of conjuncture between Jameson's two essays occurs around the figure of Andy Warhol. A long section of the essay on Chandler deals with nostalgia; not with Chandler himself producing nostalgic writing, but, rather, with the taste for Chandler among contemporary readers being a nostalgic one. Chandler, Jameson writes, evokes "a world similar enough to our own to seem very distant,"† and he argues this—in effect, a periodization of Chandler—by way of historicizing the relationship of consumers to the commercial object world. In this literary history, Chandler, with his "stable products," his "permanent industrial background which has come to resemble nature itself," lies somewhere between the inventive, creative energies of Balzac's manufactured objects and the fetishized nostalgia of Warhol's

---

* Mike Davis, "*Chinatown*, Part Two? The 'Internationalization' of Downtown Los Angeles," *New Left Review* 164 (July–August 1987), p. 87. See also his "Urban Renaissance and the Spirit of Postmodernism," *New Left Review* 151 (May–June 1985), pp. 106–14.

† Jameson, "On Raymond Chandler," p. 141.

soup cans. (Chandler, then, is a true modernist, in accordance with Jameson's later tripartite periodization of realism-modernism-postmodernism.) But consider the difference between the Warhol who emerges in this essay and the Warhol of 1984:

> The Warhol image ... [is] a fetish representing the will to return to a period when there was still a certain distance between objects ... [it] is a way of making us stare at a single commercial product, in hopes that our vision of all those around us will be transformed, that our new stare will infuse *those also* with depth and solidity, with the meaning of remembered objects and products, with the physical foundation and dimensions of the older world of need.*

The Warhol image here is endowed with depth and solidity; it entertains a powerful redemptive relation to the exterior world, both present and past. It instills desire in the viewer to extend the image's solidity to the object world around it; it is even capable of conjuring up a formerly meaningful, past, but still accessible, object world. In the 1984 postmodernism essay, however, Warhol's objects have lost any resonance to either a past world or to a context larger than themselves; they are no longer synecdochal:

> Here, however, we have a random collection of dead objects, hanging together on the canvas like so many turnips, as shorn of their earlier life-world as the pile of shoes left over from Auschwitz, or the remainders and tokens of some incomprehensible and tragic fire in a packed dancehall. There is therefore in Warhol *no way* to complete the hermeneutic gesture, to restore to these oddments that whole larger context of the dance hall or the ball, the world of jetset fashion or of glamour magazines.†

---

*   Ibid., p. 139, my emphasis.
†   Jameson, "Postmodernism," p. 61, my emphasis.

Warhol in the 1980s represents "the supreme formal feature" of postmodernism: the "emergence of a new kind of flatness or depthlessness, a new kind of superficiality in the most literal sense."

Whether or not it is true that the hermeneutic gesture can no longer be completed, it is clear that Jameson, in the 1980s, chooses not to complete it. In the Chandler essay, of course, the hermeneutic gesture is alive and well, embodied in the figure of Marlowe the detective, whose cognitive function, as we saw earlier, is rendered necessary by the proto-postmodernist space of Los Angeles:

> Since there is no longer any privileged experience in which the whole of the social structure can be grasped, a figure must be invented who can be superimposed on the society as a whole, whose routine and life pattern serve somehow to tie its separate and isolated parts together.*

Even the incorruptible, chivalric purity of Marlowe, his ability to circulate amid the human detritus of Los Angeles without being in any way tainted by it, his solitary, heroic, and exemplary purity in the face of social corruption, that quality that Chandler (and Jameson) refer to as Marlowe's "honesty," all this is granted by Jameson a purely cognitive, rather than moral, function: "the honesty of the detective can be understood as an organ of perception," and:

> the detective in a sense once again fulfills the demands of the function of knowledge rather than that of lived experience: through him we are able to see, to know, the society as a whole, but he does not really stand for any genuine close-up experience of it.†

---

* Jameson, "On Raymond Chandler," p. 127.
† Ibid., pp. 127–8.

Is Marlowe, then, the functional equivalent of the "cognitive cartographer" Jameson calls for at the end of the postmodernism essay—the cognitive cartographer who is none other than the essay's author himself? Can the figure of Marlowe help us understand Jameson's own ill-defined location within postmodernist culture? Marlowe is a modernist hero cut adrift in a postmodernist cut-and-paste world; ironic distance keeps the beautiful soul of the detective pure in a corrupt universe, a universe granted depth precisely by the detective's own ironic detachment from it. "Down these mean streets," Chandler begins a famous passage describing his detective, "a man must go who is not himself mean, who is neither tarnished nor afraid ... He is the hero, he is everything. He must be a complete man and a common man yet an unusual man."* Jameson's relation to his own attempt to "tie the separate and isolated parts" of postmodernism together raises questions. Is Jameson's desire Marlowesque, that is, does he stand outside postmodernism to explain and judge it? And isn't this an impossible task under postmodernism, when, according to Jameson, all critical distance or perspective collapses? Where does this desire come from, the desire to "give a genuinely historical and dialectical analysis" of a period defined by its sheer discontinuity and eradication of historical depth? It could not flourish, presumably, within the monolithic contours of postmodernism outlined by Jameson. Or could such a desire be nourished, as one critic suggests, "by certain oppositional forces alive within postmodernism,"† residual or emergent forces Jameson chooses in this context to downplay ("one would want to begin to wonder a little more seriously about the possibilities of political or critical

---

* Chandler, *The Simple Art of Murder*, p. 18.

† Lambert Zuidervaart, "Realism/Modernism/The Empty Chair," in *Post-modernism/Jameson/Critique*, ed. Douglas Kellner (Washington: Maisonneuve Press, 1991), p. 217.

art in the postmodern period of late capital"*) or to treat, as he has indeed done at great length (see, for example, his "Third-World Literature in the Era of Multinational Capitalism" [1986]) elsewhere? What very different account of postmodern cultural dominance would follow if the work on Third World literature was included in the panoramic perspective Jameson adopts here?

III

The work of Henri Lefebvre during the 1970s helped provide Jameson with his theory of postmodern space. It was Lefebvre who went so far as to proclaim the "urban" or spatial particularity of our time to be no mere epiphenomenal or superstructural change, but rather proof of what economists like Alain Lipietz have recently designated as a decisive shift in the way capital is working, a transition in the "regime of accumulation" and its associated mode of social and political regulation. During a mutually beneficial collaboration with the Situationists in the early 1960s, Lefebvre had begun to argue that in late capitalism practices of consumption act to legitimate and reproduce the system, regardless of an individual or group's particular beliefs or values.† Since the Second World War and the Marshall Plan in France, everyday life practices—and not abstract ideas or

---

*   Jameson, "Postmodernism," p. 60.

†   The Situationists were among the earliest theorists of postmodernism to focus on Los Angeles, and specifically the 1965 Watts Riot, which they viewed as less a race riot than a "rebellion against the commodity": "How do people make history under conditions pre-established to dissuade them from intervening in it? Los Angeles blacks are better paid than any others in the United States, but they are also the most *separated* from that high point of flaunted affluence, California. Hollywood, the pole of the global spectacle, is in their immediate vicinity." Ken Knabb, ed. and trans., "The Decline and Fall of the Spectacle-Commodity Economy," in *Situationist International Anthology* (Berkeley: Bureau of Public Secrets, 1981), p. 156.

philosophies—had come to play the functional role of ideology. In a series of books written in the 1960s and 1970s (*La révolution urbaine* [1970]; *Le Droit à la ville* [1972]; *La Production de l'espace* [1974]), Lefebvre takes up his initial concept of everyday life and reworks it in spatial terms under the rubric of what he calls "the urban." The everyday, the urban, the production of social space become in his work a constellation of concepts recoding the same basic idea: that the reproduction of the social relations of production is the central and hidden process of capitalist society, and that this process is inherently spatial.

What, then, has become of the diachronic, the historical, the dialectic in such a schema? The dialectic, effectively relegated to the dustbin of history by post-structuralism, has not, according to Lefebvre, disappeared. History, like politics, has not come to an end. The dialectic has simply been displaced—and it is this very displacement that informs what is new and paradoxical about our times.* No longer attached to temporality, no longer clinging to historicity or the temporal mechanics of thesis, antithesis, synthesis, the dialectic is to be resumed and recognized in the real, effective contradictions of space, in those lived, uneven developments that alone, for Lefebvre, have consequences—consequences like May 1968, which erupted, as he likes to remind us, in a suburban functionalized university *cité*, constructed in the middle of *bidonvilles*.

Lefebvre begins by analyzing the increasing "planification" of space under capitalism as a movement toward global homogeneity—Rimbaud's prophetic "same bourgeois magic wherever your baggage sets you down"—the unification of a planetary state system with centers or points of strength whose domination over peripheral weaker points serves to guarantee the production

---

* Henri Lefebvre, *The Survival of Capitalism* (London: Allison and Busby, 1976), p. 17.

of homogeneity. Simultaneous with the move to homogeneity, though, is one of fragmentation: space is divided up like graph paper into autonomous, Taylorized parcels with distinct, localized functions. Fragmentation occurs when the historical big city of the nineteenth century—that defined and definite object—explodes in the twentieth. The urban is not the classical city-monster defined in opposition to village or rural life but rather the ghost of that city, what hovers along its outskirts; the "urban," then, for Lefebvre, is closer to what others would call the suburban or peri-urban. For, with the emergence of global space, the city, the cradle of accumulation, the locus of wealth, the subject of history, the center of historical space, shatters, spawning in its wake a host of doubtful protuberances: banlieues, a vacation home, an autoroute, a supermarket or factory in the middle of the countryside, housing developments, *pavilions*, whole satellites of thickening small and medium-sized cities, semi-colonies to the metropolis. And amid this motley accumulation, Lefebvre's third category of hierarchy comes to light, as an increasingly conscious and treacherous strategy divides this suburban space into more or less favored zones, destined either for a great industrial and urban future, or for controlled, closely supervised decline. Guy Debord, writing at the same time, describes a similar movement:

> Economic history, which developed entirely around the city/country opposition, has succeeded to such a point that it has annihilated both terms at once. The contemporary *paralysis* of total historical development, at the profit of the sole pursuit of the independent movement of the economy, makes of the moment when city and country begin to disappear, not the *overcoming* of their division, but their simultaneous collapse.[*]

---

[*]   Guy Debord, *La Société du spectacle* (Paris: Gallimard, 1971), p. 115.

For Lefebvre, the most important spatial contradiction of our time—and this is where his dialectical method resides, in the reading of spatial contradictions—can be detected in the deterioration of urban life that has accompanied the urbanization of society. The dominant class and the state act to reinforce the city as the center of power and political decision, while the very dominance of that class and the state causes the city to explode. The boundary line is no longer to be drawn between city and country but *within* the urban phenomenon between a dominating center and a dominated periphery: the eventual "banlieu-ization" of a great part of the world, no less true in Paris than in the Third World, where peasants dispossessed as a result of the decomposition of agrarian structures pour into cities and constitute the *bidonvilles*, the shantytowns of Dakar, the *favellas*, the *ciudades perdidas* of Mexico City.

Lefebvre's discovery and analysis of this spatial structure, in large part, accompanied its production, at least in Paris. The decade between 1960 and 1970 marked a systematic and overt program of Parisian urban renewal that led to a more and more pronounced social division of urban space. Between the years of 1954 and 1974, Paris underwent the demolition and reconstruction of 24 percent of its buildable surface—a transformation equivalent in scale to the better known and more fully analyzed Haussmannian reconstruction of the city a hundred years earlier.[*] As in the nineteenth century, when recently arrived provincial unskilled day laborers—the future Communards of 1871—labored on the urban renewal projects, thus constituting both the instruments and the main victims of the transformation, the 1970s projects employed a large percentage of recently arrived foreign immigrants as an "instrument of manoeuvre" in the strategy of reconquest of central

---

[*]   Norma Evenson, *Paris: A Century of Chance, 1878–1978* (New Haven: Yale University Press, 1979), pp. 309–10.

areas by the upper classes.* The government offered incentives to employers to move what industrial jobs remained in Paris to the banlieues, while the redevelopment of substantial areas of the city, notably the Place d'Italie, eliminated most of Parisian low-income housing, causing a steady forced migration of French and immigrant workers to the outer suburbs. Algerian independence played a significant role in the *grands ensembles* boom in the early 1960s—the boom responded to the demands of a mass influx of *pieds noirs* into France and a simultaneous surge in immigration. By 1969 one in six inhabitants of the greater Paris region lived in a *grand ensemble.*† Paris *intra-muros*, peopled by the upper and upper-middle classes, became more and more a power site at the center of an archipelago of banlieues inhabited by mostly working-class people with the occasional wealthy enclave thrown in.

Substantial budgetary restrictions in the planning of the suburban communities became apparent in 1968, and many housing developments were halted in midconstruction, awaiting government subventions which all but categorically dried up after the 1973 economic crisis. Entire *cités* were left isolated and stranded in a state best described as half-built ruins, encircled by vague terrains that at one time were supposed to support an entire cultural and commercial infrastructure. The rusted carcasses of abandoned *aéroglisseurs*, and the supports for never-to-be-completed autoroutes in Nanterre and Gennevilliers testify to the endless deferment of a plan that never materialized: that of a transportational network that would link banlieue to banlieue without passing through Paris. Better to take the TGV to Lyons, as the saying goes in Paris, than the bus to Mantes-la-Jolie.

---

* See Jacques Barou, "Immigration and Urban Social Policy in France: The Experience of Paris," in John Solomos, ed. *Migrant Workers in Metropolitan Cities* (Strasbourg: ESF, 1983).

† Evenson, *Paris*, p. 238.

What are the generic options available to today's working artist that might best render the spatial dialectic described by Lefebvre, the particular kind of uneven development characteristic of our time of which the "banlieue" is perhaps the exemplary locus? Is there a space within postmodernist culture for a consciously realist mode of writing, what Jameson calls "genuine historicity," and a conception of space that is lived and historical? How, in other words, does the writer within postmodernism make history emerge—not, perhaps, so much a *representation* of history, easily subsumable into the special form of spectacle known as the "lifelike reproduction," the "image of the past" or the "period piece," but rather something quite different and jarring, namely, the *concept* of history?

French writer Didier Daeninckx has published a number of detective novels throughout the 1980s in the French *Série noire*. In the great Chandleresque division between the "formulaic" and the "authentic," Daeninckx, whose childhood reading veered between Louis Aragon and American *noir,* has cast his lot with authenticity. His setting of choice, more fully realized in his books than in any I know of, is the irregular settlements, vague terrains, and experimental decaying *cités* of what Blaise Cendrars called in the 1940s the *banlieue noire*: the north-east Parisian periphery of Seine-Saint-Denis. What interests Daeninckx is the here and now of daily life in the banlieues; his gamble is that his French readership, who rarely if ever see that reality, can be tricked, so to speak, into encountering the intolerable effects of uneven development in their own immediate surroundings by the allure of a fairly traditional and suspenseful murder plot.

The real content of Daeninckx's work then, like that of Chandler's, is a scenic one: the reader's hermeneutic activity winds its way through ramshackle buildings thrown up in three months on hasty foundations, mazes of prefabricated cubes that will lose their air of newness after the first rains; through suburbs where the municipal council thought to soften the impression of misery people feel entering the sector by giving the streets the names of Brueghel (without saying which one), Picasso, Van Gogh, and Rembrandt; through variously densely populated ruins:

> The cité République bordered the F2 highway. Its dozen or so buildings seemed to serve as an anti-noise screen for a recently constructed enclave of *pavilions*. The central building, designated B2, was a mass of 15 floors that sheltered at least 150 families. The orange and red frescoes covering the concrete walls didn't manage to confer on the mastodon the light and engaging allure desired by the decorator; the cells on the ground-floor, destined in some past life to welcome shops, had been transformed into so much debris, vague surfaces ... the square entry hall with its alignment of elevator doors recreated rather faithfully the ambiance of a metro station.[*]

The detective, Cadin, visits the parents of a victim who live in Saint-Ouen,

> in a bizarre building with a facade made of gangways whose metallic handrails, when glimpsed from the péripherique, imitated the contours of automobiles. The city government had relocated them there after the patched-up pavilion they had practically built with their own hands was included in a zone destined for renovation. They had gotten used to it little by little, the dog much less so. He had become idiosyncratic and only pissed against the entry-hall walk.[†]

But these desolate terrains are not the only setting; often just a line of trees, or some other makeshift "anti-noise" protector

---

[*] Didier Daeninckx, *Le Bourreau et son double* (Paris: Gallimard, 1986), p. 22.

[†] Didier Daeninckx, *Lumière noire* (Paris: Gallimard, 1987), p. 41.

separates the workers' *cité* from the privileged zone of the *pavilions*, designed to make the most of the "green world" fantasy of the suburbs: "The Codman-Bret *pavilions*, named after their promoter, were grouped at the centre of the village, near the grade school and the shopping centre. Each of these houses disposed of a vast garden agreeably planted with trees and flowers."* The detective in most of the stories, Cadin, is, like his continental predecessors Emile Gaboriau's LeCoq, and Simenon's Maigret, a cop; but like Chandler's private detective Marlowe, Cadin's circuit takes him, often with dizzying rapidity, back and forth between the unevenly developed zones of the suburbs, between *bidonville* and *pavilion*—through him we have access to the social territory as a whole. The detective's function, his movements, show us that the separation between zones—what Lefebvre calls fragmentation—is at once *fictive* (for one cannot completely separate the functions even though each localized function is represented as being autonomous) and *real* (for all the parcels of space, with their functions divided and Taylorized like jobs in a factory, obtain and preserve an autonomy).

In *Lumière noire*, for example, transport police murder an airline worker by mistake and launch an elaborate cover-up that extends even to Africa. For the only witness to the murder may well be a Malian worker spending the night before his expulsion from France on the seventh floor of an airport hotel reserved for those purposes by the Bobigny prefecture and the Ministry of the Interior. Investigating the murder involves a tour of the suburbs surrounding the airport; it also retraces another *international* geographical axis: the transit connecting the *foyer immigré* of Aubervilliers and the outlying districts of Bamako in Mali—quartiers that have more in common than not.

---

* Daeninckx, *Bourreau*, p. 193.

In Daeninckx's work, the detective moves frequently *between* declining and thriving areas: the juxtaposition occurs at both the urban (rich and poor suburbs) and the international (France and its former colonies) levels. And, from out of this frequent displacement comes the solution to the murder, to the mystery: a *national* crime, an ancient fact successfully repressed, a past injustice whose contamination threads its way into the present. The detective's privileged access to spatial contradictions of the present allows history to emerge: not with the purpose of giving the French "images" of their past—but rather to defamiliarize and restructure their experience of their own present.

Perhaps the most striking facet of Daeninckx's response to the postmodern crisis in narrative, is that in all of his novels the solution to the mystery rests on authentic facts, whether these be, in the case of *Lumière noire*, French minister of the interior Pasqua's 1986 decision to brutally deport hundreds of Malian workers, or, in his best novel, *Meurtres pour mémoire* (1984), the Tiananmen Square–like "disappearance" of the traces of the massacre of hundreds of Algerian demonstrators by the CRS in Paris in October 1961.* The contemporary murder masks a bloody past crime, but the crime is not, as in the novels of Chandler or

---

* Didier Daeninckx, *Meurtres pour mémoire* (Paris: Gallimard, 1984). Daeninckx's version of October 17, 1961—what amounted to the largest massacre of workers in the capital since the fall of the Paris Commune ninety years earlier —was one of the few that questioned the official police version of the peaceful demonstration of 30,000 Algerians in Paris that day. Contemporary investigations into police conduct were largely suppressed; a film made on the subject, *Octobre à Paris*, was never allowed to be released. For more information, see one of the few history books to give a (very brief) account: Bernard Droz and Evelyne Lever, *Histoire de la guerre d'Algérie (1954–1962)* (Paris: Seuil, 1982), pp. 324–5. In 1990 the first commemoration of the event took place in Paris; historian Benjamin Stora notes: "We had to wait for the political emergence of the youth produced by Algerian immigration for the date to reappear." (*Libération*, October 22, 1990). *Meurtres pour mémoire* has been translated into English by Liz Heron as *Murders in Memoriam* (Melville: Melville International Crime Publishers, 2012).

Ross Macdonald, a family affair, an Oedipal crime, a fictional, incestuous dirty secret: it is a *national* crime, an actual moment of French history the authorities—usually the police, zealous and not-so-zealous bureaucrats, and the Ministry of the Interior working in tandem—have gone to great lengths to bury.

Most popular mysteries, especially of the English variety, are devoted to solving rather than examining a problem. The detective is presented with a situation surrounded by misleading or ambiguous information; the story is an exercise in resolving ambiguity; the final scenes read with all the conclusive, reassuring clarity of *explanation*. The very *velocity* of the form, the feverish acceleration in pace of hermeneutic frenzy that plummets the reader head-forward to the final moments demands a solid, reliable closure, a reaffirmation of some comforting order and stability in the world. In Daeninckx, a different, longer temporality —deep history—comes to light in the course of the investigation that acts to prevent such closure; a past crime, often only tangentially related to the contemporary one, disrupts the hygiene of the initial national fiction. If one corpse can be properly buried at the end of the story, dozens of others have been unearthed along the way.

Le Bourreau et son double is set in a suburb called Courvilliers, located in the zone that was called in the 1930s and 1940s the "red belt," and dominated by a single factory, Hotch. A new municipal government has been recently elected on the heels of the old communist *mairie* by promising a security to its wealthier inhabitants that depends on forgetting that immigrants exist. A husband and wife are found dead in low-income housing—murder/suicide by all appearance. But the husband, Cadin discovers, worked undercover as a literacy and housing activist in the confederation of trade unions, the CGT, and against the house syndicate at the factory, and the story, in fact, is a double one: the murder victim and the new head of security at Hotch, it seems, knew one another quite well ten years earlier in a *bled* outside Oran in Algeria, and the reasons for the murder pertain as much to this earlier story as they do to the present.* Is it coincidental that the two men should end up in the same place ten years later? Not if we recall that the companies of French conscripts in Algeria were composed in large part of men drafted from the Parisian banlieue, men who worked at Babcock or Simca, who traded in a factory uniform for that of the army, nor when we remember that successful French officers in the Algerian war, returning in 1962, could make a painless transition back into a big growth sector: security assistance in the burgeoning postwar suburban factories.

And what of Daeninckx's detective, Cadin? In some ways, Cadin recalls his predecessor Marlowe: anonymous, somewhat blank, with only vague memories of a personal life the events of which are not part of any of the novels. But the distance separating Marlowe from Cadin is the distance separating the incorruptible modernist perfection of an essentially ironic hero from something like postmodern neutrality. Cadin makes his home in the transient zones he investigates without becoming fully integrated into the life there; in no way an activist or an anti-police crusader, nor, like Marlowe, imbued with chivalric purpose, he is much more a "hired man," a worker whose *métier*, at least in the early books, is an end in itself. But as his discoveries of police and state activities pile up, he is consequently assigned to more and more obscure suburbs, finally turning up in one of the last novels as a minor character, effectively silenced by the central administration, having resigned from the force after a career trajectory that increasingly came to resemble that of an immigrant worker. "They made me do a tour

---

* Activities which apparently duplicate, to a certain degree, those of the author; Daeninckx worked for many years as a cultural and literacy activist in immigrant communities in Seine-Saint-Denis.

of France," he explains to his successor in a bar. "Six months here, three months there."*

The example of Daeninckx allows us to propose a number of conclusions about the possibility of history in contemporary narrative. I take from Lefebvre and Benjamin the suggestion that the moments when everyday life becomes the most vivid or tangible are the moments when most people find themselves living more than one life. Baudelaire, for Benjamin, presided over and embodied the accelerated entry of Paris into modernism. But it was Rimbaud, as I have argued elsewhere, whose peculiar adolescent and provincial position, whose essentially *regional* perspective, allowed him to write something like the critical history *and prophecy* of that entry into modernism. Baudelaire, in other words, was *in* modernism, Rimbaud sufficiently askew from it to be able to see it.†

Daeninckx, I think, occupies a similarly regional perspective, and it is this vantage point—as well as his choice of a mass genre which immerses the reader in everyday life—that facilitates the synthesis of urban and global in his works. His peripheral perspective on Paris and environs allows the new "world city" of postmodernism—the urban condensation of the restructured international division of labor—to emerge in all the intricacy of its lived, daily, social relations.

To argue for something like a "critical regionalism" in cultural studies is fraught with dangers—not the least of which, perhaps, is the obvious one that the discourse and rhetoric of regionalism has been a mainstay of the right for decades, and has only

---

*   Daeninckx, *Bourreau*, p.140.

†   We should recall, in this light, Rimbaud's well-known critique of Baudelaire: "Baudelaire is the first seer, king of poets, *a real god!* But he lived in too artistic a world; and the form so highly praised in him is trivial. Inventions of the unknown call for new forms." Arthur Rimbaud, *Oeuvres completes* (Paris: Gallimard, 1967), p. 273.

recently begun to be reappropriated by the Left.* A "regionalist" position also runs the risk of coinciding with the recent separatist tendency to "barricade oneself within one's own subculture" of the various vernacular, regional, "identity" movements of the Left—movements whose fetishism of locality, place, or social groupuscule tends to coincide with denying or masking the totality of practices that constitute capitalism. Daeninckx's work, perhaps, suggests a limit to left fragmentation. For the moment of political accountability in his novels takes place, as we have seen, on the *national* level, and what we are shockingly jarred into realizing is a factor which everything in postmodernist culture encourages us to forget: the powerful mediating role of the national state. Economist Alain Lipietz has underlined the contradiction between the more and more internationalized character of production and the world market, and the *national* character of the "modes of regulation" that, since Fordism, have allowed for stabilization. Despite the state's need, in other words, to create a business climate conducive to attracting transnational and global finance capital, interventionism on the part of the state, particularly regarding labor control, is more crucial now than ever before. If the lived realities of postmodernism, its patterns of immigration and displacement, tend to highlight the perception of local and international experience, if the role of the state apparatus, at least in the West, seems to dwindle under the onslaught of a capitalism multi-national in its scope, it is still at the national level, the level of the state apparatus, Daeninckx reminds us, that crime is being committed. Critical regionalism, it would then seem, not only represents the privileged vantage point from which to mediate between the local and the global: it does so without losing sight of the workings of the national state apparatus.

---

* Soja, *Postmodern Geographies*, pp. 188–9.

12

Parisian Noir

Writing in 1993, at the height of the "spatial turn" in cultural analysis, Rosalyn Deutsche drew our attention to the way in which the figure of the urban theorist—her examples are Edward Soja and Mike Davis—had merged with that of the private eye in noir fiction and film. Given that the city is both scene and object of noir investigation, she commented, the analogy between the detective's disinterested search for the hidden truth of the city and the urban scholar's critique of the capitalist city practically suggests itself.* Deutsche does not go so far as to explicitly base her case on the centrality of *one* city—Los Angeles—to both the urban theory then being produced by Soja and Davis and a noir tradition that includes Raymond Chandler and *Chinatown*. Yet, if the analogy works so seamlessly, it clearly has something to do with the way it springs unbidden from the set of representations, both written and figured, that make up an imaginary particular to Los Angeles. And it is also because an earlier subterranean migration between the two figures—a transfer of practices and point of view—had already laid the groundwork for an understanding

---

* Rosalyn Deutsche, "*Chinatown*, Part Four? What Jake Forgets about Downtown," *Assemblage* 20 (1993), pp. 32–3.

of the detective himself as a kind of geographer, engaged in the mapping of social space.

The detective as social geographer emerged in early essays by Fredric Jameson, writing about Chandler.* The spatial paradigm provided by the meeting of Jameson, Chandler, and the urban particularities of Los Angeles has largely overdetermined the way in which we read detective fiction. Yet, in France, where the detective genre has emerged as one of the privileged venues for social and political critique, the narrative mechanisms and the figure of the detective have been substantially altered and put in the service of a new critical project: that of historicizing the recent past. In their reworking of aspects of the noir paradigm to provide an alternative perspective onto postwar Europe, crime-fiction writers in France, publishing in the wake of the political upheavals of 1968, demand to be read as a new kind of historiography. Their analysis of the effects of events in the recent past, offered up in widely distributed and widely read "pulp" stories, parallels and, to a certain extent, surpasses developments within the fields of critical theory and contemporary historiography.

Of all the various kinds of literary characters, the detective is one of the easiest to think of as little more than narrative scaffolding, a string or device whose wanderings link the various anecdotes, local histories, and glimpses of local color into a narrative whole. After all, what other fictional character's underdeveloped personality or lack of "roundedness" is so regularly compensated for by an all-consuming fetish—the love of orchids, for example, or the love of opera? Jameson saw the problem confronting Chandler to be the peculiarly American mid-twentieth century dilemma of how to motivate the plausible

---

* In addition to "On Raymond Chandler," see "L'Eclatement du récit et la clôture californienne," *Littérature* 49 (1983), pp. 89–101 and "Céline and Innocence," *SAQ* 93, no. 2 (1994), pp. 311–20.

narrative intersection of people from extremely different walks
of life: different classes and races, all the fragmented social sectors, all the compartmentalized private dramas that make up Los
Angeles's urban sprawl. For it was Los Angeles, the center-less,
horizontal city, that in Chandler's novels would become a futuristic
forecast of the country as a whole. The detective is the character
whose professional obligations and routine wandering oblige
him to travel between isolated parts of the city, those otherwise
hermetically sealed social spaces: in the case of Philip Marlowe,
between shabby rooming houses and elegant private clubs set
back off the street on long driveways lined with manzanita trees;
between seedy hotel lobbies and offshore gambling ships; between
the desert dry-out spas for socialites and debutantes and the
dingiest of office interiors. For Jameson, the proof that the very
content of Chandler's novels is a scenic one lies in the way we
remember certain "types" or characters in his novels on the basis
of the residences, the houses, doorframes, or interiors with which
these types are associated, rather than on the basis of their own
characterological merit or personal history. It is this essentially
scenic content that conjures up and demands the invention of a
figure who can, almost magically, unite the diverse parts of the
city and, in grasping that spatial totality, create a topography of
the social whole.

Jameson makes a strong case for the Americanness of this new
invention: the detective as social geographer whose solution to
the mystery derives from his ability to grasp a spatial totality.
In France, when a number of far-left political activists in the
1970s and 1980s turned to writing detective novels (*polars*), they
effectively steered the genre toward the depiction of a society
whose current anxieties and troubles are the result of unexpiated
historical crime. French *polar* writers like Jean-François Vilar and
Didier Daeninckx retain the almost invariably urban setting of

their North American precursors. But, in the move from 1930s Los Angeles to postwar Paris, the figure of the detective—as vehicle for knowledge, as narrative scaffolding, as instrument of perception, as consciousness—could not be transported unaltered: he must be essentially reinvented. Noir fiction had become a significant part of the contemporary struggle over the popular memory of the recent past, and particularly the popular memory of the political upheavals of the 1960s. Taken as a group, and quite unsystematically, the novels offer a new form of history and memory of the recent past that is neither commemorative nor nostalgic, and that frequently blurs the line between history and memory. In novels by Daeninckx, Vilar, Frédéric Fajardie, Gérard Delteil, Jean-Bernard Pouy, Jean-Claude Izzo, and Thierry Jonquet, among others, the causes of contemporary crime are to be found in the history of bourgeois society, and, within that history, in the events of the recent past: the Spanish Civil War, the consequences of World War II and the extermination of European Jews, May '68, but above all the Algerian War and the persistence of colonial crime and its unfinished politics.* The emphasis on colonial crime by writers of the 1970s and 1980s derives in part from the authors' own political experience: their childhood and adolescence coincided, for the most part, with the troubles in Paris and elsewhere as the Algerian War drew to an end. But their insistence, more generally, on an event-driven

* See, for example, author and editor of *polars* and former *gauchiste* Patrick Raynal's presentation of the genre as an alternative historiography in *Les Temps Modernes:* In the year 3000, archeologists looking back for the foundations of our civilization will unearth 2,500 *romans noirs.* They will find there an entire history of the previous century: the consequences or World Wars I and II, the extermination of European Jews, the colonial wars of Vietnam, Algeria, and elsewhere, racism, anti-Semitism …" Patrick Raynal, "Le Roman noir est l'avenir de la fiction. Entretien." *Les Temps Modernes* 595 (1997), p. 96. See also Elfriede Muller and Alexander Ruoff's brief but compelling survey of recent developments in French crime fiction, *Le Polar français: crime et histoire* (Paris: La Fabrique, 2002).

history of the recent past, particularly at a moment when professional historians favored the glacial narrative rhythms of the *longue durée,* has led many critics, practitioners, and readers alike to claim for the *polar* of these years the status of the novelistic form best suited to the twentieth century, and the one that offers the most accurate version of postwar history. In an introduction to fellow Trotskyist Ernest Mandel's little book on the *roman noir,* Vilar summed up what he took to be the fortuitous match between noir sensibility and the era which, in Europe at least, its adherents set themselves the task of chronicling: "The century of wars and revolutions, and thus of utopias a hairsbreadth away, is necessarily the century of trials and betrayals."* The plot, intrigue, and attitude of noir, it seemed, could be used to narrate key moments in a totality conceived of first and foremost not as spatial, but as historical.

As a practice in writing an alternative historiography, *polar* history was particularly untimely, running counter to at least two of the dominant discourses of the moment, both of which could be characterized as sidestepping any attempt to conceptualize or narrate change, and as bracketing any analysis of the recent past. Within historiography, the postwar period was dominated by the Annales school's preoccupation with nesting in the stasis of an immobile time created out of a near perfect circularity of nature and function, particularly in early modern times. Annales historians offered the excavated details of a past that was past, and that had little to do with or say to the present. The disciplinary purpose of social history more generally was limited to understanding ideologies and social movements entirely within their own particular economic and political contexts—thus flattening any possibility of event or change. While academic historians and

---

* Jean-François Vilar, "Noir, c'est noir," preface to Ernest Mandel, *Meurtres exquis: une histoire sociale du roman policier* (Paris: Breche, 1986), p. 10.

social scientists were intent on dissolving "the event" by altering
the scale of agency to geographic, if not geologic, proportions,
polar history retained "the event," the great conflagrations and
state crimes, the insurrections and emancipatory moments, as
the central organizing category by which to chronicle their era.
And if Annales-inspired history often spatialized the historical
narrative beyond the limits of the nation form, *polar* history
focused on the illusory and precarious—yet persistent—nature
of the national fiction.

As a project conducted by political activists and former activists,
polar history also departed sharply from the "ethical" discourse
then beginning to be popularized by another group of former
comrades—ex-militants that included the New Philosophers. At
the same moment in the late 1970s and 1980s, in an outpouring
of confessions, apologies, television appearances, and memoirs
timed, for the most part, to coincide with the twentieth anniversary of the May events in 1988, these *gauchistes,* well situated in
the Parisian media or en route to becoming so, took flamboyant
leave of their former political commitments.* Ex-student leaders,
anxious to both capitalize on and deny their former militancy,
invoked the language of human rights or humanitarianism to
compensate for and explain their new-found reconciliation with
the laws of economistic fatality. The discourse of totalitarianism
these writers popularized told us that an unthinkable and irreparable crime had occurred, the work of a pure and unlimited force of
evil exceeding any political, even thinkable, measure. By relying
on scale, New Philosophers used the catastrophism of Gulag and
Holocaust—forever "twinned" in their discourse and generative

---

* For fuller accounts of the reactionary context in which the New Philosophers
came to prominence, see my article "Ethics and the Rearmament of Imperialism:
The French Case," as well as Chapter 3 of my *May '68 and Its Afterlives* (Chicago:
University of Chicago Press, 2002); see also Michael Scott Christofferson, *French
Intellectuals against the Left* (London: Bergahn, 2003).

224 EVERYDAY LIFE: CULTURAL INTERVENTIONS

of a whole host of endisms (the end of art, the end of politics, the end of history itself)—to render all other actions insignificant if not suspect in nature.

Polar writers, for their part, chose a less grandiose, less heroic, and less nihilistic route through the hypocrisies of the 1980s. Writers of detective fiction, unlike philosophers, have always been associated with a kind of rote laboriousness; they lack the originality that is the mark of belles lettres. They are obliged to honor the contract between reader and subgenre writer described by Brecht—the contract that the reader's desire for a certain stereotyped format be met, that readers not have too many "high cultural demands" placed on them. *Polar* writers *did* share with their former '68 comrades a concern with crime. But in the everyday world of the *polar,* the plight of the Malian immigrant on the outskirts of Paris, say, took precedence over the victims of faraway Gulags; evil was neither absolute nor unrepresentable; agency was human and not divine; and events played out on a scale—neither geological nor catastrophic—that allowed their incorporation into a suspenseful, readable plot.

In Vilar's fiction, for example, the urban setting is used to turn his novels into the place where the revolutionary memory of Paris might well be revived *as* it is being obliterated. The city is the historical milieu par excellence, because it is at one and the same time the concentration of social power that makes historical enterprise possible, and the consciousness of the past. The space of the city and its various markers each allude to moments in a complex and differential history, to the varying timescales of staggered evolutions of institutions, ways of being, and material space. And in the case of Paris, those moments are moments of violent political struggle. It follows then that the event, in Vilar's fiction, is first and foremost that of revolutionary insurrection, just as the street is a determinant place or space of dispute and disputed power.* Everything happens as though the streets and the facades of the city keep to themselves the unconscious of the event, the insurrectional moment as trace. Layered in the interstitial spaces of the city, these traces can only be perceived by a character whose intimacy with the most minute details of the material fabric of the city, whose taste for the terrain, is matched by his own implication in the city's revolutionary history. Philip Marlowe, it is important to remember, is a literary hero without a background, and without any cultural or political substratum. The same cannot be said of Victor Blainville, *ex-soixante-huitard*, sometime journalist, sometime photographer, sometime investigator, and Vilar's recurrent protagonist. Victor Blainville experiences the city's materiality not as dumb, or unspeaking, but rather as an immense space of resonance where prior histories rub up against murders, dreams, earlier incarnations derived from detective stories, past incitations to act, the ghosts of previous struggles, each overcharged, overburdened by different historical layerings and potent affective charges. "He parked the car on the rue Daval, several yards from an apartment that, many years earlier, had served as a refuge for organizers of the Jeanson network, and then afterwards for some of Curiel's friends. I had used it as well. Cities have curious abscesses. Certain apartments with certain traditions."† A chance reencounter with the apartment he had once occupied, years after radical anticolonial activists Francis Jeanson and Henri Curiel had lived there, allows the narrator to economically allude to all the

---

* Thus what counts as an event in the recent past, for example, in Vilar or Delteil in particular, is almost entirely determined by the calendar of militant experience.

† Jean-François Vilar, *Bastille Tango* (Paris: Actes Sud, 1999), p. 46. Francis Jeanson was active during the Algerian War in establishing a network of "safe houses" throughout the city for the circulation of arms and cash by pro-Algerian militants. Henri Curiel, an Egyptian Jew whose murder in the streets of Paris in 1978 is still unsolved, was an important anti-colonial and "third wordlist" militant in France.

links that tie the third-worldist politics of the end of the Algerian War to the events of May, and the anti-imperialism of the 1970s.

On his bicycle, which is his preferred mode of transportation through the city, Victor passes "the pharmacy that Pierre Goldman hadn't attacked."* Both as readers and as inhabitants of large cities, we are accustomed to remembering a place through the crimes that were committed there—in fact, criminality is mostly figured through its association with place. But as Gregory Bateson once remarked, the letter you do not send, the milk you don't leave out for the cat—these things are also meanings. Even a "scene of the crime" for a crime that was not, in fact, committed is significant. In this case, the unattacked pharmacy serves as a shorthand evocation of the police-instigated events and frame-ups surrounding one of the more tragic (and unsolved, like that of Curiel) deaths of the post-'68 upheavals.† Yet even this poignant memory from a shared *gauchiste* political past lies in direct and curious proximity to a figure from a very different register, another kind of history, equally important for Vilar, but fictional in nature: "Returning the other way, I went down the Boulevard Richard Lenoir, past the pharmacy that Pierre Goldman hadn't attacked, crossed the overpass, thinking about a walk I'd taken along the glistening canal wharfs below, raised my hand in greeting on the other side to the apartment attributed to the Commissioner Maigret."‡ In Victor's Paris, the ghost of Pierre Goldman frequents the ghost of a fictional policeman: Georges Simenon's Maigret. And the *real* unsolved mysteries of the history of the French Left—militants like Henri Curiel and Pierre Goldman, gunned down on the streets by unknown assailants—are woven into the interaction of

*   Vilar, *Bastille Tango*, p. 15.

†   For an account of the life and murder of Pierre Goldman, see Jean-Paul Dollé, *L'Insoumis: vies et legends de Pierre Goldman* (Paris: Grasset, 1997); for Henri Curiel, see Gilles Perrault, *Un home à part* (Paris: Bernard Barrault, 1984).

‡   Vilar, *Bastille Tango*, p. 15.

the narrator's consciousness with the texture of the city, evoked, and thus remembered. The narrator's *trajet* not only moves the narrative forward, it serves as the structure for a whole network of interrelated histories, affects, and associations that, for Vilar and his protagonist, cannot help but be recalled. The *trajet* links the spaces of the city to time: it personifies temporal movement.

Issues of point of view are, of course, preeminent in the detective novel, a genre whose obsession with ways of seeing and ways of knowing constitutes its specificity. Bicycle riding, Victor's way of moving about, particularly at night, goes hand in hand with a certain kind of perception and a specific cognition. In fact, bicycle *trajets* seem to facilitate the peripheral registering of the sudden aperçu, a fugitive and fleeting impression of a history that is felt as deeply personal. The city street is elaborated in and through the narrator's mobility rather than contemplated. His perception of what has been lost is, as such, not a strict archeological super-imposition of the traces of history but rather the way in which street and *trajet* organize their own archeology, making vestiges of older times emerge without the least excavation, a moving decor of urban events, more or less recalled, instantaneously, as the product of a glance. This is not a frontal, solemn commemoration; it is not a monumental or sterile face-to-face with history. It is much closer to a playful glance.

It follows then that although Vilar's novels are saturated with an ongoing loss, what is lost does not elicit the mournfulness of the antiquarian—neither Vilar nor his narrator want the city to become a museum. For Vilar, what sutures old Paris to the Paris of Haussmann, the Paris Commune to the surrealist imaginary of the 1920s, and on to the strikes and *gauchiste* violence he participated in during the 1960s and '70s, is the tangible trace of revolution. The great civilization of Paris lies in its long experience in the matter of civil war and class insurrection; the specific texture of its urban imaginary derives from this experience. In his commitment to a political history of emancipation and its missed moments, Vilar echoes the direct identification Victor Hugo was perhaps the first to make between Paris and its revolutionary history: "Qu'a donc Paris? La révolution."* If Los Angeles caused Chandler to confront the narrative dilemma of its fragmented social geography, the city of Paris presents Vilar with a different narrative challenge. The challenge is how to tell two stories at once: the history of revolutionary violence that has unfolded in the space of the city; and the history of that other violence enacted by the economic production of urban space—all the disappearances, demolitions, and expulsions that accompany mindless urban renovation, and the generally insipid, hygienic, inevitably boring, and sterile constructions that are thrown up in its wake. The two stories are of course not unrelated. An "enlightened" modernization like the one Paris has undergone since World War II always means the destruction of certain of the tangible traces of the city's revolutionary past and usually means the forcible relocation of some of its inhabitants. Cleaning up a city like Paris, whose streets—especially those of the *faubourgs* that are the setting for Vilar's novel *Bastille Tango*—are saturated with the signs of political upheaval and popular sociabilities, inevitably means erasing the traces of its history.

Bastille Tango, published in 1986, along with Daeninckx's better-known 1985 *Meurtres pour mémoire,* perfected the "imbrication of eras" technique widely used by noir writers to show, for example, how forgotten incidents of the Algerian War thread their way into the present and persist as fascist behavior in the 1980s.† This technique allows an apparently individual crime

---

*   Victor Hugo, *Paris,* quoted in Christopher Prendergast, *Paris and the Nineteenth Century* (Cambridge: Blackwell, 1992), p. 103.

†   Muller and Ruoff, *Le polar français,* p. 47. In addition to Daeninckx's

committed in the present to reveal a historical crime that had remained hidden or obscured until then, or it shows the roots of a profound social crisis to lie in past state crimes. It provides a contextualization that unites otherwise segregated and compartmentalized temporal moments. The concern on the part of French noir writers with linking the decomposition of the present social world to unresolved residues of large-scale political events distinguishes them from their few North American predecessors —Chandler and Ross Macdonald, most notably—who made a structural use of the past in the construction of their plots. For, in the French novels, contemporary murder masks a bloody past crime, but crime is not defined, as it is in Chandler or Macdonald, as a family secret, an Oedipal or even incestuous criminal residue. Compare, for example, Macdonald's 1971 *The Underground Man* to Daeninckx's 1985 *Meurtres pour mémoire*. The books share an identical premise: a father and son are killed twenty years apart. In both novels the son's murder hides past wrongs; in the course of the investigation, past injustices come to light whose contamination has lingered or resurfaced into the present situation. Yet here the resemblance ends. In *The Underground Man*, a quasi-genetic heritage dictates that the sins of the parents must be revisited on the children. The moral of the story goes something like this: flee your parents and choose new, makeshift ones, and you may have a chance of breaking the chain of malediction from the past. "He belonged to a generation whose elders had been poisoned, like the pelicans, with a kind of moral DDT that damaged the lives of their young."* In this sense Macdonald, as Geoffrey Hartman once remarked, represents a complex reworking of one of the

---

Meurtres pour mémoire and *Le Bourreau et son double*, see Jean-Paul Demure, *Aix abrupto* (Paris: Gallimard, 1987), the Marseille trilogy by Jean-Claude Izzo, Francis Zamponi, *Mon Colonel* (Paris: Actes Sud, 1999) and *In Nomine patris* (Paris: Actes Sud, 2000) as well as Vilar's own *Djémila* (Paris: Calmann-Lévy, 1988).

* Ross Macdonald, *The Underground Man* (New York: Vintage, 1971), p. 203.

earliest instances of the genre, Horace Walpole's 1764 *Castle of Otranto,* in which a child who is heir apparent to a noble house is killed when the enormous helmet of an ancestral statue falls on him and buries him alive.* In Daeninckx and his cohort, on the other hand, crime does not, as in Macdonald, involve members of the same family, nor is it, as in Chandler, produced by the residues of the phantasmic menace sexually rapacious women pose to men. It is a national crime, an actual event in French history that bureaucratic authorities and functionaries, usually from the Ministry of the Interior, have devoted themselves successfully to keeping hidden. In *Meurtres pour mémoire,* the routine investigation of the son's murder makes visible the massacre of hundreds of peaceful Algerian demonstrators by riot police in the streets of Paris on October 17, 1961.

In *Bastille Tango,* Vilar creates a temporal palimpsest with Paris superimposed over Buenos Aires, as survivors of the Argentinian junta living in Paris and preparing to testify against their torturers in the great state trials in Buenos Aires begin to disappear once again. The punctual disappearances of some of Victor's friends are set against the background of an ongoing process that actually occurred in the early 1980s, the demolition of the Bastille quarter to build the new opera house. The novel is set midway, that is, both historically and geographically, in what Adrian Rifkin has called "the nightmare or epiphany of consumer blandness that is the reconstruction of the Paris of the *grands projets.*"† The Bastille quarter up until the 1980s had managed to resist all the various plans and projects of successive masters of rational management and urban planning; it had avoided the dreary "Hallification" of

---

*   See Geoffrey Hartman, "Literature High and Low," in *The Fate of Reading and Other Essays* (Chicago: University of Chicago Press, 1985).

†   Adrian Rifkin, "Gay Paris: Trace and Ruin," in *The Hieroglyphics of Space: Reading and Experiencing the Modern Metropolis,* ed. Neil Leach (London: Routledge, 2002), p. 125.

the center of Paris. But in the 1980s, a whole web of small streets, houses, passages, bistros, hidden courtyards, carpenters' ateliers, dance halls, profoundly laden with a popular imaginary, was brutally modified to build the new opera house. The whole area was subject to the kind of treatment that consists in razing old buildings in order to rebuild them again "*à l'ancienne*"—rebuilt to look old, in a faux-old style. This was the fate, for example, of the Tour d'Argent, the only remaining bistro whose façade existed during the actual storming of the Bastille prison.*

The pull that the Bastille neighborhood exerts on the narrator is unconscious in nature: the area has been the overdetermined terminus to any number of *trajets,* a possible definition of which is offered by Victor as "the time taken by a somewhat dreamy traversal of the city, without worrying about an efficient itinerary, made up only of remembered stimulations."† It is this unconscious centrality, a set of layered affects surrounding a walker's recurrent appropriation of the space of the city, and not any frontal political outrage or preservationist's impulse to rescue and safeguard beauty, that seems to explain why he feels called upon to record the history of the neighborhood's disappearance and its replacement with a stage set as stripped of oneiric possibility as it is of the unexpected, a planned zone that offers cleanliness, order, and freedom from scandal and anxiety. "Simmel's metropolis without the shock" is one description of the Paris of the *grands projets.*‡ "I had to take the minutes of the destruction. Without any denunciatory hidden motive. As one keeps a personal diary."§

---

* Vilar has told the story of the demolishing of the Tour d'Argent (not to be confused with the luxurious restaurant of the same name) in essay form as well in "Paris désolé," in *Paris perdu: quarante ans de bouleversements de la ville,* ed. Claude Eveno (Paris: Editions Carré, 1991), pp. 205–20.

† Vilar, *Bastille Tango,* p. 13.

‡ Rifkin, "Gay Paris," p. 125.

§ Vilar, *Bastille Tango,* p. 152.

In a nonfictional account he wrote of the renovation of the Bastille neighborhood in *Paris perdu*, Vilar makes it clear that the disappearances and changes in the built environment of the city that took place in Paris during the 1980s, the deterioration of urban life that always accompanies the accelerated urbanization of society, cannot be attributed to bad taste, or to the work of a clumsy developer. They are the symbol of a strategy: behind an apparently inoffensive operation like a simple "renovation" of a neighborhood lies an attempt to forcibly estrange people from their history and the social knowledge of the neighborhoods that had been their homes, a kind of organized urban amnesia that has as its target the revolutionary memory of the city.

In its twisting of the detective genre to function as a kind of repository of historical memory, Vilar's *romans noirs* retain very little of the pure, rational elucidation of classical Arthur Conan Doyle–era novels, devoted, as these were, to solving rather than examining a problem, and to restoring the forces of order. Very little remains of the narrative paradigm that leads the reader from ignorance to knowledge, opacity to transparency, dark to light. Rather than a solver of puzzles, Victor the photographer is much closer to the figure of the journalist, his photos a kind of reportage or report from the front. We might be tempted to trace Victor's genealogy back to another photographer-investigator, Nestor Burma, the private detective at the center of the series of novels written by Léo Malet between 1953 and 1959, the *Nouveaux mystères de Paris*. Malet's novels—he set out to write one for each of Paris's twenty *arrondissements* and completed all but five—figure squarely in both the history of the Parisian *trajet* and the history of the French *polar*. With the publication in 1943 of the novel that introduced Nestor Burma, *120, rue de la Gare*, Malet was celebrated as "the first and only French author of *romans noirs.*"* (Vilar, we should note, prefers a much earlier origin for the *roman noir*, tracing its earliest forms back to the *romans terrifiants*, born in the vicinity of the French Revolution, that recounted the subterranean conspiracies and debaucheries of the era, tales that revealed a fascinated critique of the occulted power and tyrannies symbolized by nearby castles.)† But Burma's mode of registering the city is peculiarly lacking in feeling, adding up to the most minimal accounts of his own rudimentary desires for food or sex. As seeing subjects, Victor and Nestor Burma share little in common. Unlike Burma, Victor's gaze onto the city, what he sees and doesn't see, what sees him, what *regards* him (the demolitions as a personal matter) is a kind of political positioning. As well as a method of sorts. His relationship to the city is in fact less reminiscent of Nestor Burma and Burma's Paris than it is of another photographer he readily acknowledges as a predecessor, Eugène Atget. Victor's relation to the city is an aesthetic made up of the quotidian exoticism of aleatory urban objects, the trace of insurrection or civil war, and the aftereffects of previous Parisian *trajets*—be they Victor's own, or those of Atget, Maigret, or Auguste Blanqui.

But there is a second factor at work in Vilar's use of the *métier* of the photographer for his investigator. We have said that Victor's photographs constitute a kind of journalistic reportage, often political in nature, just as much as they do a personal diary. In the detective-novel milieu of the late 1970s and 1980s, there is a marked fluidity between the activities of journalist, detective, and militant—a fluidity that effects both fictional characters and their authors.‡ Vilar, for example, has found several different yet

---

* Jean-Patrick Manchette, quoted in Alfu, *Léo Malet: parcours d'une oeuvre* (Amiens: Encaje, 1998), p. 5.

† See Vilar, preface to Mandel, *Meurtres exquis*, p. 8.

‡ This merging of the figures of militant, detective writer, and journalist is perhaps even more characteristic of Spanish noir during the period of democratic

related genres and venues by which to address his concerns with writing the recent past—in 1978, for example, at the moment of the ten-year anniversary of the events of May '68, writing a series of critical articles in the Trotskyist journal *Rouge* against the "commemoration industry" then getting into gear. Perhaps the most prominent of the 1960s militants who turned to detective writing, Didier Daeninckx, spent the years before he began to write *polars* as a journalist:

> My experience as a journalist on a daily was completely useful, even essential. From 1977 to 1982 I did investigations, I wrote hundreds of articles on the most varied and prosaic subjects. I accumulated. I loved being in the streets, looking into *faits divers*. Even with the most banal facts, the ones that appear unimportant, you always have to find an angle, a point of view that makes this or that story worth telling. You have to stay three, four hours, observing ... The important thing is the time spent observing. Your eyes become accustomed, your state of mind also becomes accustomed if you stay long enough. Photographers work that way.*

In the confusing and overwhelming years after 1968, as militant collectives disbanded and regrouped, trying to find fresh spaces and directions for struggle, many militants looked to radical journalism and to detective-fiction writing as a way of not returning back into the ranks. By the mid-1980s, when the French *polar* writers to have reached prominence—Vilar, Daeninckx, Pouy, Fajardie, and Jonquet among them—all shared a militant past

---

transition opened up with the death of Franco, beginning with the publication of Manuel Vazquez Montalban's *Tatuaje* in 1974. See Georges Tyras, "Le noir espagnol: postmodernité et écriture du consensus," *Mouvements* 15/16 (May–August 2001), pp. 74–81.

*   Didier Daeninckx, "Entretien avec Didier Daeninckx: Une modernité contre la modernité de pacotilles," *Mouvements* 15/16 (May–August 2001), pp. 11–12.

and a direct relationship to the events of May and post-May, it was clear that the *polar* had become a refuge of sorts, a place to develop an overtly political thematic at a moment when political militancy was waning, if not in the throes of a crisis. As Thierry Jonquet remarked in 1985, "The *polar's* gaze, its point of view is extremist, very scandalized. It resembles completely the militant point of view."* Many of the editors of the large number of new series of crime fiction proliferating at that time were also products of the militant culture of the 1960s.

Much of the political practice undertaken during the '68 years was based on developing a political line that was not derived from any theoretical a priori but rather inductively, from the terrain, in physical displacements that took students and intellectuals out of the Latin Quarter to workers' areas in the city where they could hear workers' own representations of their conditions, problems, aspirations, desires, unmediated by party or union officials. These investigations, or *enquêtes,* were then frequently written up in worker/activist collectives and published in radical journals like the *Cahiers de Mai.* The emphasis, in other words, was on forms of political organizing that led to encounters with people one would not meet in the normal day-to-day schedule, with overcoming the quite severe urban social segregation of the time that kept immigrants and factory workers on the outskirts of the city, far away and unapproachable. The insistence was on direct contact with workers, unobstructed by any theoretical or trade-union mediation, and on building understanding through practice— inductively, as it were. And, for many activists, this meant *trajets* of sorts to frequently unfamiliar parts of the city. Knowledge of workers must be arrived at inductively, which is to say, from the particular, beginning with the particular, empirical individual,

---

* Thierry Jonquet, in an interview published in *Le Monde*, April 21–2, 1985, cited in Mandel, *Meurtres exquis*, p. 168.

rather than deductively. In deductive reasoning consequences are drawn from an abstract, general principle—an a priori theory or profile of the working class, for example. The geography of this militant practice, as well as its underlying emphasis on induction rather than deduction, would find its way into the detective writing, alternative journalism, and documentary filmmaking of former militants.

In the case of Vilar we can see how militant experience has the secondary gain of helping solve a grave structural difficulty that plagues the detective story as much as it does the practice of militant organizing: the gap separating the detective or the organizer from "the people" around him. The detective shares with the organizer the fate of being different from the other inhabitants of the city: the detective, famously figured in Edgar Allan Poe's armchair genius Dupin, or Conan Doyle's Sherlock Holmes, possesses superior reasoning power to the people he investigates, just as greater political experience, if not theoretical education, separates the militant from those he seeks to organize. The attempt to solve that problem in a way that didn't merely paper it over was one of the defining political ideas of May culture—the attempt to unite intellectual questioning of the dominant ideological order with workers' struggle. Victor, Vilar's detective figure, is a street photographer with no particular assignment other than trade. "Taking photos is my job and a little more."* He is a highly marginal protagonist with, at best, a peripheral view onto the real. "He is not better than what he sees, but is rather a knowing part of it."† His activity—taking snapshots—makes him a professional of seeing, but it also functions as a paradigm for the illusion of disinterest that is the prevailing condition for any urban subject. His is the ordinary way of apprehending people out of the corner

---

*   Jean-François Vilar, *Passage des singes* (Paris: J'ai Lu, 2001), p. 14.
†   Hartman, "Literature High and Low," p. 139.

of your eye, the rapid glance that takes in a sweep of the contours, a few distinctive traits. The photograph, as a particular instance of a particular everyday, is the perfect device for an inductive history.

As a vehicle for knowledge, an instrument of perception, and an epistemological device, Vilar's character is light-years away from the aristocratic ratiocinations of a Dupin, secluded from everyday, mundane society. But the political biography, intentions, and experiences of a genre's practitioners do not fully explain why the tools and techniques of that genre can be refashioned dramatically at a particular conjuncture to treat themes—the Algerian War, for example—shunned by a bourgeois novelistic theory like that of the New Novel, the dominant belletristic form the French novel took in the postwar period. Nor do they explain the books' enthusiastic reception by a mass readership. A remark by Daeninckx can help us begin an account for these phenomena. Daeninckx locates the stakes of the *roman noir* in the act of exhuming the trace of historical memory in a society that "never stops erasing everything and that exists in a kind of permanent present. The *roman noir* says that traces are of a capital importance and that's why they are being hidden from us."* Daeninckx, as I read him, is suggesting that a kind of collective longing now exists for nothing so much as to be relieved of the burden of thinking and remembering at all, that in the years following World War II it is the past itself, in social and psychological terms, that became a casualty of Hiroshima and the Nuclear Age, and that the future, in turn, is ceasing to exist, devoured by an all-pervasive present. Since there is no longer any privileged vantage point from which the effects of the recent past can be reliably grasped, this historically new problem demands a new narrative invention, or, as the Russian formalists might put it, a new "motivation of the device."

---

* Daeninckx, "Entretien," p. 15.

The figure of the detective must be reinvented to become a figure who can be superimposed on the postwar era as a whole, whose routine and life pattern might serve somehow to bring separate and isolated moments together, whose optic apprehends the context that articulates historical events with each other and with the present. In this sense, the detective figure stands in, voluntarily or involuntarily, as a historical consciousness in a world where official, bureaucratic discourse hides the crime, where the past has been effaced, and the future annexed to an endless present. While he might share the urban mobility of a Philip Marlowe, the French detective of the 1970s and 1980s—"pure product of May '68 and post-May"*—is called upon less to provide a cognitive map of the social terrain than he is to show how the residues of past large-scale political events, crimes, and instances of state terrorism thread their way into the present, disrupting the hygiene of the new urban consumer blandness as much as they do the hygiene of the contemporary national fiction.

History, then, is made visible, not with the purpose of giving the French images of their past, but rather to defamiliarize and restructure their experience of their own present. What I am describing is in essence a homeopathic cure, an intervention into what Daeninckx and others point to as an "eclipse of historicity" by a subset of that ephemeral, commercially defined "product" that, if anything, has been in some very real but immeasurable way symptomatic of, if not responsible for, that very eclipse. *Polar* authors like Vilar, in my view, gamble with a readership adrift in the contemporary eradication of historical depth. How much can such a readership be tricked by the allure of a fairly traditional and suspenseful murder plot and by a page-turning pace, into a confrontation with the scandal of the present, or with the present itself *as* scandal?

---

* Mandel, *Meurtres exquis*, p. 163.

13

Elsewhere as Pastiche

The years Henri Matisse spent in the Mediterranean city of Nice during the 1920s were, from the outset, spoken of by critics as a retreat—a move tinged with an almost military connotation, as though the painter were quite literally guilty of having turned tail and fled the battlefield at the height of combat. The battlefield, of course, was Paris, center of the turmoil and tyranny of the new: new technologies, new resources, new labor forms, new industries of mass consumption. In 1920s France, Paris could claim to stand in for the whole new machine age that had served as such a powerful stimulus for avant-garde movements like cubism. Such forms of "high" culture were concentrated in the capital, leaving the provinces—and even a midsize city like Nice, which was a thriving center of the French film industry—to serve as repositories of the merely "quaint" or "charming." Given the capital's modernist presumption of its own indispensability, Matisse's retreat could only be understood as an evolutionary error, a refusal to play the game, a backward step—or, worse: a defeated withdrawal from heroic avant-garde exigencies and breakthroughs into what Jean Cocteau at the time called "a period

Henri Matisse, *Seated Odalisque, Left Knee Bent, Ornamental Background and Checkerboard* (1928), oil on canvas. Baltimore Museum of Art. Photograph: Mitro Hood.

of excessive docility."* By choosing to take up housekeeping and painting in a series of southern hotel rooms, Matisse was not swimming with the stream of history. One of modernism's ruling lions had become, in Cocteau's words, "a Bonnard kitten." And the paintings that resulted from such a cowardly retreat—the Orientalist-themed nudes and semi-nudes in interiors, known as the odalisques—could only represent capitulation to a facile and complacent middlebrow art.† Where an earlier reclining nude in the Cone Collection like *Blue Nude* had been met, in 1907, with skepticism for its modernist audacity, the odalisques of the artist's Nice period were met with an equal if not greater skepticism, one tinged with vague disdain—not for their audacity but for the reverse.

Kenneth Silver has made the point that the conservative "return to order" of 1920s France effectively weakened the prewar equation between painterly ambition and avant-garde innovation. Silver cites André Salmon, who remarked in 1920 that "the era of the virtuosos is closed."‡ But had avant-gardism and the claims of a muscular, heroic modernism really died away so quickly? Is it dead even now? As recently as two years ago, a noted contemporary scholar of Matisse, speaking about the holdings at the Barnes Foundation in Philadelphia, could be heard in an interview dismissing the Nice paintings on grounds similar to those cited by the critics of the 1920s and 1930s who had seen in them a slackening of the painter's artistic will: "Of course many of the works in the collection are great, but let's say a quarter of the works are not very good Odalisque paintings [*Laughter*], so

* Jean Cocteau, quoted in René Schwob, "Henri Matisse," *L'Amour de l'art* 1, no. 6 (1920), pp. 192–6.

† Jean Cocteau, "Déformation Professionnelle" (1919), in *Le Rappel à l'ordre* (Paris: Librairie Stock, 1926), 98–9.

‡ Kenneth Silver, *Esprit de Corps: The Art of the Parisian Avant-Garde and the First World War, 1914–1925* (Princeton: Princeton University Press, 1989), p. 234.

there's not that many interesting things to say about them."* The odalisques were once again found lacking the artistic rigor to be "great," and they seemed to fall short of masterpiece potential because of an even greater failing—their sheer quantity. Like the wretched siblings in the *famille nombreuse* in Thomas Hardy's *Jude the Obscure* (1895), the odalisques' fate has been determined by being "too menny."

But another view of the odalisque paintings becomes perceptible once we see Matisse's retreat to Nice not as defeat but as a full-throated roar on the part of the "Bonnard kitten" against the prevailing cubist-driven philosophical atmosphere in the capital. In Paris, as the "Bonnard" metonym suggests, "decoration" and "ornament" had become obscenities within avant-garde art or "high" art of any kind. They were, as Pablo Picasso's dealer put it, "not proper painting at all."[†] The retreat to Nice was thus not a failure of ambition nor an embarrassing interlude on the part of Matisse, but rather the unleashing of another kind of emancipatory ambition: toward the domestic and the decorative; toward the patterning that had appealed to him in Islamic art and that he hoped to take to a new level of formal abstraction; toward repetition practiced as a more profound and pleasurable artistic reality than the search for the singular masterpiece ("I saw myself condemned to a future of nothing but masterpieces!"[‡]); toward repetition as such as novelty, which is to say as a freedom and a task of freedom.

---

* Yve-Alain Bois, "In Conversation: Yve-Alain Bois with Alec Bacon," *The Brooklyn Rail*, March 2017, hrrps://brooklynrail.org /2017/03/art_books/Yve-Alain-Bois-with-Alec-Bacon.

† "Picasso's dealer Daniel Kahnweiler elaborated a philosophical programme for Cubism that made 'decoration' and 'ornament' dirty words, writing off Matisse's work by implication as not proper painting at all." See Hilary Spurling, *Matisse the Master: A Life of Henri Matisse, the Conquest of Colour* (New York: Knopf, 2005), p. 274.

‡ Matisse in Jacques Guenne, "Entretien avec Henri Matisse," *L'Art vivant* 18 (September 15, 1915), pp. 1–6.

The odalisques were, for Matisse, the creation of a new language, and the retreat is what it took to do it. His time in Nice
was, by all accounts, a period of profound, virtually friendless
and family-less isolation, a laboratory in which the grueling daily
schedule involved nothing but painting. It provided the material
vacuum needed to eliminate the common, idle chatter of the
Parisian art world and the frenzied rhythm of its exhibitions. The
legendary light of southern France was perhaps less important in
its intensity than in its virtually unchanging nature—the way it
helped to create a "steady-state" environment, a zone of minimal
or no interference. (To Francis Carco, who asked, "Why does
Nice hold you?" Matisse responded, "Because in order to paint
my pictures I need to remain for several days in the same state
of mind, and I do not find this in any atmosphere but that of the
Cote d'Azur."*) The intermezzo of the studio constituted a zone
of bizarre, stabilized intensity—what Gregory Bateson called a
"plateau"—a region that, as Gilles Deleuze and Félix Guattari
explain it, avoids any orientation toward a culmination or an exterior goal.† The retreat formed the basis of a social autarchy: the
enclosure of the studio held the painter, the model, the occasional
goldfish, a few plants, a bowl of fruit, a tambourine. This was a
total society, a self-sufficient cosmogony, and as such a kind of
utopia that was concerned, as all utopias are, with the pleasurable
organization of everyday life: arranging the furniture, recovering
the walls, changing the draperies, planning what to wear.

Despite their Orientalist thematics, the odalisque experiments
fail to evoke the infinite new vistas opened up by colonial adventure and the French Foreign Legion. They have much more to do

---

* Matisse in Jack Flam, ed., *Matisse on Art* (Berkeley: University of California
Press, 1995), p. 146.

† For a discussion of Bateson's formulation of the plateau, see Gilles Deleuze
and Félix Guattari, *A Thousand Plateaus: Capitalism and Schizophrenia*, trans. Brian
Massumi (Minneapolis: University of Minnesota Press, 1987), p. 22.

with a different bourgeois delight—the childlike pleasure of plenitude, of reinventing the world and filling it up such that there are
no empty corners, filling it up with so many variegated patterns
and swatches of fabric that any distinction between design and
background is blurred and, in the most interesting paintings, the
alleged subject, the woman's body, is brought to the same picture
plane as everything else—walls, ceiling, carpet—and absorbed
into the decor. The sensuality of the painting is not riveted onto
the female form but, as Peter Schjeldahl has written, "dilates to
every square inch of the canvas."* Every inch of the visual field is
filled. (As Matisse said of Cézanne, "Never a weak spot."†) This is
not the full and the void but the full and the full, a plenitude that
makes the almost miniature scale of a painting like *Seated Odalisque, Left Knee Bent, Ornamental Background and Checkerboard*
(1928), measuring only approximately twenty-one by fourteen
inches, such a surprising discovery when first viewed. It gives
the painting a life that reaches beyond the frame, and beyond the
walls that enclose these "women of the room." (The "oda" of
"odalisque" derives etymologically from the Turkish for "room.")

In the studio/laboratory, the task is to fashion a new language,
an erotic syntax, out of a highly reduced vocabulary. Here are the
elements, see what can be done with them: a woman's often nude
or partially clad body, with its movable parts (as in *Seated Odalisque, Left Knee Bent, Ornamental Background and Checkerboard*
and *Seated Odalisque, Left Leg Bent* [1926]); various draperies;
a repertory of colored costumes; and a limited number of props
(as, for instance, in *Odalisque with Green Sash* [1926] and *Reclining Odalisque with Checkerboard* [1927 or 1928]). All the desires,
anticipations, and sublimations must be expressed through a

---

* Peter Schjeldahl, "Finding Solace in Henri Matisse's Nice," *New Yorker*, July 18, 2016.
† Matisse, quoted in Spurling, *Matisse the Master*, pp. 80–1.

code whose minimal unit, of course, is the figure's posture—reclining, sitting, standing, arms raised, knee bent. In this regard, the four odalisque paintings chosen by Etta Cone (she also collected numerous odalisque lithographs and drawings) and shown in this exhibition are representative of the more than fifty that are said to exist.*

Postures can change but they are not infinite; Matisse's wager is that they can be enumerated and inventoried. Pleasure is dependent on the ordering, reordering, recombining, and restaging of the same elements over and over again in an almost hallucinatory bricolage where no one element—not even the nude female body, even if it is the stunningly rounded, sculpted, and sinuous body of Matisse's principal model, Henriette Darricarrère, the decidedly unexotic French woman featured notably in *Standing Odalisque Reflected in a Mirror* (1923)—occupies a higher order of importance than any other. In this sense, my use of the word "syntax" earlier was perhaps incorrect, for the odalisques, taken individually and in their seriality, work paratactically. That is to say that their figure is precisely that of continual variation, with no first term being repeated. Like an amplitude that never ceases to overflow, their unfolding is similar to the paratactic ordering of the "and" … "and" … "and" so favored by poet Gertrude Stein: their logic is juxtaposition, not the hypotaxis of a hierarchical or military order.

Against the avant-gardist enslavement to the "cutting edge," Matisse's new language proposes a semiotics of *friperie:* a language

---

* This essay was written for the catalogue accompanying the Baltimore Museum of Art's 2021 exhibition entitled *A Modern Influence: Henri Matisse, Etta Cone, and Baltimore.*

The exact number of odalisques is impossible to calculate without a *catalogue raisonné* of Matisse's work; Patricia Hampl estimates more than fifty were produced between 1919 and 1929 in *Blue Arabesque: A Search for the Sublime* (New York: Harcourt Books, 2006), pp. 52–3.

made out of *déchets*—the already worn, the outmoded, the secondhand. To clothe his models and drape his interiors, Matisse had shipped to him (or carted around himself) trunkloads of props and paraphernalia, theater costumes borrowed from the sets and backlots of the Nice cinema industry, and woven North African fabrics and Moroccan screens, recycled, restaged, restitched, and made over to fit.* Cocteau's criticisms of Matisse notwithstanding, it seems clear that the most fruitful comparison to the harem pants, wall hangings, and other secondhand trappings of the casbah that fill Matisse's paintings from the 1920s is to be made with that of the surrealist *objet trouvé*. Like André Breton, who is, as Walter Benjamin put it, "closer to the things Nadja is close to than to her," Matisse often seems more drawn to the decorative trappings surrounding his models than to the models themselves.† Goods made by North African craftspeople, like the outmoded found objects prized by the surrealists, are, in Fredric Jameson's words, "immediately identifiable as the products of a not yet fully industrialized and systematized economy."‡ Both sets of objects bear the traces of the artisanal work from which they are issued, as well as the traces left on their surfaces by their exchange from hand to hand in street stalls and bazaars, *marchés aux puces,* and small shops. And it is this still-palpable proximity to the human labor that produced them and distributed them, especially when compared to the depthless, plastic object world of today, that for Jameson grants their ability to unleash dreams. The same can be

---

* See especially Hilary Spurling, "Material World: Matisse, His Art and His Textiles," in *Matisse, His Art and His Textiles: The Fabric of Dreams* (London: Royal Academy of Arts, 2004), pp. 16–17.

† Walter Benjamin, "Surrealism: The Last Snapshot of the European Intelligentsia," in *Selected Writings, Vol. s: Part 1: 1927–1930* (Cambridge, MA: Harvard University Press, 2005), p. 210.

‡ Fredric Jameson, *Marxism and Form* (Princeton: Princeton University Press, 1971), p. 105.

said of the object world of the odalisques: "What prepares these products to receive the investment of psychic energy characteristic of their use by surrealism is precisely the half-sketched, uneffaced mark of human labor, of the human gesture, on them; they are still frozen gesture, not yet completely separated from subjectivity, and remain therefore potentially as mysterious and as expressive as the human body itself."* The odalisques in their rooms, surrounded by dusty, tawdry colonial trinkets, are not just silencing the phatic opinions of the Paris art world. They represent a massive effort to edit out the object world and the emerging homogenous shape of the mass society and consumer culture represented by the new technologies already becoming mainstream in 1920s France, the visual repercussions of which Matisse was all too painfully aware. As he observed: "Everything that we see in our daily life is more or less distorted by acquired habits, and this is perhaps more evident in an age like ours when cinema posters and magazines present us every day with a flood of readymade images which are to the eye what prejudices are to the mind."†

But what else do the odalisques edit out? There is no avoiding the fact that, suspended in their indeterminate time and place, they help erase the colonial present of their making. Matisse's decision to reengage with the Orientalist motif occurred at a time when finance capital already occupied the political and economic horizon and when an imperial power like France was newly energized by the war to resume an agenda focused on the exploitation of its colonial possessions. Indeed, as both Silver and Sarah Wilson remind us, the Allied victory in World War I had been taken by the French as a renewed mandate for their civilizing

---

*   Ibid., pp. 103–4.

†   Matisse, "Looking at Life with the Eyes of a Child," *Art Review and News*, February 6, 1954, p. 3.

mission.* On one level, the appeal to Orientalism could still be relied on to erase the violence of trade and expropriation and replace it with a dream of sensual revery and aesthetic diversity. In that sense Matisse's paintings in no way escape exoticism's penchant for repressing the historicity and oppression that produced the colonial context.

But the odalisques, as many have noted, are less Orientalist genre painting than they are a kind of painting of the Orientalist genre once removed. A brief historical account of the changing ways in which exoticism is practiced and understood is in order. The odalisques were a way of rewriting an earlier text of exoticism, restaging Orientalist painting in such a way as to abandon, with considerable disdain, the realistic effect, anecdotal description, spatial precision, voyeurism, and "oriental coloring" that Eugène Delacroix, for example, like so many nineteenth-century tourists and travelers before and after him, had felt compelled to use to report accurately on the strangeness he encountered in North Africa and elsewhere. Matisse replaced these artistic practices with others—the theatricality and artificiality of which sometimes verges on pastiche—designed not so much to elicit "local color" as to evoke sensation and "suggestion." In this sense Matisse stands in relation to Delacroix in the same way his contemporary, Victor Segalen, author of the 1918 "Essay on Exoticism," does to Pierre Loti, the prolific travel writer and novelist known for "going native" in the South Seas in the late 1870s. Loti and Delacroix saw travel to exotic lands as a means of gathering up "ready-made paintings" as plentiful as the magazine images saturating Parisian streets.† Reality itself provided everything

---

* See Silver, *Esprit de corps*, pp. 259–60 and Sarah Wilson, *Matisse* (New York: Rizzoli, 1992), p. 4.

† "The picturesque is plentiful here. At every step, one meets ready-made paintings that would bring twenty generations of painters wealth and glory." Eugène Delacroix, letter to Armand Bertin, quoted in Pierre Schneider, "The

that was needed; the tropics were always already picturesque, and one needed simply to avail oneself of the picturesque by traveling to meet it. A few decades later, however, Matisse and Segalen were engaging with the Orientalist motif in an effort to provide weary travelers with an elsewhere uncontaminated by industrial capitalism at precisely the moment, as Segalen complained, that one could observe a "wearing down" of exoticism's potential by "everything we call Progress."* For Matisse, as both Patricia Hampl and Ellen McBreen suggest, the exotic was better fabricated than discovered.† What does it mean that Matisse's chosen "elsewhere" was a pastiche?

Despite two stays in Morocco, in 1912 and 1913, and a trip to Polynesia, Matisse was, by his own description, a bad traveler who evinced little or no ethnographic curiosity about the people whose regions he was visiting and who, at least in Morocco, were serving as his models. "I am too hostile to the picturesque to have gotten much out of traveling."‡ His hostility to the picturesque extends to painters like Delacroix, whom he saw as dealing in it: "When Delacroix's imagination deals with a subject, it remains anecdotal."§ What Matisse did get out of traveling, however, as has been amply documented by a host of scholars and writers, is familiarity with and appreciation of cultures and aesthetic practices that overcame the sharp Western division—a division

---

Moroccan Hinge," in *Matisse in Morocco: Paintings and Drawings 1912–1913* (Washington DC: National Gallery of Art, 1990), p. 21.

   * See Victor Segalen, *Essay on Exoticism: An Aesthetics of Diversity*, trans. Yael Rachel Schlick (Durham: Duke University Press, 2002).

   † Patricia Hampl, *Blue Arabesque*, pp. 25–6, and Ellen McBreen, "The Studio as Theater," in *Matisse in the Studio* (Boston: Museum of Fine Arts Boston, 2017), pp. 114–38.

   ‡ "Je suis trop anti-pittoresque pour que les voyages m'aient apporté beaucoup." Matisse in "Matisse parle à Tériade" (1952), in Dominique Fourcade, *Ecrits et propos sur l'art: Henri Matisse 1869–1954* (Paris: Hermann, 1972), pp. 124–5.

   § Matisse, quoted in Schneider, "The Moroccan Hinge," p. 21.

that was increasing ever so dramatically during Matisse's lifetime
—between the useful and the beautiful, between articles of everyday use and works of art. His immersion in Islamic pictorial
traditions, which had begun before he first came to Nice in 1918,
served, above all, to stimulate what McBreen has characterized
as "a decorative approach to composition."*

Every viewer of these paintings knows that when looking at
harem pants on a seminude female body, braziers, or Moroccan
screens and tapestries, the painting "intends," on some level,
Africa or an indeterminate "East" as a referent. But what are we to
do with that knowledge, particularly when the paintings demand
that that very knowledge also be suspended? Matisse's odalisques
were not designed to be stared at as figures in their own right, like
those in the work of Ingres or Delacroix. Rather, they stand as a
last vestige of material reality counteracting, to a varying extent
from canvas to canvas, the viewer's pure absorption in the weave
of the painting, its compositional or relational surfaces.

The bodies function as a lure, but I doubt if anyone viewing
the odalisques in this exhibition will see them as the hoary old
stereotype demands we see them, as figures of a supine and passive
"East" awaiting ravishment by their imperial Western master. For
one thing, these women are simply too self-possessed in a literal
sense—self-contained and complete. They are women who own
themselves. Nor do I think that viewers encountering the odalisques after Susan Sontag's essay "Notes on Camp" (1964), and in
the heart of John Waters's Baltimore, will accept the modernist
criticism that these are works diminished by valuing accessorizing
—even rampant accessorizing—over substance.[24] Ours is an era,
for better or worse, that has come to terms with accessorizing
and with seriality. Modernists who resented the "relaxation" and

---

*   McBreen, "The Studio as Theater," p. 137.

"rest" of the Nice years recoiled in horror over Matisse's remark likening the satisfactions of the work of art—balance, purity, and serenity—to the relaxation a good armchair offers the body. Relaxation, in their view, was nothing more than the mark of bourgeois complacency and privilege. But this is to forget that no less a socialist artist (and fellow champion of the decorative arts) than William Morris subtitled his utopian novel, *News from Nowhere, or, An Epoch of Rest*. Morris and Matisse shared more than just a love of tapestry and textiles and an attention to sensuous detail that led them both to hand-dye their own fabrics. They shared the recognition that in their respective societies (and it is even more true today) the mere demand for something like happiness is a kind of rebellion. They recognized, too, that art can offer the counterimage of an order in which the material reproduction of life leaves no space or time for those regions we designate as "the beautiful." In Nowhere and in Nice there is space enough and time enough.

Part III. Everyday Life: The Commune-Form

14

The Survival of the Commune

This interview was originally published in *ROAR* magazine issue 1: "Revive la Commune!"

ROAR: The Paris Commune has been studied and debated for almost a century and a half. How does your book [*Communal Luxury*] add to our understanding of this world-historical event, and why did you decide to write it now?

Kristin Ross: Like many people after 2011, I was struck by the return—from Oakland to Istanbul, Montreal to Madrid—of a political strategy based on seizing space, taking up space, rendering public places that the state considered private. Militants across the world were experiencing the space-time of occupation, with all the fundamental changes in daily life this implies. They experienced their own neighborhoods transformed into theaters for strategic operations and lived a profound modification of their own affective relation to urban space.

My books are always interventions into specific situations. Contemporary events drew me to a new reflection on the Paris Commune, which for many remains a kind of paradigm for the insurgent city. I decided to restage what took place in Paris in the spring of 1871 when artisans and communists, workers and anarchists took over the city and organized their lives according to principles of association and federation.

While much has been written about the military maneuvers and legislative disputes of the Communards, I wanted to revisit the inventions of the insurgents in such a way that some of today's most pressing problems and goals might emerge most vividly. The need, for example, to refashion an internationalist conjuncture, or the status of art and artists, the future of labor and education, the commune-form and its relation to ecological theory and practice: these were my preoccupations.

The Paris Commune has always been an important point of reference for the Left but what is new about today is in part the entire post-1989 political context and the collapse of state socialism, which took to the grave a whole political imaginary. In my book, the Paris Commune reemerges freed from that historiography, and offering a clear alternative to the centralism of the socialist state. At the same time, the Commune has never, in my opinion, fit easily into the role that French national history tries to make it play as a kind of radical sequence in the establishment of the republic. By liberating it from the two histories that have instrumentalized it, I was certain we would be able to perceive the Commune anew as a laboratory of political invention.

Communal Luxury is neither a history of the Paris Commune nor a work of political theory in the ordinary sense of the term. Historians and political theorists have been responsible for most of the massive literature generated by the Commune, and in the case of the latter—whether communists, anarchists, or even philosophers like Alain Badiou—this means approaching the event from the perspective of an already-formulated theory. Communard actions become the empirical data marshaled in support of verifying the given theory, as if the material world were a sort of local manifestation of the abstract rather than the other way around.

To my mind, this amounts to summoning up the poor Communards from their graves only in order to lend gravitas to philosophizing. What I did, instead, was to immerse myself for several years in the narratives produced by the Communards themselves and a few of their fellow travelers of the period. I looked closely not only at what they did but at what they thought and said about what they were doing, the words they used, fought over, imported from the past or from distant regions, the words they discarded.

These narratives about their struggle—and we are fortunate that so many of the literate Communards chose to write something about their experience—are already highly theoretical documents. But they tend not to be treated as such by political theorists. This is why I had very little use for the existing political theory about the Commune and why, in the end, I find political theorists to be the bane of our existence to the extent that they approach instances of political insurrection from the perspective of an overarching view that tries to unify them under a single concept, theory, or narrative of historical progression. I don't think it is wise to consider historical events from an omniscient perspective, nor from the vantage point provided by our present, fat and complacent with all the wisdom of the "backseat driver," correcting the errors of the past.

I ignored all the innumerable commentaries and analyses of the Commune, many of which—even those written by people sympathetic to the memory of the Commune—consist of nothing but this kind of second-guessing or listing of errors. I had to perform a massive clearing of the terrain in order to construct the distinct phenomenology of the event and visualize it outside of the multiple projections placed on it by historians. It is the event and its excesses which teach you how to consider it, how to think and talk about it.

And, once you have paid this kind of attention to workers as thinkers—an attention I learned when I encountered and translated some of the early work of Jacques Rancière—you can't tell the story the same old way, the way, for example, it has been told by the two traditions that controlled its narration for so long: official state-Communist historiography on the one hand and the French national fiction on the other. You have to reframe and reconfigure those past experiences in order to render them significant on their own terms and to make them visible to us now, in the present.

By focusing on the words and agency of concrete individuals acting in common to dismantle, little by little and step-by-step, the social hierarchies that make up a state's bureaucracy, I've tried to think the Commune historically—as belonging to the past, as dead and gone—and, at the same time, as the figuration of a possible future. I tried to stage it as very much a part of its historical era, yet in a way that exceeds its own history and suggests to us, perhaps, the deepest and most durable demands for worldwide democracy and revolution.

The book is my way of reopening, in other words, from the midst of our current struggles, the possibility of a different historiography, one that allows us to think and do politics differently. The Commune offers a distinct alternative to the course taken by capitalist modernization on the one hand, and the one taken by utilitarian state socialism on the other. This is a project that I think more and more of us share and it's why I wrote the book.

ROAR: By choosing to focus on the afterlife of the Commune more than on the seventy-two days of "its own working existence," you manage to unearth the myriad ways in which the Commune's political imaginary actually survived the massacre and lived on in the struggles and thought of ex-Communards and their contemporaries. What do you consider to be the most important legacy of the Commune in this respect?

K.R.: I did not so much focus on the "afterlife" of the Commune as I did on its survival. In one of my earlier books, *May '68 and Its Afterlives*, my subject was indeed, as the title suggests, something more like a memory study: how the '68 insurrections were represented and discussed ten, twenty, thirty years later. And today very interesting work is being written about what some choose to see as the "afterlives" or "reactivations" of the Paris Commune: studies of the Shanghai Commune, for example, or other aspects of the Chinese Cultural Revolution, or studies that look to the Zapatistas as a kind of reactivation of some of the gestures of 1871.

Communal Luxury, however, is limited to the life span of the Communards and is centrifugal or geographic in its reach. I examine the shockwaves of the event as they reach Kropotkin in Finland or William Morris in Iceland, or as they propel the hard-pressed Communard exiles and refugees themselves into far-reaching new political networks and ways of living in Switzerland, London, and elsewhere in the aftermath of the massacre that brought the Commune to an end. The extremity and gore of that end, the Bloody Week of state violence that brought thousands of people to their deaths, has all too often proved to be an uncontrollable lure, making invisible the networks and pathways of survival, reinvention, and political transmission that came in the years immediately after, and that concern me in the latter part of the book.

There's almost a wish on the part of historians to lock the whole event up into a neat seventy-two-day episode that ends in tragedy. In that sense I wanted to examine the prolongation of Communard thought beyond the bloody carnage in the streets of Paris, its elaboration when the exiles met up with their supporters in England and the mountains of Switzerland. In so doing, of course, I am very much in agreement with Henri Lefebvre who tells us that the thought and theory of a movement is generated only with and after the movement itself. Struggles create new political forms and ways of doing as well as new theoretical understandings of these practices and forms.

On one level you could argue that it is the forms taken by that survival—a "life beyond life" as in the French word "*survie*" —that constitute the Commune's most important legacy: the very fact that its own "working existence" continued, the refusal on the part of the survivors and their supporters to allow the catastrophe of the massacre to bring everything to an end.

At a more symbolic level, though, the legacy left by the thought generated by the Commune emerges in my book in the cluster of meanings that attach to the phrase I chose for the book's title: "communal luxury." I discovered the phrase tucked away in the final sentence of the Manifesto Eugène Pottier, Gustave Courbet, and other artists wrote when they were organizing during the Commune. For them the phrase expressed a demand for something like public beauty—the idea that everyone has the right to live and work in pleasing circumstances, the demand that art and beauty should not be reserved for the enjoyment of the elite, but that they be fully integrated into daily public life.

What may seem a merely "decorative" demand on the part of decorative artists and artisans, is a call for the reinvention of wealth beyond exchange-value. And in the work of Commune refugees like Elisée Reclus and Paul Lafargue and fellow

travelers like Peter Kropotkin and William Morris, what I am
calling "communal luxury" was expanded into the vision of an
ecologically viable human society. It's striking that the work
of Reclus, Lafargue, and their friends is now at the center of
the attention of ecological theorists who find there a level of
environmental thought that died with that generation in the
late nineteenth century and was not resuscitated again until
the 1970s with figures like Murray Bookchin.

This is all exciting work, but it often fails to take into account
how the experience of the Commune was part and parcel of
the ecological perspective they developed. The experience of
the Commune and its ruthless suppression made their analysis
even more uncompromising. In their view, capitalism was a
system of reckless waste that was causing the ecological deg-
radation of the planet. The roots of ecological crisis were to
be found in the centralized nation-state and the capitalist economic system. And they believed a systemic problem demands
a systemic solution.

ROAR: Following up on the previous question, you particularly
emphasize the profound impact of the Commune on Marx's
thinking at the time. Could you briefly discuss how the events
of 1871 informed, changed, or deepened Marx's understanding
of capitalist development and the transition to a post-capitalist
society?

K.R.: Marx knew about as much as it was possible for someone
to know about what was transpiring in Paris streets that spring
given his distance and the veritable wall of censorship—"a
Chinese wall of lies" in his terms—mounted by the Versaillais
to prevent accurate information from reaching French people
in the countryside and foreigners alike. He looked at the Commune and was astonished to see for the first time in his life a
living example of unscripted non-capitalist life in the flesh—the

inverse of dailiness lived under state domination. For the very first time, he saw people actually behaving as if they were the owners of their lives and not wage slaves.

In *Communal Luxury*, I chart the profound changes the Commune's existence brought to Marx's thinking, and, more importantly, to his path: the new attention he paid in the decade following the Commune to peasant questions, to the world outside Europe, to pre-capitalist societies, and to the possibility of multiple routes to socialism. Seeing, for the first time, what non-alienated labor actually looked like had the paradoxical effect of strengthening Marx's theory and causing a break with the very concept of theory.

But it must be said that I am less concerned with relating the Commune to the intellectual trajectories of Marx or some of the other well-known fellow travelers I discuss in the book, than I am in weaving together the thought, practices, and trajectories of contemporaries like Kropotkin, Marx, Reclus, and Morris, shoemaker Napoléon Gaillard, and other lesser-known figures into the relational web the event produced—a kind of "globalization from below."

The socialist imaginary in the immediate wake of the Commune was fueled not only by the recent insurrection, but by elements that include medieval Iceland, the communist potential of ancient rural peasant communes in Russia and elsewhere, the beginnings of something called anarchist communism, and a profound rethinking of solidarity from what we would call today an ecological perspective.

ROAR: You note how the Commune was really a shared project that "melted divergences between left factions." Likewise, you yourself have little patience for sectarian squabbles that overemphasize the split between Marx and Bakunin, or between communism and anarchism, in the wake of the insurrection.

What was it about the Commune that allowed these various tendencies to find common cause, and what—if anything—should the Left take from this experience today?

K.R.: Life is too short for sectarianism. It is not that sectarianism didn't exist under the Commune and in its wake. In fact, the Left in the years immediately after the Commune is usually seen to be fiercely riven by the quarrel between Marx and Bakunin—a quarrel between Marxists and anarchists that is said to be responsible for the end of the First International, and a quarrel that is often tiresomely rehearsed today between those who believe economic exploitation is the root of all evil and those who believe that it's political oppression.

What I chose to do in my book was to push Marx and Bakunin, those two old graybeards whose quarrel has been for so long all any of us could see or hear from that era, off the stage or at least to the sidelines for the moment in order to see what else there was to be seen. And what I discovered was a whole host of very interesting people who were neither slavishly loyal to Marxism nor to anarchism, but who made adroit use of both sets of ideas.

This seems to me to resemble very closely the way militants today go about their political lives, perhaps because some of the most sectarian types from both sides have left the scene. Even so, my book has had its share of sectarian attack—for insufficient towing of the Marxist line and of the anarchist line, in about equal numbers!

ROAR: Many contemporary movements seem to harken back to the spirit of the Commune in their own struggles. Do you believe we are experiencing a revival of the communal imaginary in our times? How would you account for the return of occupation-based political strategies and this renewed interest in the politics of urban space?

K.R.: I think there is clearly a revival of the communal imaginary today, but I don't agree with you that it is centered in the politics of urban space. The city today all too often presents young people with three choices: no work, badly paid work, or meaningless work. Many have chosen to move to the countryside to lead lives that interweave struggle and social cooperation. When I think about the various struggles today, particularly in France which is the context I know best, they are often in rural areas, and are concerned with defending a way of life deemed "archaic" under capitalist modernization. Occupiers seek to create a form of regional self-sufficiency that does not entail retreating into a self-enclosed world, or eddying in isolated pools of self-referentiality.

This is a desire that emerged very strongly, by the way, in the period following the Commune, and I discuss at some length the many interesting debates on this subject that took place in the Jura mountains in Switzerland between refugees and their supporters all too aware of the dangers of isolation. From what I know of the current communal occupations of territories and terrains, occupiers and Zadistes claim a certain lineage not only with the Paris Commune but with more recent struggles like the Larzac in the 1970s and important figures from that era like Bernard Lambert. It was Lambert, after all, who stood upon the Larzac plateau in 1973 and proclaimed to the thousands of people who had traveled there from all over France and beyond to support local farmers in their fight against being expelled from their land by the French army, that "never again will peasants be on the side of Versailles."

When Lambert in his classic text, *Les Paysans dans la lutte des classes,* situated urban workers and peasants in the same place vis-à-vis capitalist modernity, he was mobilizing exactly the same rhetorical strategy that one of the main figures in my book, Communard Elisée Reclus, does in his 1899 pamphlet, "A mon frère, le paysan." And it's the identical strategy underlying an even earlier pamphlet addressed to (but never received by) French in the countryside by besieged Communards in April 1871, "Au Travailleur des campagnes." To quote Lambert: "Paysans, travailleurs, même combat."

Today, the existence of zads—*zones à defendre,* or "zones to be defended"—and communes like Notre-Dame-des-Landes in France or No TAV outside of Turin, settlements that occupy spaces given over by the state to large infrastructural projects judged to be useless and imposed, mark the emergence of something like a distinctly alternative and combative rural life. This is a rural life opposed to agribusiness, to the destruction of farmland, to the privatization of water and other resources, and to the construction by the state of infrastructural projects on a Pharaonic scale. We see here a real defiance with regard to the state. And at the same time the rural world is being defended as a space whose physical as well as cultural realities oppose the homogenizing logic of capital. By refusing to move they are placing themselves at the center of combat.

The current remobilization of the commune-form, as I understand it, seeks in part to block the ongoing creation of a territorial network of privileged financial metropolitan centers whose development comes at a price: the destruction of the links that tie those centers to their immediate outskirts and surroundings. It is those outskirts, rural or semi-rural in nature, that are then destined to decline in a kind of prolonged desert-ification, as finance capital sucks more and more personnel and resources into the work of transporting at higher and higher speed, and on a larger and larger scale, communication, goods, and services between the designated loci of wealth.

Militants today often see themselves as fighting a distinctly new and neoliberal reality, but I don't think it matters much whether we view neoliberalism as a distinctly novel phase of capitalism or not—the capitalist world they oppose was already substantially analyzed by Henri Lefebvre in his *Production of Space*, a book that came out, I believe, in the early 1970s. There he showed how the increasing "planification" of space under capitalism was a movement in three parts: homogeneity, fragmentation, and hierarchy.

The production of homogeneity is guaranteed by the unification of a global system with centers or points of metropolitan strength that dominate peripheral weaker points. Simultaneously, though, space becomes fragmented the better to be instrumentalized and appropriated: it comes to be divided up like graph paper into autonomous, Taylorized parcels with distinct localized functions. And an increasingly conscious and treacherous strategy divides all the rural and suburban zones, the satellites made up of small and medium cities, the banlieues and the bleak spaces left behind by the decomposition of agrarian life—all these semi-colonies to the metropolis— into more- or less-favored zones with most, of course, being destined for controlled, closely supervised, often precipitous decline.

Such contemporary struggles and occupations are, like the Paris Commune—of necessity—locally based. They are bound to a particular space and as such demand a specific political choice. They share all the concerns and aspirations that are place-specific in kind. But they are not localist or localizing in their aims. Communards, we should recall, were fiercely anti-state and largely indifferent to the nation. Under the Commune Paris wanted to be an autonomous unit in an international federation of communes.

In this regard the Commune anticipated in act all kinds of possibilities such that even the projects it could not undertake and that remain at the level of a wish or an intention, like the federating project, retain a profound meaning. Site-specific struggles like Notre-Dame-des-Landes and No TAV are much better placed today to achieve the kind of international federation that Paris under the Commune had no time to achieve.

15

The Wind from the West

What continues to give what we call "the sixties" their power is the way that any attempt to narrate those years, to commemorate them, curate them, or even allude to them in passing, functions, almost invariably, as a glaring indicator of *what is being defended now*. Last October, because of a book I wrote almost twenty years ago concerning the construction of the official memory of the French '60s, I was invited by the Macron government to come to the Elysée Palace to discuss President Macron's intention to "celebrate," throughout the entire upcoming year, the fiftieth anniversary of May '68. What, precisely, I wrote back, did the president intend to celebrate? If the answer I received—"the end of illusions, the modernization of France, the closing down of utopias"—was not a surprise, the angry breach of protocol on the part of Macron's counsellor when I declined the invitation, was. Apparently, a summons to the palace was to be thought of as a command performance.

Later, I learned that a couple of other historians in France had received a similar invitation and that they, like me, had chosen to decline. Left with only his fervent supporter, Daniel Cohn-Bendit, in tow to function as the master of ceremonies of any celebration,

President Macron chose wisely to abandon the idea and devote his commemorative energies to the centennial anniversary of the end of World War I and other more neutral topics.

Commemorations are killers. But they are a preeminently French exercise. President Sarkozy, who presided over the fortieth anniversary of May, had announced his intention to liquidate all existing memories of the upheavals as part of his presidential campaign. This, in the end, was an attitude on the part of the state to be preferred to Macron's wish to absorb and celebrate, since it gave a bit of vim to the deadly ritual of the commemoration ten years ago. In Paris this year,* May '68 was everywhere: the date and accompanying images screaming out from kiosks, on posters announcing museum exhibits and competing colloquia, film series, memoirs, and special issues of everything from mainstream magazines to scholarly journals. Yet the commemoration framing and fueling the proliferation of references seemed to drain those references of any compelling interest.

There was one exception. Only once did some aspect of the '68 years break through the commemorative fog to enter directly, and with a high measure of political necessity, into the figurability of the present moment. This occurred early in the year when people found their attentions drawn to the sudden reinvocation in the media of the ten-year struggle that began in 1971 in southern France—the battle by farmers in central France known as the Larzac. Suddenly, people old enough were dusting off their memories of summer evenings of solidarity spent on the Larzac plateau, and young journalists were scurrying to bone up on the intricacies of sheep farming. The Larzac was a ten-year battle that began when 103 sheep-farming families attempted to block the state expropriation of their land to serve as an army training

---

* 2018.

ground. Over the course of the decade, hundreds of thousands of French people and others made their way to the Larzac plateau to show their support for the farmers' ultimately victorious battle. This was the first time that such a large number of French people had displaced themselves and traveled such a long distance for political reasons.

The sudden reawakening of interest in the Larzac struggle had everything to do with the victory in January of this year of what was the longest-lasting ongoing battle in postwar France: the occupation of a small corner of the countryside in western France outside of Nantes whose purpose was to block the construction of an international airport. What had begun around 1968 when the site was chosen for a new airport with a few farmers in the village of Notre-Dame-des-Landes refusing to sell their land, had become in the last ten years a full-fledged occupation known as the zad: a motley coalition of farmers, elected officials, townspeople, naturalists, and occupiers who had succeeded up until then in blocking progress on any construction. Like the sheep farmers in the Larzac forty years ago, the zad attracted tens of thousands of supporters over the years to the site to help build their communal buildings and habitations, to share in collective farming and banquets, and to defend the wildlife and wetlands as well as the alternative and semi-autonomous, secessionary way of life that had developed there. And, in January 2018, the zad won. President Macron announced a definitive end to the airport project. The state had, in effect, collapsed in the face of tenacious opposition. That fact alone caused the all-too-familiar feelings of fatality and powerlessness that so strongly permeate the recent political climate to be gloriously lifted. In the euphoric months following the Macron administration's announcement, the Larzac reemerged to be parsed and examined as a possible precedent, a model of sorts, a way that the occupiers and farmers of the zad might continue to farm collectively in the manner they had become accustomed to, with the land remaining under their collective control. Suddenly, the Larzac was understood as not just an afterthought or a waning moment of the long 1960s, but as a site whose deepest aspirations could only be fulfilled in the present, in the form of the communist experiments at the zad. (The zad brought the Larzac back to people's minds, and not, for example, another significant struggle from the 1970s at the Lip factory in Besançon, in a way that made it clear that Lip now represented the closing down of a particular political strategy: factory occupation. While the Larzac—ironically, given the widespread perception of farmers as backward-looking, clinging desperately to the old—was from the future.) Since there was to be no airport at Notre-Dame-des-Landes, and the farmland and the wetlands had been preserved, why couldn't the Larzac serve as a precedent?

That hope was to prove very short-lived for reasons I will go into at the end of this essay. But what the new visibility of the Larzac early this year in turn made possible was a new perception of the decade of highly exemplary, even Homeric battles that began in 1966 when peasants and farmers outside of Tokyo, nimbly supported by the far-left members of the National Student Union, the Zengakuren, fought the state expropriation of their farmland to be used for the building of the Narita airport. It became possible to see that battle, known as Sanrizuka, together with the Larzac, for what they truly were: the most defining combats of the worldwide 1960s.

The zad and other recent land-based territorial struggles, in other words, help us to see the Larzac and Sanrizuka (Narita) struggles as the battles of the second half of the twentieth century that reconfigure the lines of conflict of an era. Another way of saying this is that the 1960s, whatever else they were, are another name for the moment when people throughout the world began to

realize that the tension between the logic of development and that
of the ecological bases of life had become the primary contradiction of their lives. Henceforth, it seems, any effort to change social
inequality would have to be conjugated with another imperative
—that of conserving the living. What these movements of the
long 1960s initiated and what the zad confirms is that defending
the conditions for life on the planet had become the new and
incontrovertible horizon of meaning of all political struggle. And
with it came a new way of organizing, founded on the notion of
territory as a praxis produced by space-based relations. Sixty-eight
was a movement that began in most places in the cities but whose
intelligence and future tended toward the earth/Earth.

This is perhaps a major shift in the way we consider the 1960s,
but I have experienced once before how a shift in the political
sensibility of today can give rise to a new vision of the past. This
was at the moment when the 1995 labor strikes in France, followed
by anti-globalization protests in Seattle and Genoa, awakened new
manifestations of political expression in France and elsewhere and
new forms of a vigorous anti-capitalism after the long dormancy
of the 1980s. It was this revitalized political momentum (and NOT
any obligatory commemoration) that led me to write my history
of May's afterlives.[*] The workers' movements had dislodged a
sentiment of oblivion, if not triviality, that had settled over the '68
years, and I felt the need to try to show the way the events, what
had happened concretely to a staggeringly varied array of ordinary people throughout France, had not only receded from view,
but had in fact been actively "disappeared" behind walls of grand
abstractions, fusty clichés, and unanchored invocations. The
reemergence of the labor movement in the 1990s jarred the 1960s
loose from all the images and phrases put into place in France and

---

[*]   See Kristin Ross, *May '68 and Its Afterlives* (Chicago: University of Chicago
Press, 2002).

elsewhere by a confluence of forces—the media, the institution of the commemoration, and the ex-*gauchistes* converted to the imperatives of the market. Today, when Bernard-Henri Lévy, André Glucksmann, Bernard Kouchner, and Alain Finkielkraut no longer dominate the airways in France with the ubiquity they still commanded even a mere ten years ago, it is difficult to remember the monopoly such self-appointed and media-anointed spokesmen held as lone interpreters of the movement. These men, and a few others (we have their equivalents in the United States), all of whom could be relied upon to reenact at the drop of a hat the renunciation of the errors of their youth, were those I called in my book the official memory functionaries or custodians. It was they who took on the pleasurable task of affirming, symbolizing, and incarnating an essentially generational movement the better to criticize its goals and foundations. Using the movement as a target of opportunity, they in effect made themselves the guardians of the temple they were in the midst of destroying. By the twentieth anniversary of the May events—the peak of their power—they had successfully presided over a three-part effacement of the memory of the movement: the effacement of history by sociology, politics by ethics, and ideology by culture. The voice of the counterrevolution was taken in France to a remarkably homogenous degree to be the voice of the revolution.

But the labor strikes of the winter of 1995 not only succeeded in forcing a government climb-down over the issue of changes to the pensions of public sector workers, they also helped wrest control of the memory of '68 from the official spokespeople and reminded people what all the combined forces of oblivion, including what we can now see as a kind of Americanization of the memory of French May, had helped them to forget: that May '68 was the largest mass movement in modern French history, the most important strike in the history of the French labor movement, and the only "general" insurrection Western, overdeveloped countries had experienced since World War II.

Rereading my book about May's afterlives, I was surprised to see that the seeds of the new argument I sketched out at the beginning of this essay were already there in its pages. In what was for me a very uncharacteristic venturing into the realm of prophecy, I found that I had suggested back then that there would come a day when an autodidact farmer like Bernard Lambert would emerge as a far more powerful figure of '68 politics in France than Daniel Cohn-Bendit. And that what occurred offstage in Nantes that spring would someday be seen to be more significant, more powerful than what occurred center stage in Paris. *Nantes plutôt que Nanterre*. The wind from the west. "The Wind from the West" was the name of a farmer's journal coedited by Lambert published in 1967 and '68. It's not often that what emanates from the west can command our attention in a positive way, but I'll try in what follows to show why I think that the kinds of solidarities that developed in the Loire-Atlantique region in western France and in analogous land-based struggles throughout the world are at least as interesting to consider, and possibly more, as any of the solidarities that come to mind when we talk, say, about "the global south." To return to my prophecy, I think that day has come, Cohn-Bendit's day is indeed over, and Lambert, with his call to "decolonize the provinces," his day has come, and it is only now, in the wake of the zad, that we can begin to measure the significance of that summer day in 1973 when Lambert, high atop the Larzac plateau, addressing the tens of thousands of people who had come from all over France to support sheep farmers in their battle with the army, proclaimed that "jamais plus les paysans ne seraient des Versaillais." (Never again will country people be on the side of the Versaillais.)"*

---

* Bernard Lambert, speech at Larzac, summer 1973. Film, Christian Rouaud,

Lambert's reference to the Paris Commune is suggestive and appropriate, for the history I wish to trace in western France is in part nothing more than the continuing reemergence of vernacular commune forms. Consider the events of May-June 1968 proper in Nantes, widely remembered under the name of the "Commune de Nantes." There, the central strike committee was made up of a coordinated alliance between three distinct social groups— farmers, students, and workers. It is not accidental that such a three-part alliance should occur only in Nantes and nowhere else in France. For the Loire-Atlantique region can lay claim to being the birthplace of a new agrarian left that had its origins in the Paysans/Travailleurs movement of the 1960s and '70s and its creation of new disruptive practices outside the confines of existing nationally led unions. As Lambert put it in an interview, "We had lost the habit of asking our spiritual fathers in Paris how we were supposed to think about the actions we were taking."[*] This group, led by Lambert, was founded in response to the very direct and directed influx of industrial and finance capital into French agriculture after 1965, and it was they who were responsible for organizing the march of some 100,000 people, mostly farmers, in villages throughout Brittany and the Loire-Atlantique on May 8, 1968, behind the slogan "The West Wants to Live."

In this sense, Lambert's 1970 text, *Les Paysans dans la lutte des classes*, which was the first to place farmers and urban workers in the same structural situation vis-à-vis capitalist modernity, and this amid a general call for the establishment of "a real regional power," bears comparison with canonical revolutionary texts like Fanon's *Les Damnées de la terre*, or de Beauvoir's *Le deuxième sexe*, in its conjuring up of a genuinely new political subjectivity.

Paysan et rebelle. Un portrait de Bernard Lambert, Pathé Télévision, INA Entreprise, France 2 et France 3 ouest, 2002.

[*] Bernard Lambert, Françoise Bourquelot, and Nicole Mathieu, "Paroles de Bernard Lambert: Un Paysan révolutionnaire," *Strates* 4 (1989), p. 6.

A new subjectivization emerges in the pages of Lambert's book to accompany that of woman or the colonized in the form of the "paysan"—or defender of the earth.

What I'd like to do now is return to the four movements and moments I've briefly evoked: the zad in Notre-Dame-des-Landes and its struggle that continues today, even after the airport victory; the two protracted land wars of the late '60s and early '70s—the Larzac and Sanrizuka in Japan—and the Commune de Nantes in May and June 1968, and consider them each, as well as the constellation they form, in the light of three practices they share, above and beyond their use of occupation as a form of direct action. The first such practice is the act of defending per se, embodied in the figure of the "paysan" whose name, etymologically, means "someone who defends a territory" and prominent in a word that has only just entered the French dictionary two years ago, namely "zad," or "zone à defendre." Japanese farmers in Sanrizuka, taking a tip from North Vietnamese peasants in their war with the United States, went so far as to bury themselves in underground tunnels and trenches to prevent the entry of large-scale construction machinery into the zone. At a moment when the state-led modernization effort had made accelerated industrialization the sole national value in Japan, farmers countered with their conviction that the airport would destroy values *essential to life itself*. In Notre-Dame-des-Landes, farmers who refused to sell their land, many of whom had been active in the Paysans-Travalleurs movement and who were among those who drove their tractors into the city center in May 1968, were joined by nearby townspeople and a new group after 2008: squatters and soon-to-be occupiers. With the arrival of the first squatters, the ZAD (zone d'aménagement différé) became a zad (zone à défendre)—the acronym had been given a new combative meaning by the opponents to the project, the administrative perimeter of the zone now designated a set of porous battle lines, and the act of defending had replaced the action we are much more frequently called upon to do these days—namely, resist. Why does the history of the zad show us that defending is more generative of solidarity than resisting? *Resistance* means that the battle, if there ever was one, has already been lost and we can only try helplessly to resist the overwhelming power we attribute to the other side. *Defending*, on the other hand, means that there is already something on our side that we possess, that we value, that we cherish, and that is thereby worth fighting for. African Americans in Oakland and Chicago in the 1960s knew this well when the Black Panther Party of *Self-Defense* designated black neighborhoods and blackness itself as of value and worthy of defending.

What makes a designation of this kind interesting and powerful is that it enacts a kind of transvaluation of values: something is being given value according to a measurement that is different from market value or the state's list of imperatives, or existing social hierarchies. In the case of the Larzac, a spokesman for then minister of defense Michel Debré characterized the zone chosen for army camp expansion as essentially worthless, a desolate limestone plateau, populated, in his words, by "a few peasants, not many, who vaguely raise a few sheep, and who are still more or less living in the Middle Ages."* As for the land designated for the airport at Notre-Dame-des-Landes, it was regularly described in initial state documents as "almost a desert." These descriptions could only have been the echo of the familiar colonial trope indicating a perceived scarcity of population preceding invasion, since the area chosen in the latter instance was in fact wetlands—an environmental category unrecognized as having any value at all in the 1970s.

---

* Cited in Stéphane Le Foll, "Les Paysans cultiveront le Larzac jusqu'en 2083," *Le Monde*, July 18, 2013.

So the gesture of defense begins frequently by proclaiming value, even and especially a kind of excessive value, where it hadn't been thought to exist before, in a manner I've discussed elsewhere that the Parisian Communards called "communal luxury."* In 1871 Eugène Pottier and the Artists' Federation under the Commune overturned the hierarchy at the core of the artistic world, the hierarchy that granted enormous privilege, status, and financial advantage to fine artists (painters and sculptors)—a privilege, status, and financial security that decorative artists, theater performers, and skilled artisans simply had no way of sharing under the Second Empire. Why should the labor of artisans not have the same value as the work of fine artists? The federation, which gathered together "all the artistic intelligences, in complete independence from the State," produced a manifesto that ends with this phrase: "We will work cooperatively towards our regeneration, the birth of communal luxury, future splendors and the Universal Republic." What Pottier and the other artisans meant by "communal luxury" was something like the creation of "public beauty": the enhancement of the lived environment in villages and towns, the right of every person to live and work in a pleasing environment. This may seem like a small, perhaps even a "decorative," demand, made by a handful of mere "decorative" artists. But what they had in mind actually entails not only a complete reconfiguration of our relation to art, but to labor, social relations, nature, and the lived environment as well. It means a full mobilization of the two watchwords of the Commune, namely decentralization and participation. It means art and beauty deprivatized, fully integrated into everyday life, and not hidden away in private salons or centralized into obscene nationalistic monumentality.

---

*   See Kristin Ross, *Communal Luxury* (London: Verso, 2015), pp. 39–66.

This was, in other words, a full dismantling under the Commune of socially determined and ancient categories of artistic practices that began by proclaiming the value of artisanal work and decorative art. Shoemaker Napoléon Gaillard, or rather *artiste-chaussurier* Gaillard, as he insisted on calling himself, reinvents himself as barricade strategist and architect, constructing both a knowledge and an art of street defense, just as he performed in his trade a knowledge and an art of the shoe. Anti-Communards called Gaillard a "vain shoemaker," spoke contemptuously of him as the "père des barricades," and nicknamed the enormous barricade he had constructed on the Place de la Concorde "the Chateau Gaillard."

They complained that he considered his barricades "works of both art and luxury." As indeed he did, arranging to have himself photographed in front of his creations—in effect, signing them. Communal luxury as practiced during the Commune (or on the zad) is thus a way of constituting an everyday aesthetics of process, the act of self-emancipation made visible.

Paris Commune, Barricade de la Place de la Concorde (c. 1873)

Photo by Auguste-Hippolyte Collard

Photo by Kristin Ross

Communal wood-working studio at the zad

And, from here, we can now begin to track the development of something like the end of luxury founded on class difference and examine how such an idea opens out onto perspectives of social wealth that are entirely new, perspectives best amplified by the work of William Morris. What seems initially like a decorative demand on the part of decorative artists is in fact the call for nothing short of the total reinvention of what counts as wealth, what a society values.

Today, as we witness states redistributing wealth to the rich in the name of austerity, it is interesting to consider how much a phrase like "communal luxury" defies the logic underlying austerity discourse. By designating something that had no value before in the existing hierarchy of value to be of value and worth defending, one is not calling for equivalence or justice within an existing system like the market (as in an austerity regime or in the demand for fairer distribution). One is not calling for one's fair share in the existing division of the pie. Communal luxury means that everyone has a right not just to his or her share, but to his or her share *of the best*. The designation calls into question the very ways in which prosperity is measured, what it is that a society recognizes and appreciates, what it considers wealth.

And what it is that is being defended, of course, changes over time. To return to the Larzac, Sanrizuka, and the zad at Notre-Dame-des-Landes, these are what the Maoists used to call "protracted wars"—struggles that keep changing while enduring and whose strikingly long duration has everything to do with the non-negotiability of the issue. Farmland is either farmland or it has become something else: housing developments, say, or an army training ground. But where once what was being defended might have been an unpolluted environment or farmland or even a way of life, what is defended as the struggle deepens comes to include all the new social links, solidarities, affective ties, and new physical relations to the territory and other lived entanglements that the struggle produced.

And as new, creative ways are found to inhabit the struggle, it becomes apparent that the state and capitalism do not have to completely collapse in order for people to begin living relatively free lives. Alternative collective and practical ways of going about satisfying basic needs, both material and social—housing, food, education, health care—can be created in a relative independence from the state, a kind of lived and livable secession that is frequently called "dual power"—the second of the practices or strategies I wish to discuss. Lenin used the phrase to describe the practical help offered on a daily basis by the network of soviets or workers' councils in 1917 that coexisted with, and formed a kind of alternative to, the provisional government. He was describing what was in fact a transitional political conflict that had to be resolved, an unstable and temporary situation where workers' councils competed with the state for power. But the term has also come to refer to working alongside state structures, becoming less and less reliant upon them, in an attempt to render state structures redundant. And this, of course, requires the active cultivation of new capacities and collective talents to adapt to new circumstances. In the US 1960s, with their school breakfasts and other community grassroots organizations, the Black Panthers, to all intents and purposes, turned their communities into dual power communes.* They knew that by operating at the level of everyday life and not ideology, by substantially transforming everyday life, in effect re-owning it by and through political struggle and becoming fully accountable for it, they were making revolution on a scale people could recognize.

In France, the events of May and June 1968 in Nantes, even if ephemerally, offer the best illustration of the paths opened by such a dual power strategy. After the Sud Aviation workers outside of Nantes occupied their factory, providing the spark that ignited the general insurrectional strike across the country, links that had been established earlier by the Paysans/Travailleurs movement allowed farmers to feed strikers at cost or sometimes for free. A popular government in the form of a central strike committee in the town hall was set up in Nantes for several days at the end of May and the beginning of June. At the same time, in the neighborhoods, using networks already in place, an organization of collective food distribution from nearby farms sprang up to deal with the most pressing problems of day-to-day life.

Everything began at the end of the second week of the strike in a Nantes neighborhood that was 95 percent working-class, les Batignolles, where the wives of the strikers met together in neighborhood associations ... and decided to organize food distribution themselves. Walking through the neighborhood with a

---

* See former Black Panther party member Lorenzo Kom'boa Ervin's 1993 text, "Anarchism and the Black Revolution," https://libcom.org/library/anarchism-black-revolution-lorenzo-ervin.

loudspeaker, they summoned people to an informational meeting
... After the meeting, a delegation of one hundred women went
to the nearest factory to contact the strike committees. After
that a food and provisions committee was created by uniting the
three workers' neighborhood associations. The committee made
direct contact with the tamers' unions in the closest village: La
Chapelle sur Erdre. A meeting made up of fifteen farmers from
the union and a delegation of workers and students decided to
form a permanent alliance to organize a distribution network
with no intermediaries.*

These initiatives were in turn linked to the central strike committee which, operating from the town hall, could well appear
as a kind of parallel administration. Forty years later the prefect
of Nantes himself attested to the accuracy of a term like "the
Nantes Commune" to describe the situation that had developed
in the region.† "If, everywhere in France, the interruption in the
functioning of large-scale public services tended to paralyze the
action of the legal authorities, it seems to be the case that only
in the Loire-Atlantique region did forms of parallel administra-
tions appear, animated by the strikers."‡ And, as Yannick Guin,
author of *La Commune de Nantes*, points out, "The influence of
these parallel circuits was so considerable that the population
wanted to prolong the experiment."§ This was particularly the
case in the poorer areas of the city, where workers' families were
most effected by the strike and where a farmers' milk cooperative
distributed 500 liters of milk a day for free after May 26. That the
population should want the experiment to endure should come

---

    * Extract from the journal "Les Cahiers de Mai," special Nantes edition,
June 1968.

    † Jean-Emile Vie, cited in *Ouest-France*, May 9, 2008.

    ‡ Jean-Emile Vie, cited in Sarah Guilbaud, *Mai 68 Nantes* (Paris: Coiffard
Editions, 2004), p. 97.

    § Yannick Guin, *La Commune de Nantes* (Paris: Maspero, 1969), p.133.

as no surprise. When questions of existence and subsistence are no longer being posed at the individual level, who wouldn't want such a state of affairs to continue?

The power source in "dual power" is of the same type that abounded during the Paris Commune of 1871—power that comes not from a law enacted by parliament, but from the direct initiative of the people from below, working in their local areas. But the Communards in 1871 were separated by vast armies and what Marx called "a Chinese wall of lies" from any comrades they may have had in provincial cities or in the countryside. When Peter Kropotkin rewrote the experience of the Paris Commune in *The Conquest of Bread*, he imagined the whole Ile-de-France and the surrounding *départements* given over to vast vegetable gardens to feed the revolutionary city. Proximity to and involvement with the means of subsistence is essential not only to establishing a lived intimacy with the territory, it is also essential to a movement's duration. The active participation of a sector of Nantes farmers in May 1968, bringing food to the occupied factories and campuses, created the perspective, if not the reality, of a fight with duration. The farmer/student/ worker coalition in Nantes enacted however briefly a kind of dual power that projected Nantes '68 well beyond a riot or a general strike into well-nigh Kropotkinian dimensions, filling in the outlines of what life might look like if the infrastructure of a city and its surroundings were managed autonomously by an insurrectional commune.

The Nantes coalition is also an exemplary if short-lived manifestation of the process that the authorial collective at the zad, the Mauvaise Troupe, call in their book "composition"—and this is the third aspect of these movements I want to highlight. "Composition" is a continuation of sorts of the relational subjectivity often said to be at the heart of '60s politics. Henri Lefebvre, for example, used to say that May '68 happened because Nanterre students were forced to walk through Algerian *bidonvilles* to get to their classes. The lived proximity of those two highly different worlds—functionalist campus and immigrant slums—and the trajectories that brought students to organize in the *bidonvilles* and Algerian workers to worksites on campus, these precarious and ephemeral meetings, beset with all the incertitude, desire, empathy, ignorance, and deception that mark such encounters, are at the heart of the political subjectivity that emerged in '68. They are the laboratory of a new political consciousness.

A relational subjectivity of that sort clearly developed during the struggle against the Narita airport, as a coalition came into being under skies crisscrossed by American domination, in the form of the encounter between farmers, who began by hunkering down to defend their way of life but learned in the process the true violence of which the state was capable, and radical urban students and workers who had never before given a thought to where and how the food they ate was produced. In the Loire-Atlantique region in the late 1960s, the central imperative motivating farmers in the Paysans/Travailleurs movement was the desire to break out of corporatism and achieve dialogue with other social groups. This was the moment when farmers in France began, perhaps for the first time, to consider the problems of agriculture and the countryside in global political, rather than merely sociological, terms. They wanted to self-affirm as a social group, but in a noncorporatist manner, to respond to problems that the whole country, and not just farmers, confronted: the problem of the use of space, of alliances with workers, of weapons production, of the fate of the land—land ownership and land usage—in general. The movement organized long marches (including a march to the Larzac) in reaction against the national Paris-based Farmers Union, the FNSEA, that had demanded that their march on Paris be stopped at Orleans, so that they didn't "stir up any shit" in the capital. And, equally importantly, so that they didn't come into contact with the "urban riff-raff"—i.e., revolutionaries.*

The force of the Larzac movement lay in the diversity of people and disparate ideologies it brought together: anti-military activists and pacifists (conscientious objectors), regional Occitan separatists, supporters of nonviolence, revolutionaries aiming to overthrow the bourgeois state, anti-capitalists, anarchists, and other *gauchistes,* as well as ecologists. But, where the Larzac movement indeed gathered together a diversity of social groups and political tendencies under its umbrella, at no time was the fundamental leadership of the farmer families who had spearheaded the movement ever in question. Sympathizers who supported the farmers politically and financially, usually from afar but sporadically in vast demonstrations of hundreds of thousands of people who had voyaged to the plateau, were supporting the visceral attachment of the farmers to the same land and the same *métier.* At the zad, with its improbable assortment of different components made up of old or historic farmers, young farmers from the area, petty-bourgeois shopkeepers in nearby villages, elected officials, occupiers, and naturalists, however, no such group was or is in a leadership position. This has created a very different kind of movement, one that in its desire to hold together the diverse but equal components that make it up, requires, as one zad dweller put it, "more tact than tactics."†

Composition, in that sense, was born with the zad. The kind of social base it creates is distinct: essentially a working alliance, involving mutual displacements and disidentifications, that is also

---

*   Bernard Lambert, cited in Lambert, Bourquelot, and Mathieu, "Paroles de Bernard Lambert," p. 10.

†   Mauvaise Troupe Collective, *The Zad and No Tav: Territorial Struggles and the Making of a New Political Intelligence,* ed. and trans. and with a critical preface by Kristin Ross (London: Verso, 2018), p. xxii. For an extended discussion of how "composition" worked at the zad, see pp. 87–115.

the sharing of a physical territory, a living space. Composition is the mark of a massive investment in organizing life in common without the exclusions in the name of ideas, identities, or ideologies so frequently encountered in radical milieux. If the zad is perhaps the best example of an open conflict that has managed to endure, to build for itself duration in the midst of struggle, then it has everything to do with this process.

Composition is really nothing more than the fruits of an unexpected meeting between separate worlds, and the promise contained in the becoming-commune of that meeting. It is thus a space or process where even antagonisms create an attachment. "Composition" could be said to be the way that autonomous forces unite and associate with each other, sometimes complementing each other, sometimes contradicting each other, but always, in the end, dependent on each other. When it works, these different elements strive to recognize each other and work together to pursue common desires that surpass each of them, rather than trying to resolve their differences. Rather than trying, that is, to convince each other or convert the other to the superiority of one's ways, whether this be sabotage, filing legal briefs, cataloguing endangered species, or frontal violence with the police. This is especially important in a movement whose enemies try ceaselessly to divide and conquer by setting one group up against another. The strength of the movement derives precisely from its diverse makeup, which in the case of the zad has allowed it to express itself through various kinds of actions, from highway blockages using tractors to legal maneuvering to violent demonstrations.

Composition creates and maintains *solidarity in diversity*, solidarity among people of disparate ideologies, identities, and beliefs whose coming together and staying together adds up to no final orthodoxy, just a continuing internal eclecticism. That eclecticism and the disagreements it produces can be exhausting, often aggravating. So why make the effort? Because the power of the movement resides in a certain excess—the excess of creating something that is more than the sum of ourselves—something that only the composition between our differences makes possible.

The goal is not to make the whole territory over into one's image. Elisée Reclus and Peter Kropotkin knew this well when they wrote of the dangers of self-enclosed, intentional communities, withdrawn from the world and made up only of the faithful. "In our plan for existence and struggle," wrote Reclus, "it isn't a little chapel of like-minded companions that interests us—it's the world in its entirety."* The goal, as the naturalists might say, is to conserve diversity. To conclude by returning to our earlier discussion, it is the diversity of the territory that is now what is being defended.

Afterword

Within months of abandoning the airport project at Notre-Dame-des-Landes, the Macron government, whose agenda this spring was nothing short of smashing all political opposition of any kind, whether it be from the universities, the postal service, the SNCF, or the zad, ordered, at the cost of 400,000 euros a day, a military-style invasion of 3,000 police and soldiers in tanks into the zad, destroying numerous dwelling-places and communal buildings.† Government intransigence, combined with the military occupation of the zone that has still not completely ended to this day,

---

*   Reclus, cited in Ross, *Communal Luxury*, p. 119.

†   As I write, a similar military invasion of the *zone à défendre* in the Hambach Forest has begun in western Germany, where occupiers dwelling in sixty treehouses for the last six years had successfully protected what remains of a 12,000-year-old forest from becoming an open-pit soft coal mine.

created an insurmountable division among the occupiers between those willing to negotiate with the government to find a way to stay and continue in some form the collective experiments of the zad, and those who brooked no dialogue whatsoever with the state. These latter were forcefully expelled by the government from the zone. For those occupiers who remain, a different phase of the struggle has unfolded, as they try to secure the different habitations and practices they developed over the years. Among these practices is one whose roots in the Commune de Nantes of 1968 could not be more explicit. La Cagette des terres is a network operating from the zad since 2017 to "feed the struggles" of the Nantes region quite literally, using vegetables, bread, and cheese produced collectively from the zad. Whether these movements be more punctual, like the strike by postal workers in the city, or more long-term, like the occupation by students of buildings at the University of Nantes they demanded to be turned into refugee housing, or the various migrant squats or workers' *cantines* in the area, the network has already made its presence and solidarity known. Besides the immediate goal of simply helping movements to endure at the day-to-day subsistence level, the goal of La Cagette des terres is to strengthen the links between the city and the countryside, to reinforce the circulation *between* struggles more generally, and, beyond that, to experiment with forms of food distribution other than those dictated by capitalist economy.*

---

* Those interested in joining the network as a farmer, deliverer, or subscriber, see LA CAGETTE DESTERRES-Réseau de ravitaillement des luttes du Pays nantais, lacagettedesterres.wordpress.com.

16

The Internationalism of Improbable Alliances

Where are the internationalisms, or better, transnationalisms that might compete pragmatically with the universal culture produced by the tireless circulation of global capital? Posing this question made me think back to the early discourse that accompanied the onset of neoliberal globalization in the 1980s and '90s, and that predicted the eventual withering away of the nation-state, presumably worn down by the onslaught of financial transactions and the circulation of commodities. In response to that onslaught, some people then felt called upon to look for ways to try to strengthen and fortify the welfare state against the destructive imperatives of the economy. Now, however, it seems clear that no such weakening of the nation-state ever really transpired, and that if anything many aspects of the state's functions—particularly its police functions—have instead been built up and fortified precisely to protect and facilitate the easy flow around the world of capital and commodities, business executives, tourists, and all the networked elites. The nation-state and global capital are not enemies but mutually enhancing partners, and both continue to function, separately and in closer cahoots with each other now more than ever before, to channel our behavior into set patterns and, above all, to manage our relations with each other and the environment.

But another imaginary and disruptive history exists which is neither the national fiction nor the transnational flow of global capital, and that is the *commune-form*. Though it may initially seem a paradox, a new alternative internationalism, or what might be called "solidarity in diversity" at a global level may now be being forged on the basis of local instantiations of the commune-form. Communal practices imply staying in place and standing in the way, and, in so doing, creating pragmatic alternatives *in the here and now* that take the form of distinct, more or less self-reliant and semi-autonomous, semi-secessionary zones or territories created in the interstices of capitalist logic, the zones it forgot. Taking a position, in other words, is not just central to the issue—it is the issue.

In 2016, I was invited to the site of the longest-lasting political struggle in postwar French history, the occupation of a small stretch of farmland and wetlands outside of Nantes whose aim—an ultimately successful one—was to block the construction of an international airport at the site. The inhabitants of the zad asked me to discuss with them the continuities and discontinuities between the 1871 Paris Commune and what was then occurring at Notre-Dame-des-Landes. They were interested—as I am—in the form and practices of "free communes," in questions of decentralization and ways of creating a regional self-sufficiency that is not a closing-in on itself, that is in fact built on new kinds of associations, cooperation, and interdependencies. Their interest in the nineteenth-century event reconfirmed something that I had argued in my book *Communal Luxury*: that the return after 2011 throughout the world to a political strategy based on seizing space or rendering space public had caused the Commune to enter forcefully into the figuration of the present as a laboratory of political invention, a kind of usable archive of legacy ideas and practices.

I accepted the invitation to the zad and for me that visit and the many that followed were extraordinary. There was a kind of physical density and physical intensity there made up of bodies in action, the palpable sense of a world—physical dwellings as much as a space of collective social transformation and experiment being built together, a proximity of the animals and the outdoors, as well as a number of notable absences—habitual money relations and wage labor, to name two—that for me was more memorable than any theoretical exchange we might have had. But we actually did try to talk about the Paris Commune, and we discussed it as an integral part of its own historical moment but also in a way that allowed it to exceed its own history and suggest to us possible futures—a kind of anticipation-in-act of all kinds of possibilities. Even the projects the Communards couldn't complete—like federation or an enduring regional self-sufficiency, for example— projects that were forced to remain at the level of an intention or a dream, could then be seen to have profound significance for contemporary struggles like Notre-Dame-des-Landes.

In my more hopeful moments I like to think of the 1871 Paris Commune and contemporary persuasive forms of social experimentation like the zad as forming historical bookends of sorts around the whole era of what Arthur Rimbaud called "bourgeois magic": the era of capitalist accumulation and over-productivity.* What today's political experiments in living differently show is that developing strategies in common with people who have different modes of political action is not only possible but desirable when the shared enemy—the capitalist international and its

---

* "La même magie bourgeoise à tous les points où la malle nous déposaera!" (The same bourgeois magic wherever your suitcase sets you down!) Arthur Rimbaud, "Soir historique," *Oeuvres completes*, p. 201.

various manifestations—is clearly designated and when solidarity
extends to all the different groups who have allied together. This
is solidarity, in other words, not in spite of but because of the
diversity of the groups.* The zad's continuing existence, as much
a shared territory as a movement, with both aspects held equally
dear, is a forceful reminder that to gain ground in the fight against
enclosure—for this is what the fight is all about—we actually
need to gain ground, that is, we need to put our feet some place,
to remain some place, to retreat into and defend some place, even
if it is only, as in the case of the Parisian Communards, a city
exhausted by months of siege and deprivation; or for the *gilets
jaunes,* the traffic circle meeting place surrounded by big-box
stores at the edge of town; or for the zad, a semi-arable stretch of
land which the government insisted on describing, much to the
surprise of the farmers living and cultivating there for decades, as
a "desert." Access to as well as the shared use and communal care
of the land, is at the heart of the matter, something Communard
Arthur Arnould recognized in 1878 when he wrote: "The social
revolution must have a collective character, that is to say, it must
proceed with the restitution of the soil and all the instruments of
labor, capital or otherwise into the hands of the collective."† To
the extent that it lies outside of a logic of accumulation or expropriation, "restitution" is a very interesting word, and "restitution
of the soil" a fitting slogan for many place-specific struggles
across the globe. It suggests a symbiotic relationship that has
nothing to do with collectivizing in the old Soviet style nor with
nationalization. It suggests an ongoing process of relearning
and reinventing practices designed to preserve land in view of

---

* This is what zad inhabitants call "composition": see Mauvaise Troupe Collective, *The Zad and No Tav: Territorial Struggles and the Making of a New Political
Intelligence,* trans. Kristin Ross (London: Verso, 2018), pp. 151–220.

† Arthur Arnould, *Histoire populaire et parlementaire de la Commune de Paris*
(Lyon: Editions Jacques-Marie Laffont, 1981), p. 290.

future generations, a solidarity not only with the dead but with those to come.*

Space-specific, grounded struggles have a kind of refreshing flat-footedness about them. David Harvey has suggested that this is because the fact of being bound to a particular space creates an either-or dialectic—something quite distinct from a transcendental or Hegelian one.† Demands, concerns, and aspirations that are place-specific in kind create a situation that calls for existential change and political choice—one is either for the airport or against it. In the words of Karl Marx to Vera Zasulich writing in the context of an earlier rural battle against the state, "It is a question no longer of a problem to be solved, but simply of an enemy to be beaten … it is no longer a theoretical problem … it is quite simply an enemy to be beaten."‡ A fifty-seven-kilometer tunnel will either be drilled through the Alps for a high-speed train line between Turin and Lyon or it will not. An airport will either be built in farmland or it will not.

One of the major effects of the world that capitalism creates is to make us disconnected from the living, transforming us into people without places, endlessly uprooted and uprootable according to the vicissitudes of the economy. And the idea that there is only one world is, in fact, the essence of capital—the world as it exists is the lone referential basis for what is possible. The zad is one answer to the question of how to cultivate a point of view that is not that of the economy, how to get out of the impasse of political economy and its critique. For even the critique of

---

*   For a sense of the stakes in the zad's continued communizing of the land since the abandonment of the airport project, see "Prise de terre(s)," *lundimatin* 209, September 23, 2019.

†   David Harvey, *Spaces of Hope* (Berkeley: University of California Press, 2000), pp. 164–75.

‡   "Marx-Zasulich Correspondence: Letters and Drafts," in Teodor Shanin, *Late Marx and the Russian Road: Marx and the Peripheries of Capitalism* (New York: Monthly Review Press, 1983), p. 116.

political economy, as the *Bogues* collective reminds us, keeps us locked in the unique world of capital and thus participates in the eradication of the plurality of worlds. When we say that the zad makes dwelling or inhabiting into a more forceful political act, we are saying that to think our lives from the perspective of where we live, inhabiting a place and being inhabited by it, is one way to cultivate a point of view that does not begin and end with economic productivity.*

In Valparaíso, Chile, at the end of 2017, the Chilean Supreme Court voided the permit to construct an enormous shopping mall that would have covered the entire historic harbor seafront, bringing to a close a ten-year battle between inhabitants and developers. North American–style shopping malls in Chile, like airports in Spain, have mushroomed everywhere, ushered in by way of the tried-and-true language of modernization, job creation, and economic profit. But this one dwarfed all the others in scale: 162 luxury boutiques, convention centers, even a theme park. An unlikely alliance of dock workers, artists, urbanists, and students saw the commercial center clearly for what it was: a space designed not for them but for tourists and visiting business executives, and thus a pillage of the common good. Though it took ten years of concerted actions, legal maneuvers, and improvisations, they succeeded in defending their city and its seafront.

If what matters for the world of economic productivity, agribusiness, international airports, and shopping malls is a smooth and seamless transit of people and commodities between substitutable spaces, then the making of a territory has everything to do with a logic of difference and possibility, autonomy and self-determination. Old, rather unfashionable notions like "aura" and "authenticity" associated with singularity and identity come

---

* For a discussion of territorial struggles as a way to think beyond the impasses of political economy and its critique, see *Bogues* 6 (Summer 2018), pp. 14–15.

back into play. But with a difference. For, if the zad has an aura, it has been constructed over time by the actions of many, its "authenticity" created through the possibilities of common life that place-based social relations perpetuate, even amid a striking diversity of beliefs and identities. The making of a territory is the making of a place that, precisely, lacks fungibility: it cannot be exchanged for any other. Where once the zad's fight was with the airport, it soon broadened into a battle with the world the airport represents: a world of class division that identifies human progress with economic growth and defines human needs in terms of markets and the submission of all the world's resources to markets. Preventing one's territory from becoming a mere node in a global capitalist system, a space of pure transit where people do nothing more than pass through, is a way of stabilizing in time—and perhaps even, with luck, a lifetime—a way of life that lies at least partially outside of and against the state and the market. We make our community by defending it.

You may begin by defending the land, in other words, but you end up defending the way of life that mounting the defense has nourished. This, I think, is where the importance of the social experimentation around new ways of living communally lies. What is now being defended includes all the new social links and entanglements, as well as the new physical relation to the territory —what Gaston Bachelard calls its "muscular consciousness." Defending the territory now entails defending the collective life project that had emerged there, a project that includes the very concept of territoriality itself to the extent that it fuses the spatial and the social while nurturing a certain autonomy and will to self-determination.* The territory offers the possibility of acting on

---

* See Arturo Escobar, *Territories of Difference: Place, Movements, Life, Redes* (Durham: Duke University Press, 2008), p. 68.

the real in a manner that is at once convivial, transgressive, and pragmatic. It creates mobilization out of demobilizing.

What is revolutionary about the zad and its inhabitants is not so much their opposition to the airport as their discovery over time of *what it is that they were for*, what they had to defend—and this comes largely from the experience of anchoring themselves in a symbiotic entanglement of people and place best summed up by a slogan frequently encountered at the zad: "Nous ne défendons pas la nature: Nous sommes la nature qui se defend." (We are not defending nature: we are nature defending itself.) A slogan that to my mind more or less rephrases geographer and Communard Elisée Reclus's statement: "L'homme est la nature prenant conscience d'elle-même." (Humanity is nature becoming conscious of itself).* And which is also reminiscent of Gustav Landauer's: "La part de la nature que nous sommes nous-mêmes se transforme." (That part of nature which we ourselves are is transformed.)†

In each of these sayings, physical phenomena and human phenomena that are customarily thought separately are here strictly intertwined in a dialectic of dependencies and reciprocities geared toward maintaining the earth as commons.

In the town of Langouët in Brittany, the enemy's name is Monsanto and the town's mayor has taken on the task that neither the European Union nor the national government would perform, that of defending the town's inhabitants from toxic levels of pesticides. When levels of glyphosate thirty times the recommended level showed up in the urine of the town's children, the mayor

---

*   Elisée Reclus, epigraph to *L'homme et la terre* (1905); reissue (Paris: La Découverte, 1982).

†   Gustav Landauer, "Das dritte Flugblatt: Die Siedlung," *Der Sozialist*, May 1, 1910, rpt. in *Der Sozialist*, December 1913; trans. Gael Cheptou as "La Colonie," *A contretemps: Bulletin de critique bibliographique* 48 (May 2014), acontretemps. org/spip.php?articles41.

responded by banning the use of pesticides within 450 feet of any dwelling. His ordinance was subsequently struck down by a judge representing the state who ruled the mayor "incompetent" to make such a decision. But forty other mayors of small towns, from the Alps to the Atlantic, have since passed similar ordinances.

The possibility of extension represented by those forty other mayors or by the numerous zads that have taken shape in Europe and beyond, suggests the beginnings of an answer to the question of what any local instantiation of the commune-form could possibly have to do with internationalism. Each time and place that a particular defense of the living is implemented, it attains the status of an example, changing our ideas of what is possible by giving us practical illustrations of what can be if economic rationality is not the rationality that prevails. A world organized for trade and profit need not be the only world. In this way each instantiation provides for us the act of self-emancipation made visible.

Another way to answer this question lies in tracing the very real and sometimes subterranean trajectories and meetings, the fabric of lived solidarities and socialities that link together forms of action across vast distances. These can sometimes make for surprising moments like the one I experienced in the Rohanne forest at Notre-Dame-des-Landes when I took a fork in the path and came face-to-face with six Mexicans—visitors from Chiapas, I later learned. A great deal of energy is in fact spent in creating, intentionally, such intersections in thought, sociability, and transmission of knowledges across regional, often national divides. At times, though, a relational web may be created almost fortuitously. Japanese farmers on the outskirts of Tokyo in the 1970s, fighting to prevent their land from becoming the Narita airport, became the subject of Breton documentarist Yann Le Masson's 1973 film, *Kashima Paradise*. Screened in Nantes in the mid-1970s, could the film's depiction of the Japanese struggle have inspired the farmers of the Paysans/Travailleurs movement, those whose refusal to sell their land launched the long saga of the zad, to pursue a similar path? Whether fortuitous or intentional, the political praxis of the groups refusing the world created by capital includes amplifying the occasions for extension, constructing paths and places to meet and exchange what are, for the most part, very practical solutions to the difficult problems associated with living differently. Their efforts, as I see it, constitute a kind of lived "globalization from below."

And, thus, a fuller answer to the question would have to come to terms with the fact that these struggles are themselves the sign of the need to come up with a different perspective on the question of internationalism. The first and only real *Internationale* took form, of course, in the nineteenth century with the creation of solidarity between workers, the recognition that workers shared interests across national differences. Now, however, as André Gorz and others have made clear, the world of work—looking for it, performing it, identifying with it, being defined by it—the world that gave meaning to the lives and actions of the members of the First International and that gave birth to the idea that there was one and only one social group destined to create communism—that world is no longer a world we share. What we do share is a common enemy: the capitalist international. And what the commune as a political and social medium offers that the factory does not is a broader social scope—one that includes women, the unemployed, the elderly, animals, children. It comprises not only the realm of production but both production and consumption, and is in practice, at least in part, a collective existential exit, on a human scale, from the world of salaried labor, consumer gratification, and, perhaps most importantly, an exit from even the most frayed belief in capital's promise of unending growth. It bears the mark of a massive investment instead in organizing life in common in opposition to a shared enemy but without the exclusions in the name of ideas, identities, or ideologies so frequently encountered in radical milieux. The commune-form's creation of another space, another temporality, and alternative ways of being with each other, whether in Notre-Dame-des-Landes, New Lebanon, New York, or Chiapas, exemplifies a process that goes far in fulfilling the old surrealist mating of the political and the poetic, Marx and Rimbaud: "Transformer le monde, a dit Marx; changer la vie, a dit Rimbaud. Ces deux mots d'ordre pour nous n'en font qu'un." (Transform the world, said Marx; change life, said Rimbaud. These two slogans for us are the same thing).* The scale of the state's military offensive against the zad in 2018 after the decision to abandon the airport project is one measure of the threat the powers that be perceive in such a collective exit from the capitalist international—the threat, too, represented by the appeal the world they are building has held to the thousands of people who came there in support, with some of these deciding to stay put and make a life there.

---

* André Breton, "Position politique du Surréalisme," speech delivered at the Writer's Congress, June 1935.

Acknowledgments

Chapter 1. "Introduction to *Yale French Studies* 'Everyday Life.'" Originally published as "Introduction," cowritten with Alice Kaplan, in *Yale French Studies* (1987). Reprinted with permission.

Chapter 2. "Lefebvre on the Situationists: An Interview." A shorter version was published in *October* 79 (Winter 1997) © Kristin Ross.

Chapter 3. "The Sociologist and the Priest." *Sites* 1: 1 (1997) © Taylor and Francis. Republished by permission.

Chapter 4. "Introduction to Jacques Rancière, *The Ignorant Schoolmaster.*" Originally published as "Translator's Introduction" in Jacques Rancière, *The Ignorant Schoolmaster*. Stanford University Press, 1991. Reprinted with permission.

Chapter 5. "Historicizing Untimeliness." *Jacques Rancière: History, Politics, Aesthetics,* eds. Gabriel Rockhill and Phillip Watts. Duke University Press, 2009. Reprinted with permission.

Chapter 6. "Yesterday's Critique, Today's Mythologies." *Contemporary French and Francophone Studies* 12: 2 (2008) © Taylor and Francis. Reprinted with permission.

Chapter 7. "Democracy for Sale." *Democracy in What State?,* eds. Giorgio Agamben et al. Columbia University Press, 2011. Reprinted with permission.

Chapter 8. "Shopping: An Introduction to Emile Zola's *The Ladies' Paradise.*" Originally published as "Shopping," in Emile Zola, *The Ladies' Paradise.* University of California Press, 1992. Reprinted with permission.

Chapter 9. "Jacques Tati, Historian." *Jacques Tati Box Set: The Criterion Collection,* 2014. Reprinted with permission.

Chapter 10. "Schoolteachers, Maids, and Other Paranoid Histories." *Yale French Studies* 91 (1997). Reprinted with permission.

Chapter 11. "Watching the Detectives." *Postmodernism and the Rereading of Modernity,* eds. Francis Barker, Peter Hulme, and Margaret Iversen. Manchester University Press, 1992. Reprinted with permission.

Chapter 12. "Parisian Noir." *New Literary History* 41: 1 (Winter 2010) © 2010 *New Literary History,* University of Virginia.

Chapter 13. "Elsewhere as Pastiche." *A Modern Influence: Henri Matisse, Etta Cone, and Baltimore,* eds. Katherine Rothkopf and Leslie Cozzi. Baltimore Museum of Art Exhibition Catalog, 2021.

Chapter 14. "The Survival of the Commune." *Roar* 1 (Spring 2016).

Chapter 15. "The Wind from the West." Originally published as "The Long 1960s and 'The Wind from the West.' " *Crisis and Critique* 5: 2 (2018).

Chapter 16. "The Internationalism of Improbable Alliances." Originally published as "L'Internationalisme des alliances improbables." *Lignes* 61 (2020).

Index